KT-406-615

THE UNIVERS

WITHDRAWN FROM
THE LIBRARY

UNIVERSITY OF
WINCHESTER

KA 0168870 7

Places in the Primary School

In loving memory of my dear aunt, Alwina Wiegand

Places in the Primary School:
Knowledge and Understanding of Places at Key Stages 1 and 2

Patrick Wiegand

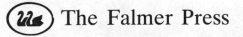 The Falmer Press

(A member of the Taylor & Francis Group)
London • Washington, D.C.

UK   The Falmer Press, 4 John St, London WC1N 2ET
USA   The Falmer Press, Taylor & Francis Inc., 1900 Frost Road, Suite 101, Bristol, PA 19007

© P. Wiegand 1992

All rights reserved. No part of this publication may be reproduced, stored in a retrieval system, or transmitted, in any form or by means, electronic, mechanical, photocopying, recording, or otherwise, without permission in writing from the Publisher.

KING ALFRED'S COLLEGE
WINCHESTER

375.91 WIE | 01688707

First published 1992

A catalogue record for this book is held by the British Library

Library of Congress Cataloging-in-Publication Data are available on request

ISBN 0 75070 052 1 cased
ISBN 0 75070 053 X paperback

Set in 10/12pt Times
by Graphicraft Typesetters Ltd, Hong Kong

Printed in Great Britain by Burgess Science Press, Basingstoke on paper which has a specified pH value on final paper manufacture of not less than 7.5 and is therefore 'acid free'.

Contents

Note on National Curriculum Documentation

Reference is made throughout the text to National Curriculum (England and Wales) core and foundation subject documentation. The references used are to the latest subject documents available at the time of going to press. These are:

DES (1989a) *English in the National Curriculum*, London, HMSO
DES (1989b) *Mathematics in the National Curriculum*, London, HMSO
DES (1989c) *Science in the National Curriculum*, London, HMSO
DES (1990a) *Technology in the National Curriculum*, London, HMSO
DES (1991) *History in the National Curriculum*, London, HMSO
DES (1990c) *Modern Foreign Languages for Ages 11 to 16*, London, HMSO
DES (1991) *Geography in the National Curriculum*, London, HMSO

List of Figures

Acknowledgments

I would like to thank the following friends and colleagues for their help:

Eunice Gill, Tony Dale, Jenny Thomas and Adrian Smith of Oxford University Press for teaching me about the production of books and atlases.

Andrew Convey and Margaret Whiteside for putting me in touch with a number of helpful colleagues.

The headteachers, teachers and pupils who participated in a number of investigations referred to in this book.

Elspeth Cardy of the Central Bureau for Educational Visits and Exchanges for providing information about school links.

Simon Asquith and Diane Shorrocks for reading parts of the typescript and for making valuable suggestions.

David Tucker for the loan of materials relating to the Inuit and for the opportunity to discuss distant places with himself and his students at North Riding College.

Many of my PGCE and MEd students for the opportunity to discuss ideas in relation to teaching about places and for the use of some of their taped interview material.

Jorma Ojala for ideas on activities relating to distant places.

Ian Biercamp for materials relating to Children's International Summer Villages.

The audio-visual service of the University of Leeds.

I would especially like to thank Helen for painstakingly transcribing the tapes on which much interview data was based.

I would also like to thank the following for permission to reproduce material previously published elsewhere: The editors and publishers of *Education*

Acknowledgments

3–13, *The New Era in Education*, *Geography*, *Teaching Geography* and *Primary Geographer* for permission to reproduce parts of my articles in those journals; David Marshall, Editor of *Campus World*; Hartwig Haubrich, Henk Meijer, John Murray (publishers); Dervla Murphy, Richard Hook, Oxford University Press; Children's International Summer Villages; Brian Goodey and the Centre for Urban and Regional Studies, Birmingham; and the National Curriculum Council.

Chapter 1

Knowledge and Understanding of Places in the National Curriculum

Pupils should develop their knowledge and understanding of places in local, regional, national, international and global contexts. They should develop:
(i)   a knowledge of places;
(ii)   an understanding of the distinctive features that give a place its identity;
(iii) an understanding of the similarities and differences between places;
(iv)   an understanding of the relationships between themes and issues in particular locations. (DES (1991) *Geography in the National Curriculum*, p. 7)

Introduction

What impact do dramatic international events have on children? What images do children have in their minds about distant places? What are children's attitudes towards foreigners and to what extent are those attitudes formed by books or television or even their own travel experiences?

This book is about these and other related questions. It examines the evidence for what children know and feel about their own country, other countries and people who live far away. It looks at the ways in which children acquire information about distant people and places and the ways in which such information may be distorted and misleading. It identifies opportunities within the National Curriculum for England and Wales for teaching about other countries and cultures and makes suggestions for curriculum planning and classroom activities in the primary school. At one level, the text is a handbook to Attainment Target 2 in the National Curriculum for Geography (Knowledge and Understanding of Places) at Key Stages 1 and 2. However, its scope is broader than that. Although written by a geographer, the approach is cross-curricular. There are for example many opportunities for teaching about places in the core subjects of mathematics, English, science and technology as well as in the foundation subjects of the National Curriculum. There is also a strong 'place' component to the cross-curricular themes of education of citizenship, environmental education and economic and industrial understanding. The study of places is also closely related to the cross-curricular dimension of preparing children for life in a multicultural society. In most primary schools 'places' will form the subject matter of topic or project work. This may be in the form of projects devoted to particular localities (including the home area), regions, or countries or in the form of thematic topics with a significant place dimension (such as homes or clothes or food around the world). This book examines ways in which such integrated approaches can be initiated and developed.

Most of the examples used in this book are of *distant* places. This is not only because of the attention paid to localities beyond the United Kingdom in the National Curriculum documentation but also because of the author's conviction (which I had better declare at the outset) that some form of education for international understanding is necessary in primary schools.

Why is the Study of Distant Places Important?

My initial teacher training was in Durham in the late 1960s. During the first week of the first term I met a fellow student who came from Hartlepool. As a Southerner, I was much intrigued when other students from the North-east took great delight in teasing him with the curious question 'What about the monkey?' I later learned that during the Napoleonic Wars a ship carrying a menagerie was sunk off the North-east coast of England. The only survivor was a monkey who managed to swim ashore. The patriotic townsfolk of Hartlepool, mistaking the animal for a Frenchman, hanged it in the town square. I understand that visitors to the town today are still well advised to exercise some discretion when referring to this incident ...

The story raises a number of issues that remain relevant today. No monkeys have been hanged recently (to my knowledge) in Hartlepool, or anywhere else for that matter. But international misunderstanding and conflict continues. And unhelpful images continue to be held about foreigners. This book was written during a time of mounting tension in the Middle East and was near completion when war broke out in the Gulf. A difficult and complex international situation was not much helped at the time by the reinforcement in the tabloid press of negative images of Arabs that have been prominent in Western Europe at least since the times of the crusades. The interplay between images, attitudes and national events can be further illustrated in the context of the United Kingdom by the 'Ridley affair' of July 1990. In an interview with *The Spectator* magazine, the then Trade Secretary, Nicholas Ridley suggested that a more economically and politically united Europe would fall prey to German domination. He was reported as saying that 'this rushed takeover (of Europe) by the Germans on the worst possible basis, with the French behaving like poodles to the Germans is absolutely intolerable'. He was further reported as saying 'I'm not against giving up sovereignty in principle but not to this lot. You might as well give it to Adolf Hitler, frankly.' His subsequent resignation was followed by a new crisis — the revelation of a confidential minute of a Chequers meeting chaired by the Prime Minister which had considered the 'German national character'. The meeting, attended by the Foreign Secretary and academic experts on Germany, apparently discussed supposed national characteristics of Germans, concluding that these were *'angst, aggressiveness, assertiveness, bullying, egotism, inferiority complex and sentimentality'*. Relationships with Europe were further strained in the autumn of that year, fuelled again by the tabloid press (this time, for example, with *The Sun*'s 'Up yours, Delors' campaign against the European Community) and provoking the leadership crisis in the Conservative party. Confused notions of national characteristics, race and stereotypes, together with straightforward chauvinism and prejudice play an important part in both national and international affairs.

We need to be aware of the ways in which our minds can be scratched by the images we hold of other people. One of the aims of this book is to try to present a sort of 'natural history' of the popular images of distant people and places that *children* appear to hold and the processes responsible for their formation. I hope that the identification of these images will enable readers to help their pupils acquire richer and less biased ways of looking at the world.

The National Curriculum Geography Working Group's views on what the subject has to offer young children (which received little dissent at the time from the geography education community) is given below (my emphasis):

We believe that geographical education should:
(a) stimulate pupils' *interest* in their surroundings and in the variety of physical and human conditions on the earth's surface;
(b) foster their sense of *wonder* at the beauty of the world around them;
(c) help them to develop an informed *concern* about the quality of the environment and the future of the human habitat; and
(d) thereby enhance their sense of *responsibility* for the care of the earth and its peoples. (DES, 1990d)

Of course, not all of these aims will be met solely by the study of *distant* places. The child's immediate surroundings, the local environment and the home country are important too. Children gradually need to confront issues relating to their own national identity as well as developing knowledge and understandings of the wider world. A major message of this book however is that teaching for international understanding needs to begin *early*. The nursery is not too soon, as by the age of 3 and 4 many pre-school children seem already to display strong (and often negative) views of other cultures. It is also important to remember though that the distinction between near and far is blurred for many children. Young children may perceive *all* places that are not 'here' as being remote.

Before the introduction of the National Curriculum in geography, it was generally agreed that although there was good work in primary schools relating to the local environment, the study of distant places had received too little emphasis.

> The study of unfamiliar places deserves greater attention than it is often given. Pupils should begin to explore similarities and differences between their local area and more distant places. (DES, 1986, p. 13)

> Work related to other places in the British Isles and the world was limited. The almost total absence of a national and world dimension to the work in many cases highlighted the need for schools to consider a broader perspective. (HMI, 1989, p. 12)

This absence of the study of distant places in the primary school curriculum may have been the result of a number of factors, including the previously widely-held assumption that children do not have much direct experience of foreign countries and that therefore geographical work is best restricted to studies of the immediate locality. A summary of the deliberations of an international UNESCO seminar held in 1950 to consider the contribution of geographical education to international understanding expressed a commonly held view of the time:

> There is some doubt as to the age when it is wise to study more than the local environment of the school. It is, however, generally accepted that stories of children in other lands should not be introduced until after the age of 7, and that there should be no definite study of the world as a whole until after the age of 9. (Scarfe, 1951, p. 34)

However, since that time, not only have opportunities for children to gain experience of the wider world increased hugely (through, for example travel and television); it is also more widely recognized that children's own interests may take them beyond the immediate locality. Many children may in fact be much more interested in 'volcanoes, Australian aborigines and coral islands than plotting the distribution of lamp posts or making a map of the cycle sheds' (Storm, 1970, p. 5).

What is significant about official statements on primary school geography from the mid-1980s is that they stressed the importance of the study of distant places in the *early* primary years. Her Majesty's Inspectorate, for example, acknowledge the important role of holidays, television and books in stimulating children's interest in faraway places (DES, 1986) and point to evidence that even the youngest children are able to undertake work concerned with what places are like, how locations affect what people do and how people have used and adapted to their surroundings (DES, 1986). It is this recognition of distant places in the curriculum for key stages 1 and 2 which now poses the greatest challenge for those planning geographical work in the primary school. Many teachers will in fact find themselves having to prepare distinctively geographical work for the first time.

What more particularly does the study of places in the primary school aim to achieve? Setting aside the development of cross-curricular intellectual and social skills and competencies such as oracy, literacy and numeracy, the following goals (DES, 1990d) are a useful starting point:

* the acquisition of a framework of knowledge about locations and places. This enables children to fit 'new' place knowledge into their developing mental maps of their own country and of the world;
* an understanding of the variety of characteristics of the Earth's landscapes and climates;
* an understanding and appreciation of the variety of ways of life of people;
* an understanding of the relationships between people and environments; that the environment influences people and that people can use and alter their environment in different ways;
* an understanding that human activities are influenced by location (where you are influences what goes on there);
* an understanding that people, places and environments are interrelated;
* the development of a 'sense of place' — a feeling for what it might be like to live in a particular place.

These aims involve what has come to be seen as a basic trilogy of geographical education: the acquisition of knowledge, the development of skills and the formation of attitudes and values, even though these three are more closely interconnected than is often acknowledged.

From Near to Far

A useful model (figure 1.1) for considering knowledge and understanding of places has been provided by Goodey (1973). The model is useful because it differentiates between two sorts of experience in relation to places. The

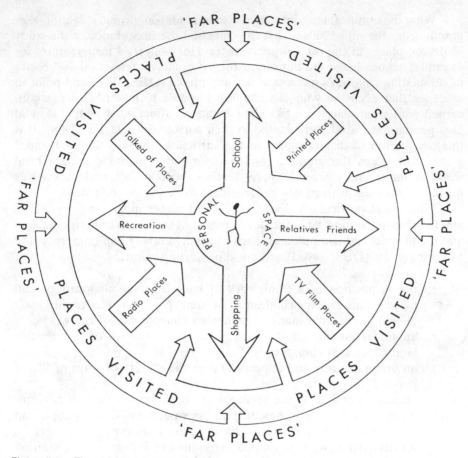

Figure 1.1: The child in information space

Source: Goodey, 1973, p. 7

first is *direct* experience, obtained through first-hand encounters. Children are located in their own 'personal space' which they experience directly through play and interaction with their immediate surroundings. With age the extent of their 'known world' increases as they attend school, visit friends and relatives and go on holidays. But they also come to know places through *indirect* experience. This vicarious (or 'second-hand') experience is obtained through, for example, television and books. The distinction between these two types of experience is, however, more apparent than real. Children have, for example, direct experience of foreign influences in their local environment, through shop products, architecture and the experiences of their peers. Nevertheless, the perceptual map that results from such experiences is unique to each individual and depends on the individual's movements, perceptual abilities and the information received.

There are two principal aspects to the way information about distant places is transmitted — what places get mentioned and what the information about each place consists of (Burgess and Gold, 1985). The selection of places reported by the news media is biased. Some places are mentioned more than others and some places are not mentioned at all. This seems to hold true for a number of countries and at a variety of scales (Cole and Whysall, 1968; Walmsley, 1982). The typical method used in investigations such as these is to count up the number of mentions of separate places in a particular newspaper or news bulletin and map those places so that each country is shown in a size proportional to the number of mentions it has received. The content of place information is also frequently distorted through 'promotional literature'. Travel brochures have been known to be economical with the truth. One plus one, it has been said, equals, according to many estate agents, a spacious three, and with some imagination, four. Place promotion however, is an important part of regional economic development as well as of tourism. In order to attract businesses to the target location advertisers may have to work hard to counteract widespread myths and stereotypes held about places — for example that Milton Keynes is an undesirable place to live or that Wigan is a music hall joke.

Much work has been done in recent years on the nature of children's understanding of their immediate locality. Some evidence suggests that children remember landmarks that are of particular interest or importance to them in finding their way around their home area (Siegal and White, 1975). They then relate information about routes to these landmarks and subsequently form 'minimaps' which eventually become coordinated into some larger and more complete mental representation of their environment. On the other hand, very young children do appear to be able to remember routes without paying much prior attention to significant landmarks at all (Darvizeh and Spencer, 1984). The whole field of children's increasing spatial awareness and competence has been fully and clearly explored by Spencer, Blades and Morsley (1989). But how far does the immediate locality extend? The definition of this area has generally been referred to as the child's 'home range' and has been investigated in some detail by Hart (1979). Gender, for example, appears to make some difference to the extent of children's knowledge and experience of their immediate locality. Hart's investigations showed that the home range of boys was substantially greater than that of girls. Parents generally allowed boys more freedom to explore the neighbourhood and were more inclined to turn a blind eye when they went 'beyond bounds'.

International Understanding

'International understanding' is perhaps the most convenient label to apply to children's knowledge and understanding of distant places, but the term

needs further clarification. It is also sometimes called international education, although that term refers more usually to education that takes place *in*
other countries, (as, for example, in international schools). Note too, that
the abbreviation EIU, which formerly stood for Education for International
Understanding is now used more widely in the National Curriculum literature for Economic and Industrial Understanding. The term 'international
understanding' was made popular by the 1974 UNESCO *Recommendation
Concerning Education for International Understanding, Cooperation and
Peace and Education Relating to Human Rights and Fundamental Freedoms*.
This recommendation states that the following objectives should be the
guiding principles of the educational policy of all member states:

(a)   an international dimension and a global perspective in education
      at all levels and in all forms;
(b)   understanding and respect for all peoples, their cultures, civiliza-
      tions, values and ways of life, including domestic ethnic cultures
      and cultures of other nations;
(c)   awareness of the increasing global interdependence between
      peoples and nations;
(d)   abilities to communicate with others;
(e)   awareness not only of the rights but also of the duties incumbent
      upon individuals, social groups and nations towards each other;
(f)   understanding of the necessity for international solidarity and
      cooperation;
(g)   readiness on the part of the individual to participate in solving the
      problems of his (sic) community, his country and the world at
      large.

The significance of this statement is that it includes not just knowledge and
awareness of distant places but also empathy for the people of other countries and their ways of life and preparedness for action towards making the
world a better place in which to live. The United Kingdom is, of course, a
signatory to this recommendation and key organizations within the UK that
have promoted international understanding are the Council for Education in
World Citizenship (for a full discussion of this body see Heater, 1984) and
the Standing Conference for Education for International Understanding.

   Education for international understanding is more than just a school
'subject'. It is a reform *movement* which consists of a number of identifiable
conceptualizations or sub-movements with such labels as world studies,
development education and peace education. Heater (1980), Hicks and
Townley (1982) and Lynch (1989) have each identified a number of such
sub-movements and discussed the relationships that exist between them.
Capps (1986) has also presented an account of the evolution of the working
concepts of global and multicultural education. Each of these separate
reforming initiatives has attempted to influence the education system by

setting up its own teacher networks and publicising what it regards as good practice. This work has been facilitated by teacher centres (such as the network of Development Education Centres) and many of these centres have published resources for use in the classroom. Each identifiable part of the larger education for international understanding community tends to have its own membership, conferences, literature and journals, but many of these groups share a set of common goals and aspirations and there is in fact much overlap between them. Indeed, in recent years there has been much greater emphasis on their common concerns and various attempts have been made to subsume separate traditions under a single label such as 'Earth-rights' (or education 'as if the planet really mattered') by Greig, Pike and Selby (1987) and 'global multicultural education' (Lynch, 1989). Development, environmental issues and peace are now more often regarded as being interconnected and interdependent both in the world political arena and the classroom.

What now follows is a brief account of each of these main initiatives and approaches, to illustrate how some of the networks are sustained. I shall begin with geography because of its established status as a foundation subject in the National Curriculum.

Geographical Education

'Geography is, perhaps, the most obvious subject for the promotion of Education for International Understanding' (Council for Education in World Citizenship, 1987). However, prior to the introduction of the National Curriculum, geography in primary school had suffered 'much neglect' (DES, 1990d) and HMI reports on primary education in the 1970s and 1980s consistently pointed to generally unsatisfactory standards of work. Common observations during this period were that the work was superficial, repetitive and that available resources were barely adequate. Geography appears, in the pre-National Curriculum era at least, to have been principally taught in association with other subjects as part of topic or thematic work. Whilst such topic work in itself was often seen by HMI to be 'reasonably satisfactory', there was a tendency for the distinctive contribution that geography can make to be lost and opportunities for developing geographical skills (such as those relating to maps and atlases) were rarely taken. HMI frequently indicated their concern that a 'continuous experience' of geography was missing and raised the question of inadequate progression in the children's work and weak differentiation of tasks for pupils of different abilities. (see, for example, HMI, 1989). In particular, the monitoring of children's progress has received very little attention and recent work on assessment in the humanities (Blyth, 1990) is to be welcomed.

The National Curriculum does much to strengthen the position of geography in the primary school and the specification of attainment targets and levels of attainment will be helpful to teachers planning topic work. Teacher support in geographical education is available from the Geographical Association (see appendix) which has a growing list of publications for primary teachers and a journal (*Primary Geographer*) offering suggestions for classroom activities. The Geographical Association's (free) annual conference at Easter includes a 'primary day' at which there are workshops and seminars and a comprehensive publishers' exhibition of resources for teaching.

Broad accounts of the current state of the art in geography in the primary school may be found in Mills (1988), Blyth (1984), ILEA (1981) and Bale (1987).

World Studies (or, in America, Global Studies)

The central organizing concept of world studies is interdependence. It emphasizes the need to see the world as a single, interrelated system or 'global village', because the human and environmental problems we face are recognized as being interconnected at a world scale. World studies includes:

(a) studying cultures and countries other than one's own, and the ways in which they are different from, and similar to, one's own;
(b) studying major issues which face different countries and cultures, for example those to do with peace and conflict, development, human rights and the environment;
(c) studying the ways in which everyday life and experience affect, and are affected by, the wider world. (Fisher and Hicks, 1985, p. 8)

But world studies is not defined by content alone. It is a vigorously proselytizing movement supporting 'active' teaching methods such as role play, games and simulations. These experiential activities, it is claimed, help pupils to learn more about the world by understanding more about human nature.

The term 'world studies' has gained currency in the UK principally through the work of the *World Studies Project* set up by the One World Trust from 1973 to 1980. Its characteristic approach of pupil-centred activities may be seen in publications such as the influential *Learning for Change in World Society* (1977). The World Studies Project was followed by the joint Schools Council/Rowntree Trust Project *World Studies 8–13*, which has been fully described in Hicks and Townley (1982) and Fisher and Hicks (1985). Also of significance in the field of world studies through its courses and publications is the Centre for Global Education at the University of York (see appendix), which publishes the *World Studies Journal* (see also, for example, Pike and Selby, 1988). An excellent survey of the scope and justification for world studies is provided by Heater (1980).

The European Dimension in Education

In the early 1990s, education about Europe began to figure more prominently in school curricula in Great Britain. There had been massive political and social changes in Eastern Europe and much publicity for the forthcoming single market of the European Community. Greater attention was being paid to European affairs in the media (such as the publication of *The European* newspaper and the Europe section of *The Guardian*). But what is 'Europe'? The concept is both geographically and politically diffuse. The definition of Europe in most British people's minds is probably the European Community but increasingly the concept has come to be seen more broadly, to include not only the countries of Eastern Europe but also the Soviet Union (especially following Gorbachev's 1989 reference to 'our common European home' as the Cold War drew to a close.)

Perhaps the clearest statement of the 'European dimension' in education and its objectives is to be found in the resolution of the Ministers of Education meeting within the European Council (European Council, 1988). This resolution set out a number of measures which were designed to:

— strengthen in young people a sense of European identity and make clear to them the value of European civilization and of the foundations on which the European peoples intend to base their development today, that is in particular the safeguarding of the principles of democracy, social justice and respect for human rights;
— prepare young people to take part in the economic and social development of the Community and in making concrete progress towards European union, as stipulated in the European Single Act;
— make them aware of the advantages which the Community represents, but also of the challenges it involves, in opening up an enlarged economic and social area to them;
— improve their knowledge of the Community and its member states in their historical, cultural, economic and social aspects and bring home to them the significance of the cooperation of the Member States of the European Community with other countries of Europe and the world.
(European Council, 1988)

This resolution determined that member states should each set out in a policy document how they would incorporate the European dimension in schools and colleges, encourage initiatives that would foster the European dimension, strengthen its profile in teaching materials and give it greater emphasis in teacher training. The inclusion of the European Dimension in the National Curriculum and in the criteria for the approval of courses of initial teacher training is the practical expression in England and Wales of this resolution.

However, the major difficulty with the European dimension in education for many people is that its scope for international understanding is limited by definition to Europe alone! It is also not always clear whether the objectives of such study are instrumental or enriching:

> Is European Awareness, including the development of language skills, principally concerned with buying and selling, manufacturing and earning one's living? Or is it also a means of understanding and enjoying the cultural and social achievements of other countries and thus part of a general education and personal enrichment? (Slater, 1990, p. 4)

The European dimension in the United Kingdom is supported by a number of initiatives at both community and government level. One of the best examples of such initiatives is the pilot project funded by the Department of Education and Science to generate policy models for the promotion of European awareness in schools and colleges in twelve local education authorities (*ibid*). The experience of the twelve pilot authorities suggests that as there is no clear definition of what European awareness *is*, an important starting point for LEAs wishing to develop policy is to clarify for themselves a working definition and rationale for European awareness before examining carefully existing opportunities for its development in the school curriculum. Several local education authorities now have policies and specialist advisors for European education.

Advice and information about the European dimension is provided by the United Kingdom Centre for European Education (UKCEE) (see appendix). This is a grant-aided organization which is part of a network of centres in each Community country which seeks to promote a European perspective in education. As well as dealing with requests for information from schools and member organizations, it supports conferences, seminars and curriculum development and has published a termly bulletin called EUROED NEWS, designed to disseminate throughout the UK, information on teaching about Europe. This was replaced in 1991 by a new journal: EDIT (The European Dimension in Teaching). Since 1989 the UKCEE has been part of the Central Bureau for Educational Visits and Exchanges.

There have been a number of attempts to develop teaching materials and strategies for teaching about Europe within the EC. Perhaps the most notable is the Europe in the Primary School project (see Bell, 1979, 1987 and Bell, 1989; Bell and Lloyd, 1989; Bell, Miles and Ovens, 1989). This is a project which aimed to encourage teacher-based studies on practical problems arising from teaching about Europe in primary school classrooms. The work is described as action research units designed to stimulate cooperation between teachers and teacher trainers.

The study of Europe in primary schools was weakened by the Secretary of State when he reduced the programme of study for Key Stage 2 following the National Curriculum Council's consultation report. The Geography working group and the National Curriculum Council itself had recommended the study of two contrasting regions within a European Community country. Only one *compulsory* European locality now remains — at level 5, i.e. for only the most able children in primary schools.

Development Education

Development Education deals with the conditions of progress and the means to achieve a better quality of life. It had its origins in concern for the Third World and the publication of the Brandt Report in 1980 was especially influential in alerting teachers to its curriculum priorities. However, the term 'development' has increasingly been broadened. Many people now feel that there has in the past been too much preoccupation with *economic* development and prefer to widen the thrust of this movement to include human welfare expressed more comprehensively. 'The object of development education is to enable us to comprehend and participate in the development of ourselves, our community, our nation and the world' (National Association of Development Education Centres, 1980). The term 'third world' could be used therefore to describe not just economically poor nations but also those groups who are marginalized in *wealthy* countries, for example people who are unemployed as well as elderly, homeless, poor or oppressed people.

Development education also includes a consideration of how the more economically developed nations might develop further. It is concerned to indicate how the West can learn from non-Western perspectives on development and to show that what is appropriate development in one context is not necessarily appropriate in another.

Development education has largely been facilitated by a number of resource and information centres which provide speakers, courses, audio visual aids and publications. Many were established and financed by committees drawn from a variety of voluntary agencies. The Development Education Centre at Birmingham is especially active. It produces a newsletter, *The Elephant Times*, and set up a Primary School project in 1983. This project, still current in 1991, has developed teaching approaches and resources for primary schools as well as providing in-service support for teachers. The project is evaluated and reviewed in Combes (1990) and its most substantial publications (*Theme Work*, *Hidden Messages* and *A Sense of School*) are based on ideas developed by the project team (McFarlane, 1986). The Centre for World Development Education (see appendix) has a broader focus. It aims to stimulate interest and awareness about development both within the education system and amongst the public at large. It plays a coordinating role for many non-governmental organizations and distributes publications.

Multicultural Education

Multicultural education is principally concerned with the development of better community relations in a domestic, i.e. national context. In Western Europe it grew from the increasingly multiethnic character of (especially) city areas as a result of mass migration in the 1950s and 1960s. Its main imperatives are equality of opportunity, a commitment to counteracting prejudice and an attempt to view cultural diversity as a positive attribute of society. It has generated more tension than other educational reform movements because its focus of concern is more immediate — and local. Such tension has been maintained by the presence of endemic racism in society but multicultural education is much strengthened by official support at the Department of Education and Science. As a result, multicultural education probably has more currency in everyday teacher talk than the other education reform movements described in this chapter. Preparation for life in a multicultural society has been identified by the National Curriculum Council as an important cross-curricular dimension. It is, of course, equally relevant (some would say more so) for children and schools not located in urban and multiethnic areas. For an excellent source book on developing anti-racist education in predominantly white primary schools, see Epstein and Sealey (1990).

Multicultural education is relevant to the study of distant places because one of its approaches has been to teach more about the customs, traditions and countries of origin of UK ethnic minority groups. But this view has not always been espoused by some members of minority communities who have preferred not to locate the curriculum too strongly in their past. Some writers have claimed that multicultural education has been guilty of narrow parochialism, restricting attention to one nation only and omitting the global dimension (Lynch, 1989). The Swann Report on the education of children from ethnic minority groups makes its own position quite clear on this issue:

> In our view, an education which seeks only to emphasise and enhance the ethnic group identity of a child, at the expense of developing both a national and indeed an international, global perspective, cannot be regarded as in any way multicultural. (Secretary of State for Education and Science, 1985, p. 32)

There are a number of organizations promoting anti-racist education. The Commission for Racial Equality helps enforce the legislation of the Race Relations Act, 1976 and is a principal source of information and advice. It publishes material relating to racism and multicultural education in schools.

Environmental Education

Environmental education studies the planet as a life-support system and the threats that are posed to it. Teaching and learning about the environment is currently characterized by the recognition that *local* environments are part of the *global* ecosystem and that the world's environmental problems (for example North Sea pollution or acid rain) cannot be solved by nations acting in isolation from one another.

The attention of the world was drawn to a more holistic global concern for environmental issues after publication of the declaration by the United Nations Intergovernmental Conference on Environmental Education in Tbilisi, USSR, in 1977 and the publication by the International Union for the Conservation of Nature (IUCN) of the *World Conservation Strategy* (1980). Both of these documents emphasized the interdependence of human and physical systems, for example:

> By adopting a holistic approach rooted in a broad interdisciplinary base, it, (i.e. environmental education) recreates an overall per-spective which acknowledges the fact that natural environment and man-made environment are profoundly interdependent. It helps reveal the enduring continuity which links the acts of today to the consequences of tomorrow. It demonstrates the interdependencies among national communities and the need for solidarity among all mankind. (Tbilisi declaration, 1977)

Objectives in environmental education often centre on what can be done to create environment-friendly values in children and foster the development of political decision making strategies. The provision of education about, for and through the environment in England and Wales was much strengthened by the definition of environmental education as a cross-curricular theme. However, the virtual total removal of pupils' exploration of attitudes and values from the environmental geography attainment target by the Secretary of State against the advice of both the National Curriculum Geography Working Group and the National Curriculum Council led most observers to doubt the Government's commitment.

The Council for Environmental Education (see appendix) is a coordinating body for more than fifty environmental and educational organizations. It has a regular *News-sheet* and publishes the *Review of Environmental Education Developments*. Friends of the Earth and the World Wide Fund for Nature provide support for schools on global environmental education.

Human Rights Education

Human rights education deals with the concept of justice. It developed from the American Civil Rights Movement and its cause has been fuelled by oppression in (amongst other places) South America, the Soviet Union and South Africa. Its relevance to the study of distant places is that human rights are the responsibility of everyone, not just those living in the countries where such gross oppression occurs ('No man is an island . . .'). Teachers in the United Kingdom have been slow to espouse human rights education and where they have, they have concentrated more on civil and political rights (such as freedom of speech) than social and economic rights (such as the right to food and shelter). The 'set text' for Human Rights education is the Universal Declaration of Human Rights as presented to the General Assembly of the United Nations in Paris in 1948 (United Nations, 1948). Its thirty articles deal with individual freedoms relating, for example, to education, marriage, property, thought and religion. Some years later, UNESCO formulated a recommendation concerning Education for Human Rights and Fundamental Freedoms (1974). This outlines the major aims and objectives of Human Rights education, including an international dimension to all forms of education which embraces understanding and respect for all peoples, their cultures, civilizations, values and ways of life. Significantly, it also stresses duties and responsibilities as well as rights.

Further suggestions for teaching and learning about human rights in schools are taken up by the Council of Europe Committee of Ministers (1985). This particular formulation stresses intercultural and international understanding. A case for the centrality of human rights in education is made by Lynch (1989).

Peace Education

Peace education not only emphasizes interrelationships between nations but also the propensity of people to be violent. It attempts to sharpen awareness about the existence of conflict within and between individuals as well as nations. Much peace education therefore is related not only to the study of other countries but also to human relationships at the level of the individual and the group. Increasingly, peace educators have looked not just at 'negative peace', that is at ways in which wars can be avoided, but 'positive peace', that is ways in which social justice may be created within and between societies. Peace education, like world studies, is particularly associated with the use of learning situations that involve active participation as well as cooperation between learners. This quality of the relationships between learners is considered to be an important part of learning about peace. This is based on the premise that individuals need to learn about themselves, their personalities and aggressive inclinations and to explore how they can live harmoniously with other people.

Peace education in Britain has received much criticism from the political right, most notably from Cox and Scruton (1984) and Scruton (1986).

Their contentions that peace studies is, for example, indoctrinatory, likely to inculcate guilt and is non-beneficial have been refuted by White (1988).

Peace education has been much strengthened in Britain by the centre for Peace Studies at St. Martin's College, Lancaster, and in particular the writings of David Hicks (see for example a general work on issues, principles and classroom practice in peace education, 1988).

Citizenship

The definition of citizenship is somewhat problematic. The Report of the Commission on Citizenship (1990) found a good starting point in a definition by Marshall (1950) which includes a strong social element reflecting a particularly British view of the concept. According to Marshall, citizenship is

> a status bestowed on all those who are full members of a community. All who possess the status are equal with respect to the rights and duties with which that status is endowed. (*ibid*, p. 28)

Three elements of rights are involved in this definition: *civil* rights necessary for individual freedom, the right to *participate* in the exercise of political power and a range of *social* rights ranging from rights to welfare and sharing in the cultural heritage of society. The emerging definition of citizenship adopted by the National Curriculum Council (1990) has its roots in the Law in Education project of the 1980s in the United Kingdom. Like environmental education, this theme is seen by the National Curriculum Council to have a strong global and international aspect. Pupils should, for example, develop knowledge and understanding of the national, European and worldwide community and study the diversity of cultures in other societies. They should also study the means by which other countries ensure the rights of their citizens and how attempts have been made in the twentieth century to promote international and global cooperation.

Places Across the National Curriculum

As we have seen, there have been a number of different approaches to teaching and learning about places. Each of these has added its own distinctive perspective to the literature and the stock of resources available to the teacher. The educational aims and preferred classroom activities of these various sub-movements have been compared by Richardson (1974). According to Richardson, there are three underlying political and ideological stances which cut across all the approaches identified above. These are:

    (a)   conservative-classical
    (b)   liberal-progressive
    (c)   radical-socialist

The conservative-classical approach tends to be characterized by a nationalist perspective and a didactic or transmissive teaching style. The purpose of this type of education according to Richardson is to foster loyalty to one's *own nation*. Those who adopt the liberal-progressive stance tend to use enquiry based learning methods and aim to foster loyalty to the *global* community. The radical-socialist position engages pupils in experiential learning such as empathy-raising activities. The aim here is to develop in pupils the will and the skills to become politically active in achieving *global justice*. These three ideological stances underpin the research into children's understanding of people and places described in chapters 2 and 3 as well as the classroom activities described in chapter 6.

As has been implied, each approach requires a greater or lesser degree of commitment by the teacher to the idea of a global education. But where is the study of places to be found in the National Curriculum for England and Wales? Figure 1.2 lists some references in the core and foundation subject documentation (Statutory Orders and working party reports) available at the time of writing. Particular reference is made to distant places. The number and letter codes refer to subjects, Attainment Targets and Levels of Attainment. Note that some children will achieve level 5 by the end of Key Stage 2, but by no means all.

Places at Key Stage 1

The unit of place that is emphasized at Key Stage 1 is that of the *locality*. This is a small area, at a scale understandable by very young children. In the case of the local area it would be the immediate vicinity of the school and where the pupils live. At Key Stage 1 pupils have to increase their understanding of localities in, and beyond, their own country. The statutory orders for geography say that pupils have to study:

* the local area
* a locality in the United Kingdom which offers a contrast to the local area
* a locality beyond the United Kingdom.

More specifically, pupils should be taught:

* to name where they live
* to identify and name familiar features in the locality of their school
* to name the country in which they live

Pupils should be able to:

Level 1

* observe and talk about a familiar place (Gg/1/1b)
* state where they live (Gg/2/1c)
* demonstrate an awareness of the world beyond their local area (Gg/2/1d)
* name the country in which they live (Gg/2/1e)
* listen attentively to stories and poems (including examples from different cultures) (Eg/1/1)

Level 2

* use geographical vocabulary to talk about places (Gg/1/2a)
* name the countries of the United Kingdom (Gg/2/2a)
* identify features of a locality outside the local area and suggest how these might affect the lives of the people who live there (Gg/2/2c)
* describe similarities and differences in land use, landscape and weather between the local area and another locality specified in the programme of study (Gg/2/2d)
* listen attentively to stories and poems (including those from other cultures) and talk about them (Eg/1/2)
* make simple judgments about familiar artifacts, systems or environments, including those from other cultures (DT/4/2b)

Level 3

* name the features marked on maps A and C (see figures 1.3a and 1.3c) (Gg/2/3a)
* demonstrate that they know the location of their local area within the country in which they live (Gg/2/3b)
* compare features and occupations of the local area with the other localities specified in the programme of study (Gg/2/3d)
* describe contrasting weather conditions in parts of the world (Gg/3/3a)
* pupils should be able to generate a design specification and draw from information about other cultures to help in developing their ideas (DT/2/3c)

Level 4

* use the index and contents pages to find information in an atlas (Gg/1/4e)
* name the features marked on maps B and D (see figures 1.3b and 1.3d) (Gg/2/4a)
* describe how the landscape of a locality outside the local area has been changed by human actions (Gg/2/4b)
* describe the geographical features of the home region (Gg/2/4d)
* describe how the daily life of a locality in an economically developing country is affected by its landscape, weather and wealth (Gg/2/4e)
* specify location by means of coordinates (Ma/11/4)
* know that in other cultures people use design and technology to solve familiar problems in different ways (DT/1/4f)
* comment upon existing artifacts, systems or environments, and those from other cultures, including appearance and use of resources (DT/4/4c)

Level 5

* name the features marked on maps E and F (see figures 1.3e and 1.3f) (Gg/2/5a)
* explain how the occupations, land use and settlement patterns of a locality outside the United Kingdom are related to environment and location (Gg/2/5c)
* demonstrate an awareness that the globe can be represented as a flat surface (Gg/1/5e)
* understand that the differences in physical factors between localities, including differences in seasonal and daily changes, are reflected in the different species of plants and animals found there. (Sc/2/5)
* understand that artifacts, systems or environments from other cultures have identifiable characteristics and styles and draw upon this knowledge in design and technology activities (DT/4/5)

Figure 1.2: Some references to places in the National Curriculum

Figure 1.3:   The 'World to be Known' of the National Curriculum (a) The British Isles

Figure 1.3: The 'World to be Known' of the National Curriculum (b) Europe

* that their country is part of the United Kingdom, which is made up of England, Wales, Scotland and Northern Ireland
* to identify features of, and talk about, places outside the local area
* to investigate the use of land and buildings in the local area
* to investigate features of localities outside the local area; identify the features of, and talk about, places outside the local area; and investigate how these features might affect people's lives
* to identify and describe similarities and differences between their local area and other localities.

Where possible, teaching should build on direct experience of visits made (for example on holiday) but children should also have the opportunity to

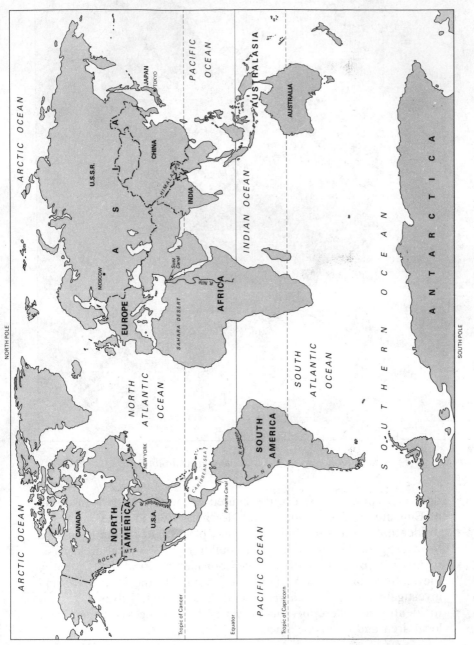

Figure 1.3: The 'World to be Known' of the National Curriculum (c) The World

Figure 1.3: The 'World to be Known' of the National Curriculum (d) The British Isles

Figure 1.3:   The 'World to be Known' of the National Curriculum (e) Europe

use simple maps, atlases and globes, as well as stories, videos, photographs and pictures in order to find out more about distant places. The observational skills of using photographs (for example, to find out about plants and animals in other places, as well as to consider similarities and differences between their own way of life and that of others) are central to science at Key Stage 1. Children are also to investigate in science, ways of making and experiencing sounds by using simple musical instruments from a variety of cultures.

In English, all 3 profile components (speaking and listening, reading and writing) have scope for teaching and learning about distant places. Children should listen and respond to stories, rhymes, poems and songs, and these are specifically to include examples from different cultures. The

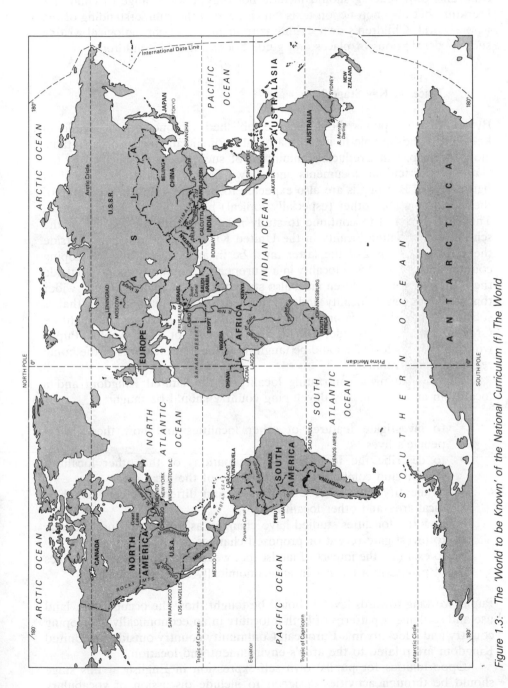

Figure 1.3: The 'World to be Known' of the National Curriculum (f) The World

children's own reading should include not only a wide range of children's literature but also non-fiction texts which deepen their understanding of the whole world. Children's own writing is to include non-chronological writing such as descriptions of places and guide books for other children.

Places at Key Stage 2

By Key Stage 2 pupils should have established a framework of locational knowledge and be able to identify a number of specific places on a suitable globe or map. An irreducible minimum of such places is specified in the National Curriculum documents and shown in the 'world-to-be-known' of figure 1.3a–f. But pupils are also expected to be able to locate on a map of the world or globe, other (especially topical) places that they learn about. They are expected to continue to study in some depth the locality of the school, a contrasting locality in the United Kingdom and a locality outside the UK. For levels 2–4 the latter must be in an economically developing country and, by level 5, a locality in a European Community country outside the UK. By level 4, children must also study the 'home region'. This is wider than the immediate locality and is intended to encompass an area that is substantial in either area or population. Examples of such regions might be Greater London, Tyneside, Devon and Cornwall or East Anglia. Pupils working towards level 5 should be taught how the main features of the home region are interrelated.

Pupils studying a contrasting locality in the United Kingdom and a locality in an economically developing country should be taught:

* to investigate features of other localities and how these affect people's lives
* to describe the features and occupations of the other localities studied and compare them with those of the local area
* to identify and describe similarities and differences between their local area and other localities
* how the localities studied have changed as a result of local actions
* to investigate recent or proposed changes in a locality
* to examine the impact of landscape, weather and wealth on the lives of people in a locality in an economically developing country

Pupils working towards level 5 should be taught: how the occupations, land use and settlement patterns of both a locality in an economically developing country and a locality in a European Community country outside the United Kingdom are related to the area's environment and location.

Opportunities for pupils' own self-expression in English at this stage should be through activities designed to include discussion of vocabulary that is specific to place (such as words for local and distant places, types of natural environment and buildings) and occupations. This vocabulary is extensive and ranges from elementary descriptions of landscape (such as 'mountains' and 'valleys', through more difficult concepts such as 'rolling hills' to specific place concepts such as 'savanna' and 'tundra'. The terminology of patterns and distributions as shown on a map is similarly complex and needs careful attention to its development. Practice will be needed in using descriptions such as 'sparsely' or 'densely' populated. Fiction, non-fiction and poetry provide opportunities for the study of distant places as seen through the eyes of other people and the English statutory orders make specific reference to fiction from other cultures. First hand accounts of exploration and good travel writing are sources of stimulation to readers. Folk tales and fables might include translations from original sources. Pupils are also to be shown how to 'search read' a text for (for example) a geographical fact. Pupils' non-chronological writing at Key Stage 2 should include opportunities to produce extended written texts such as guide books to places. There is also scope in the study of distant places though for imaginative as well as factual writing.

Work in mathematics relates to international understanding through, for example Attainment Targets 10 and 11 (shape and space) and 12 and 13 (handling data). For Key Stage 2 children need to be able to sort two-dimensional shapes. Cut-out country outlines could be used for this purpose and for the development of mathematical language of size and shape. Many mathematical concepts built on this early language development such as distance, direction, area, size and scale are crucial to international understanding. Children are also required to be able to extract information from tables and lists and to enter and access information using a simple database. They also need to be able to construct and interpret bar charts and graphs. At Key Stage 2 children can design a data collection sheet for information about other countries, store this information in a computer database and subsequently interrogate it. They can also investigate the probability of, say, rainfall and temperature in different parts of the world, basing their decisions on climate graphs. Reference is made in the mathematics programme of study for Key Stage 2 to the need for children to be able to specify location by coordinates. The location of places successfully in atlases depends on being able to handle coordinates properly.

In science, for Key Stage 2 children should explore and investigate at least two different localities and the ways in which the animals and plants that live there are suited to their location. They should also be able to follow a simple model of the solar system to explain day and night, the seasons and time zones.

In technology (design and technology capability) pupils are required to learn about other environments and cultures. Pupils should be taught, for example, at Key Stage 2 to consider the needs and values of individuals and groups from a variety of backgrounds and cultures when appraising artifacts, systems and environments made by others. The programme of study makes much explicit reference to the design and technology of other cultures, for example, Islamic art, Greek theatre design, crop irrigation techniques in other countries. Children should be able to draw from information about materials, people, markets and processes in other cultures in order to develop their ideas in design and technology.

Selection of Content

Although the National Curriculum provides much directional guidance there are still some aspects of teaching and learning about places that remain at least partly unresolved. One such issue relates to the selection of curriculum content.

Consider, for example, the 'framework of locational knowledge'. This framework is seen as an essential structure into which children can fit 'new' places as they become known. As shown above, some of this place knowledge is quite clearly specified and has been identified on maps in the National Curriculum documents (figures 1.3a–f). But the selection of other places to be studied remains at the discretion of the teacher. Some guidance is provided — for example a locality must be chosen for study from 'outside the UK' or 'an economically developing country'. But within the limited freedom allowed, what principles should determine the selection of places for study? Hard choices may have to be made if limited time is available. Are some places 'more important' than others? And how do you judge that importance? Is it something to do with area or population or wealth or whether there are, or have been, strong links with Britain through tourism or trade or because they happen to be near us? To what extent would you agree that children living outside London should study part of the capital as their 'contrasting locality in the UK'? Are there some countries of which a study would be more instructive for 'international understanding'? Places could, for example, be selected on the basis of whether or not they are 'like' our own. But what are the dimensions of like us/not like us? Landscapes? Economy? Political system? Or places could be selected on the basis of the experience of children in the class. If many children have been to Spain, or have family connections with India, those places might be good as starters, to be balanced later with the study of a place which few children in the class know about. But what about world coverage? Should every Continent be represented in the places selected for detailed study? Balance has to be achieved between doing more places in depth at the expense of 'world coverage' or giving a broader (but correspondingly shallower) view of the world and its peoples. Should countries chosen for study be those most often in the news because of their seemingly endless social and political problems such as the countries of the Middle East or South Africa? Yet another criterion might be the availability of information. Some countries are very successful at promoting themselves and in making materials available for teachers. (The Information and Documentation Centre for the Geography of the Netherlands or the Japan Education Centre are examples of organizations that provide high quality materials.) But detailed case study information about some countries is almost impossible to obtain. The teacher's own travel experience is clearly a significant factor in selecting curriculum content but we tend to travel selectively and a curriculum comprised of distant places which are based entirely on Miss's holiday slides is clearly undesirable.

'Coverage' of the world has always been a problem for geographers in school and the freedom (albeit limited) of teachers to choose places selected for study in the primary school reawakens some of those issues.

A 'Sense of Place'

One of the intentions for geography in the National Curriculum was that children should develop a 'sense of place' — that is a feeling for the 'personality' of a place, together with a sense of the range of diversity of places around the world (DES, 1990d). This diversity is a result of landscape, economy, culture and political systems and pupils should be able to identify ways in which specific places differ from their own home area.

But what exactly is 'a sense of place' and what does it mean to 'know' about places? An attempt is made in this book to describe the sorts of information and knowledge that children have of distant places but the terms 'information' and 'knowledge' are deceptive. This book is about what children *believe* to be true about faraway places. It is about the subjective impressions and beliefs they hold. These may come from their own travel or from the media, from their peers, from stories, from parents. The images children have may be clear or muddled, stable or fleeting, probable or improbable. They may refer to 'facts' or 'attitudes'. What makes the study of these images more complicated (and more interesting) is that they cannot be measured against some adult, end-state, 'accurate' image of the world for no one image, whether held by an individual or a group, can be 'truer' than another. We each see and construct our own picture of how we think the world is through our own assumptions, experiences and values.

The study of people's knowledge and understanding of their environment (both near and far) is complex, and the terms used to describe it (such as 'environmental cognition', 'environmental knowing' and 'environmental perception') have been applied in a confusing variety of ways. (Good summaries of the field which also illustrate its complexity may be obtained in Hart and Moore, 1973; Cohen, 1985; Moore and Golledge, 1976; Downs and Stea 1977).

Many such studies deal with 'maps in minds' and have been principally concerned with how people function in the urban environment. Several different disciplines, such as geography, psychology, sociology, anthropology and urban planning, have contributed to this field. Kevin Lynch's seminal *Image of the City* (1960) was written within the field of urban planning. His book deals with how people 'read' the urban environment in order to find their way around it. Particular features of towns for example appear to form a coherent pattern in people's minds helping them to remember routes. In human geography, work on the perception of natural hazards and landscapes has demonstrated that what was *believed* to be true (rather than what was actually true) about the nature of the environment influenced the behaviour of people in it. For example, farmers perceive with greater or lesser accuracy the likelihood of drought in their region and seem to make crop decisions based on this, often faulty, perception rather than on the basis of more scientific 'evidence' such as rainfall records. Historical geography provides further examples of how images of the environment have affected behaviour in the past. The 'Great American Desert' (Bowden, 1976) existed for years in the minds of those first white explorers of the central parts of the USA before it was shown that no such desert existed. First accounts were recorded at a time of very low rainfall and this early evidence about what is now some of the most productive ranch and farmland in the continent was translated into descriptions of desert on early maps of North America. What underpins all such studies is the fundamental argument that:

(a) images of the environment exist in the minds of individuals and groups;
(b) that these images can be accurately identified; and that
(c) these images in some way influence people's actual behaviour.

Two examples may be used to illustrate different research traditions in the process of investigating the world that exists inside people's heads. The first is from that branch of geography known as behavioural geography.

Gould and White, in a highly influential book, *Mental Maps* (1974), asked people in a number of European countries to record their preferences in rank order for other countries in Europe. The preference systems of different national groups appeared to be distinctive. The Swedes for example, expressed a strong preference for other Scandinavian countries as well as Switzerland, France and Britain. Their view was almost identical to that of the British, who also shared the Swedish dislike of Eastern European countries. The Italian sample, on the other hand, revealed a strong preference for countries with Latin languages (such as France and Spain) whereas the French were the most divided amongst themselves in their opinions about residential desirability of other European countries and in their views of Eastern Europe in particular. The spatial preferences of people investigated in studies such as these have been used to provide answers not only to location decisions about, for example, where to live but also to the planning of social investment — such as applying differential salaries to different places in order to attract people to less desirable areas.

The quantitative analysis of Gould and White, in which data is ranked, grouped and summed may be compared with a contrasting *phenomenological* approach. Phenomenologists argue that there is no objective world independent of human experience. 'All knowledge proceeds from the world of experience and cannot be independent of that world' (Relph, 1970, p. 193). Phenomenologists attempt to describe rather than to measure and explain. They try not to impose their own conceptual structures on what is studied but instead endeavour to achieve empathetic understanding of how individuals make meanings. Rowles' study of 'the geography of growing old' (1980) is an example of how such researchers attempt to identify people's 'private geographies'. Rowles undertook an in-depth study of five elderly individuals, seeking to immerse himself in the 'worlds of their lived experience'. Although the physical surroundings of these elderly men and women were now dilapidated and they had become themselves frail, Rowles showed that they lived 'worlds in their heads' far removed from their present circumstances:

> Stan mused on the Poland of his boyhood; Evelyn during reflective monologues participated in the affairs of a son in Arizona; all the participants frequently reminisced on events in the neighborhood of the past. (*ibid*, p. 60)

The distinction between these two approaches is an important one (Johnston, 1987). The first treats people as responders to stimuli. It tries to find out how people respond to the information they have about places and goes on to build models that can predict the likely impact of the images people hold on their behaviour. One possible end product of this sort of work is to change the environment so that people respond in a particular preferred way. The second approach treats the person as an individual who is constantly interacting with the environment. It tries to understand the nature of that interaction and to reveal it to the individual in ways that will allow the individual to become aware of the processes at work. This distinction has significance for the teaching of distant places in the primary school and relates to the aims of such teaching. One is to predispose children to think positively about other places and people. This may involve deliberate selection of stimuli on the part of the teacher and an attempt at management of pupil response. The other is an attempt to get the pupil to understand more about the processes by which places are known and attitudes are developed.

Arguably the most important book on the nature of places and how we 'know' them is Relph's *Place and Placelessness* (1976). Relph draws a distinction between experiencing places as an *insider* and as an *outsider*. These terms are applied to places in much the same way as in everyday speech. To be an insider is to have deep personal knowledge of a place and to experience a sense of belonging. Being an outsider means viewing places in a colder, more detached way. But within each of these two forms of experiencing places are levels of intensity, according to the degree of emotional involvement we might feel towards places. Thus Relph makes a classification of ways of knowing places, although it is of course possible to know places in more than one way at the same time. In the list that follows I have added exemplars of my own experiences of place to Relph's classification:

as an existential insider

To know a place like this is to know that *this* place is where you belong. It is a sense of deep attachment. To my mind it is not necessary to have had a long acquaintance with such places to experience them with existential insideness. In the pursuit of family history I visited the village of Altenfeld in Thuringia some years ago in (what was then) East Germany. Previously my known 'roots' extended back only to my grandfather. In one day I gained a family history going back to 1625, a churchyard full of dead Wiegands and a village full of (albeit distant) relatives who wanted to shake my hand. I was 'home'.

as an empathetic insider

This involves being open to the potential meanings of a place, recognizing them but not necessarily sharing them. Relph gives the example of appreciating the symbolism of a sacred place without necessarily believing in that particular religion. My children have shown me around their schools on parents' day. I have seen their classrooms, where they sit, the view they have from the window. I can feel the importance of these places for them because like everyone else, I can still recall the images of similar places once well known to me. But these places are *theirs* not mine.

as a behavioural insider

This is knowing a place by being in it and recognizing that it has distinctive characteristics that make it *this* place rather than any other. I know that when I'm in France it feels different from being in Germany. Of course it's partly the language, but its also the architecture and maintenance of the buildings, something about the rhythm of everyday life. I don't necessarily prefer one to the other and perhaps sometimes the differences are more illusory than real. Perhaps too I take special care to look out for what I perceive as being distinctively different, but nevertheless the configuration of sights, sounds, smells make for a distinctiveness.

as a vicarious insider

It is possible to experience places in a vicarious or 'secondhand' way without actually visiting them at all but for the experience to be nevertheless one which is deeply felt. The degree to which we are able to do this depends on our experience of other places as well as our imagination. We know what it is like to be *there* because we know what it is like to be elsewhere. I have not (yet) been to the United States, but I have (I think) a fair sense of what it must be like to be in New York. Not only have I seen (too many) episodes of *Kojak* and *Cagney and Lacey* but I have an idea of the land use and layout of the city as well as an indication of the likely temperatures in summer and winter. Furthermore, the experience of seeing American police dramas set in other US cities leads me to have an entirely different feeling about New York from that for, say, Los Angeles or Chicago.

as an incidental outsider
This way of 'knowing' a place pushes the place itself into the background. The place is known only because it is the location for a particular activity. Encounters with places in this way are only incidental. I have sometimes given a lecture or run a workshop in a particular teachers' centre with, regrettably, little real feeling for the locality or community. Much though I have enjoyed working with the colleagues involved, the 'place' itself consisted only of a classroom. This experience perhaps resembles that of airline flight crews whose 'travel' consists of seeing the world's tarmac and departure lounges.

as an objective outsider
Here, places are seen objectively as a collection of attributes rather than fused with personal meaning. When I taught geography I was sometimes guilty of presenting places as 'examples' of, say particular arrangements of land use or industrial or agricultural activity. With inadequate visual material and no time spent on attempting to build the 'personality' of a place (good geography teachers use travellers' tales, literature, music ...) regional studies become sterile lists. For many pupils, Dundee is 'jute, jam and journalism'. No more than that.

as an existential outsider
This involves total lack of belonging, a sense of alienation from place. Oxford is a city I visit often. But I know few of the colleges and many are closed to casual visitors. Most of the college buildings appear to turn inward and are accessible only by a small entrance guarded by a porter's lodge. Thomas Hardy in *Jude the Obscure* writes about such apparent rejection of an individual by a place. Jude leans against the walls of one of the colleges in Christminster and feels excluded from the activity within.

As well as providing a classification of the ways in which we can know places, Relph distinguishes between two attributes of places themselves: place and placelessness. The key concept here is *authenticity*. This is an elusive concept but places gain authenticity by being lived in and by being created over time unselfconsciously. One might think of a small nineteenth-century terrace house built of local stone. It might retain some characteristics of the original design and purpose but these have been modified to take account of the needs of successive occupants. Once such places acquire nostalgic value however and are consciously preserved or even artificially recreated they become inauthentic. Inauthenticity makes itself apparent when places look alike and feel alike. One city centre shopping mall for example resembles any other with the same air conditioning, Muzak and collection of predictable chain stores.

Achieving a sense of place therefore appears to be a somewhat complex goal. It involves building a framework of locational knowledge so that children know where places are. It involves providing as far as is possible, accurate 'pictures in their heads' about the nature of places and it involves an approach that fosters positive attitudes so that children are better able to appreciate what is distinctive in other localities, regions, cultures and ways of life. It has been thought by some that the concepts involved are too abstract. But much of the evidence presented below refutes this. And in any case, children's interests need to be taken into account. They are, after all, generally hugely interested in the seemingly 'difficult' concepts of, for example, space and dinosaurs. International *mis*understanding also appears to be established earlier in childhood than has been hitherto recognized. There is a dialectical relationship between children's experience of the near and the distant, between the familiar and the remote and between the directly and the indirectly experienced. What sorts of understandings about the wider world do children come to school with and how do these seem to change with maturity? The next chapters explore these issues more closely.

Chapter 2

Developmental Approaches
to the Concept of Place

and in his brain ... he hath strange places cramm'd with observation ... (*As You Like It*, II, vii, 38)

This chapter attempts to identify some ways in which children's knowledge and feelings about their own country and others changes during the primary school years. The literature in this field is complex and sometimes contradictory. This is partly because the studies reviewed here extend over a period of fifty years in several different countries and against a background of greatly changing international affairs, during which time ideas of nationhood and patriotism have become more or less salient for each country concerned. But it is also because the subject matter itself is inherently difficult to study. There are, for example, great methodological problems in attempting to identify just what children know and feel about entities (such as countries) which are conceptually fairly difficult to handle.

Much of the research related to the development of international understanding in children that is discussed below (particularly that in the 60s and 70s) has been influenced by the ideas of Jean Piaget. His theory of human development offers a fairly detailed account of *stages* through which children pass and which indicate how and when children are 'ready' to learn. Attempts to teach forms of understanding that are more appropriate to a later stage than the one the child is currently at are likely to be unsuccessful. Piaget's primary view of the workings of the mind is that 'thought is internalized action'. According to this view young children differ from adults in that they are unable to perform 'logical operations'. They have a different type of thought process and pass through a number of 'intellectual revolutions' on their way to achieving adult thought. This 'image of childhood' (the term is used by Wood, 1988) may be compared with a different, more recent perspective on children's learning — that of the child as an 'information processor'. This view represents the child's mind in a way rather similar to an information processing device in a computer. According to this perspective, children are not necessarily *incapable* of performing logical operations mentally. It is rather that they simply don't yet have enough expertise. The speed at which they deal with new information and the ways in which they store and retrieve it are not as efficient as the organizational strategies used by adults. This alternative view of the mind has been adopted by those interested in international understanding principally in the context of examining stereotypes that children hold of other peoples and will be discussed more fully in the next chapter.

It may be best to start by looking at an early paper by Piaget with Weil (1951). This is necessary, not only because the original paper is from a rather inaccessible journal, but also because the ideas it contains have underpinned much of the work in this field. Piaget's general theory can then be discussed in the light of more recent critiques before we move on to examine in more detail some particular components of international understanding.

The Piagetian Model of Understanding Places

Children's understanding of places is the result of a complex relationship between development in the cognitive and affective domains. Piaget and Weil discuss this interrelationship in the development in children of the idea of the 'homeland' and of relations with other countries. The key concept in cognitive and affective understanding of others is 'reciprocity'. Essentially, reciprocity is the ability to look at the world from someone else's point of view. It is investigated by strategies such as asking questions like:

'If you did not belong to any country, which one would you choose to belong to?'

'If I were to ask a German boy the same question, which one would he choose?'

Piaget argues that (for example) a British child might choose to be British if he/she was without nationality, making the choice on the basis of perhaps greater knowledge, or preference for the familiar. But is the child able to see that a German child might go through the same reasoning and choose to be German rather than British? Reciprocity is achieved once children are able to see that others make decisions based on how it seems to *them*, which is not necessarily the same as how things might seem to *us*.

Piaget and Weil point to what they see as a paradox in children's understanding of their homeland. This is that before understanding cognitive and affective aspects of their *own* country, children must make considerable progress in 'decentring', that is, acquire an understanding of points of view that are different from their own. This is not a smooth process but one in which children pass through clearly identifiable stages. This involves them at each stage in making adjustments to their existing ideas. These adjustments are called 'assimilation' and 'accommodation'. The child begins with the assumption that his/her ideas are the only ones possible (this stage is termed *egocentricity*), and passes through a stage of *sociocentricity* (where the prevailing attitudes of those in the child's immediate surroundings are accepted) to a stage of *reciprocity* whereby the point of view of others is understood.

Piaget and Weil asked a number of children which country they preferred, and why. Based on an analysis of their answers, three stages of development were identified.

During the first stage the young child expresses a preference for any country that takes the fancy at the time. Favourite countries are chosen by whim:

Switzerland is best because they have pretty houses.

Italy is best because they have the best cakes.

During the second stage children express preferences for their own country according to some personal criterion. This is often family loyalty:

I like Switzerland best because I was born there.

I like Switzerland best because its my own country.

At the third stage children defend their preference by referring to what Piaget and Weil call 'collective ideals of the national community'. These are abstract criteria which are more widely shared than the personal criteria underlying preferences at stage 2:

I like Switzerland best because we never have any war here.

I like Switzerland best because it's a free country.

How do children's ideas of *other* nations develop? According to Piaget and Weil, in the same way as they do for the homeland. The critical stage comes when children 'decentre' from their own original, egocentric attitude and give way to the ideas or traditions of family and society. This stage is *en route* to 'reciprocity' which requires independence of judgment. To test for reciprocity, Piaget and Weil asked each child what a foreigner was and whether they themselves could become one. Children's responses at each of the three stages outlined above can be summarized as follows (after Davies, 1968):

Questions: Do you know what a foreigner is?
Could you become one?
Is a Frenchman a foreigner in France?

Stage 1 (7/8 years)

Answer: (a) 'I don't know.'

       (b) A Swiss would never be a foreigner; there are Swiss *and* foreigners.

Stage 2 (7/8–10/11 years)

Answer: A Swiss living in another country will be treated as a foreigner, but he remains not exactly comparable with other people. A Frenchman is not a foreigner living in France but in Switzerland he is.

       (*Question*: Is he still French then?)

       Yes, but a little bit Swiss too.

Stage 3 (10/11 years plus)

Answer: A foreigner is anyone out of his own country.

Piaget and Weil conclude that children's discovery of their own nationality and their understanding of other countries is a gradual process of progressing from egocentricity to reciprocity. Cognitive reciprocity is achieved when children are able to understand that a foreigner is 'anyone out of his or her own country'. Before reaching that point they are likely to claim that they themselves could never become foreigners. Affective reciprocity is achieved when children understand that one country is not 'better' than another, that there are good and bad people everywhere, that everyone sees the world from his or her own perspective. However, this journey towards reciprocity is subject to setbacks at each stage.

Piaget and Weil's paper concludes by setting the main agenda item for teaching about distant places and people:

> the main problem is not to determine what must or must not be inculcated in the child; it is to discover how to develop that reciprocity in thought and action which is vital to the attainment of impartiality and affective understanding. (Piaget with Weil, 1951, p. 578)

Critiques of the Piagetian Approach

It has to be said, however, that Piaget's work is not without its critics. Although his ideas are powerful, there are substantial objections to his methodology.

In a critical examination of the 1951 study Jahoda (1964) commented that replication of Piaget's work was difficult because there is no adequate definition of the criteria used to assign children's responses to stages of development. Many critics of Piaget focus on the experimental conditions under which his research was conducted. Think about the young child's perception of what he/she is being asked to do in such situations. The actual vocabulary and grammatical structures used by the experimenter are of crucial importance in analyzing the child's response. So too is the normal pattern of interaction expected (by the child) between children and adults. For example, children come to expect that a follow-up question from an adult usually implies that their answer to the initial question was wrong (Blank, Rose and Berlin, 1978). Similar doubts on some of Piaget's experiments were expressed by McGarrigle and Donaldson (1974), who described how children's answers to test questions were considerably different if the nature of the experimental testing was interrupted by a 'naughty', but (to the child) plausible, teddy bear who 'messed up' the experiment, breaking the normal rhythm of the child's social interpretation of the experimenters' questions. As regards the study of reciprocity in children, we simply don't know enough about the effects of question sequences such as:

Which country would *you* choose?

Now suppose I asked a *German* boy the same question . . .

and whether the responses would be different if the questions were asked in, say, reverse order. The contextual features of Piaget's tasks and the way they influence children's responses continue to attract attention (for example, Eames, Shorrocks and Tomlinson, 1990).

Piaget appears to have interviewed children individually but Doise, Mugny and Perret-Clermont (1975) established that children performed at a higher level if they worked in *groups* of two or three. When they took the views of their peers into account children were more readily able to de-centre. Cognitive development and social development are in fact closely interrelated. This can be easily demonstrated by Bruner and Goodman's (1947) investigations into children's comparative perceptions of magnitude and value. Children were asked to make comparisons between things they perceived as being valuable and things they perceived as being worthless. The judgments children made of the sizes of a number of coins were compared with their judgments of the sizes of cardboard discs. Judgments of the weight of jars of sweets were also compared with their judgments of the weight of jars of sand. The social value that children place on coins and sweets affects their estimation of how big or heavy they are. The perceived differences between the smallest and the largest coins was much larger than corresponding judgments for cardboard discs. A jar of sweets seems heavier than a jar of sand of the same weight. Their eyes, as their mothers might have said, were bigger than their stomachs.

Cognitive Aspects of Space and Place

This book belongs to N. Molesworth,
St. Custard's,
England,
Europe,
The World,
The Universe,
Space.
(Willans and Searle, 1958)

Most of us have experienced at some point in childhood the sudden realization that parts of the world can be fitted together in a 'nesting' arrangement — like those Russian dolls that fit one inside another. In early childhood, children have little idea of the 'continent — country — county' relationship. Children need to acquire some understanding of these relationships in developing their awareness of places. Although the National Curriculum only calls upon children to '*state* where they live' at level 1 (Gg/2/1c), some understanding is called for at level 3 where children must demonstrate that they know the location of their local area within the country in which they live (Gg/2/3b).

The groundwork for establishing a framework for children's understanding of the relationship between such geographical units was established by Piaget in *The Child's Conception of the World* (1924). After questioning Swiss children, Piaget was struck by their responses to questions such as: 'Are you Swiss?'. A frequent response was, 'No, I am Genevan' (i.e. from Geneva). Further questioning revealed that 'three-quarters of the children up to the age of 9 denied the possibility of being *both* Swiss and Genevan'. Other children knew that Geneva was in Switzerland but denied that they themselves were Swiss. The difficulty, according to Piaget, was not lack of information by the children, but being unable to schematize, i.e. represent for themselves the relationships between the areal units involved: Geneva and Switzerland. Even with the aid of a diagram (a large circle representing Switzerland, and smaller circles inside representing Geneva, Vaud and other towns), children would claim that one could be both Genevan *and* Vaudois since both Geneva and Vaud are in Switzerland.

Piaget went on to identify three stages of development in the evolution of the idea of a country. In the *first* stage (up to about nine years), a country to children is simply a unit, along with towns and districts and, the children presume, of the same size as these. Children may be able to *say* 'Geneva is in Switzerland' but answers to further probing questions reveal they conceptualize them as being the same.

A country is another town.

Switzerland is further away than Geneva.

The *second*, intermediate, stage is the one already described above.

I'm not Swiss, I'm Genevan.

In this stage, Geneva is viewed rather like a piece of land enclosed in a foreign country. You cannot be both Genevan and Swiss at the same time. There is a vague, partial and fluctuating understanding of the correct relationship between the part and the whole.

The final, *third* stage marks the advent of correct schematization.

Geneva is in Switzerland.

One can be Genevan and Swiss at the same time.

Later investigations have extended Piaget's work on children's understanding of the relationships between cities and countries. Jahoda (1962) questioned Glaswegian children aged 6–11 about the spatial relations of Glasgow, Scotland and Britain. He identified four stages of development (although acknowledged that the definition of these was problematic). The first part of the investigation was based on verbal questioning of children:

1   In the first identified stage, children had no conception of Glasgow as a 'unitary whole' — Glasgow was thought of as being some vague nearby entity but not usually including where they themselves actually were. It was 'round the corner' or 'beside the playground'.
2   In the second stage, children had some conception of Glasgow as a unitary whole but no conception of it as part of Scotland — children were aware of being 'in' Glasgow, but with little idea of also being in Scotland. They themselves were 'here' but Scotland was 'away in the highlands'.
3   In the third stage, children understood that Glasgow was part of Scotland but had no conception of Scotland as being part of Britain — Children could *say* that Glasgow was in Scotland but further questions revealed only partial understanding — 'Britain includes the countries of Glasgow, London and France'.
4   By the fourth stage, the Glasgow — Scotland — Britain relationship was correctly expressed.

Jahoda then made use of cut out shapes to represent, respectively, Britain, Scotland, England and Glasgow. Britain was represented by a black piece of card, England and Scotland by smaller pieces of white card and Glasgow by a small brass disc. Children had to arrange the shapes as in figure 2.1 to demonstrate that they had a correct understanding of the spatial relationships between these places. How did their performance on this test compare with their performance on the verbal test? Almost three-quarters of

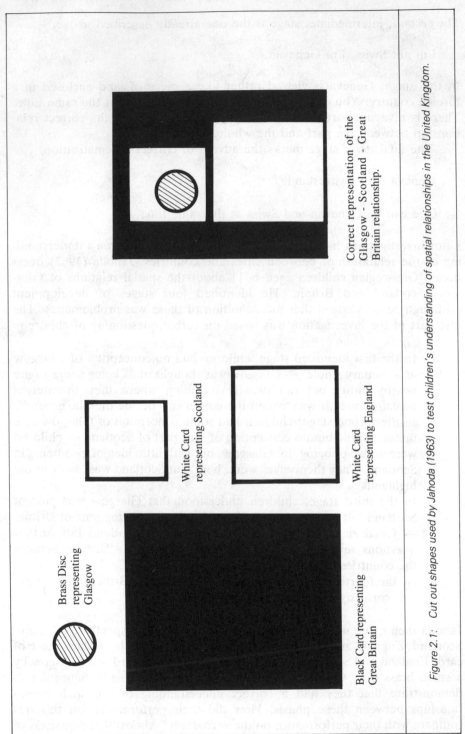

Correct representation of the
Glasgow - Scotland - Great
Britain relationship.

White Card
representing Scotland

White Card
representing England

Brass Disc
representing
Glasgow

Black Card representing
Great Britain

Figure 2.1: Cut out shapes used by Jahoda (1963) to test children's understanding of spatial relationships in the United Kingdom.

the children previously identified as being at stage 3 were still unable to complete the shape arrangement correctly. Although, therefore, these children were able to make verbal statements to the effect that 'Glasgow is part of Scotland', the spatial test revealed an inadequate grasp of the part-whole relationship involved. Children appeared to schematize these relationships later than their initial answer might suggest. There are a number of implications here for teachers. For example, that children's understanding of the spatial relationships between countries, counties, towns, and so on is gradual and partial and that physical apparatus (such as jigsaw puzzles or maps that can be built up by superimposing symbols) might be useful in order to develop an understanding of basic geographical units and their interrelationships. Jahoda's study reveals the gap between being able to say your address (as in Gg/2/1c) and having an understanding of the spatial units that addresses describe.

It may be helpful at this point to set children's understanding of the spatial relations of countries within the context of their ideas of the scale of the world as a whole. The Leicester Polytechnic Development Education Project (Allison, Conway and Denscombe, 1982), for example, attempted to find out what ideas primary school pupils had of the scale of the Earth. Pupils were invited to imagine they were going to travel around the world and asked about the means of transport, the distance and the time they thought it would take. 'Reasonable' combinations of answers were used to assess their grasp of scale.

> ... the 6-year-old pupil who answered that she would travel by aeroplane, that the distance was 101,510 miles (sic) and that it would take a month might be seen to have a reasonable grasp of the scale. The pupil who wrote that he would travel by bike, that the distance was 518 miles and that he would spend four days on the journey, by contrast, would seem to have little real grasp. (*ibid*, p. 14)

Answers generally showed that primary children had a very vague understanding of the dimensions of the world. Distances and times were usually hugely exaggerated. Puzzled readers may like to know that the equatorial circumference of the world is in fact approximately 25,000 miles or 40,000 km!

It is also worth noting at this point the findings of some investigations into children's understanding of the Earth as a cosmic body. These are relevant to children's understanding of place because of the implications as to how people 'on the other side of the Earth' live. Are Australians, for example, 'upside down'? Why don't they fall off? Nussbaum and Novak (1976) provided children with some problem situations relating to the Earth. Children were shown a large globe and a small doll that could be stuck onto its surface. They were to imagine that the doll was a real girl and that she

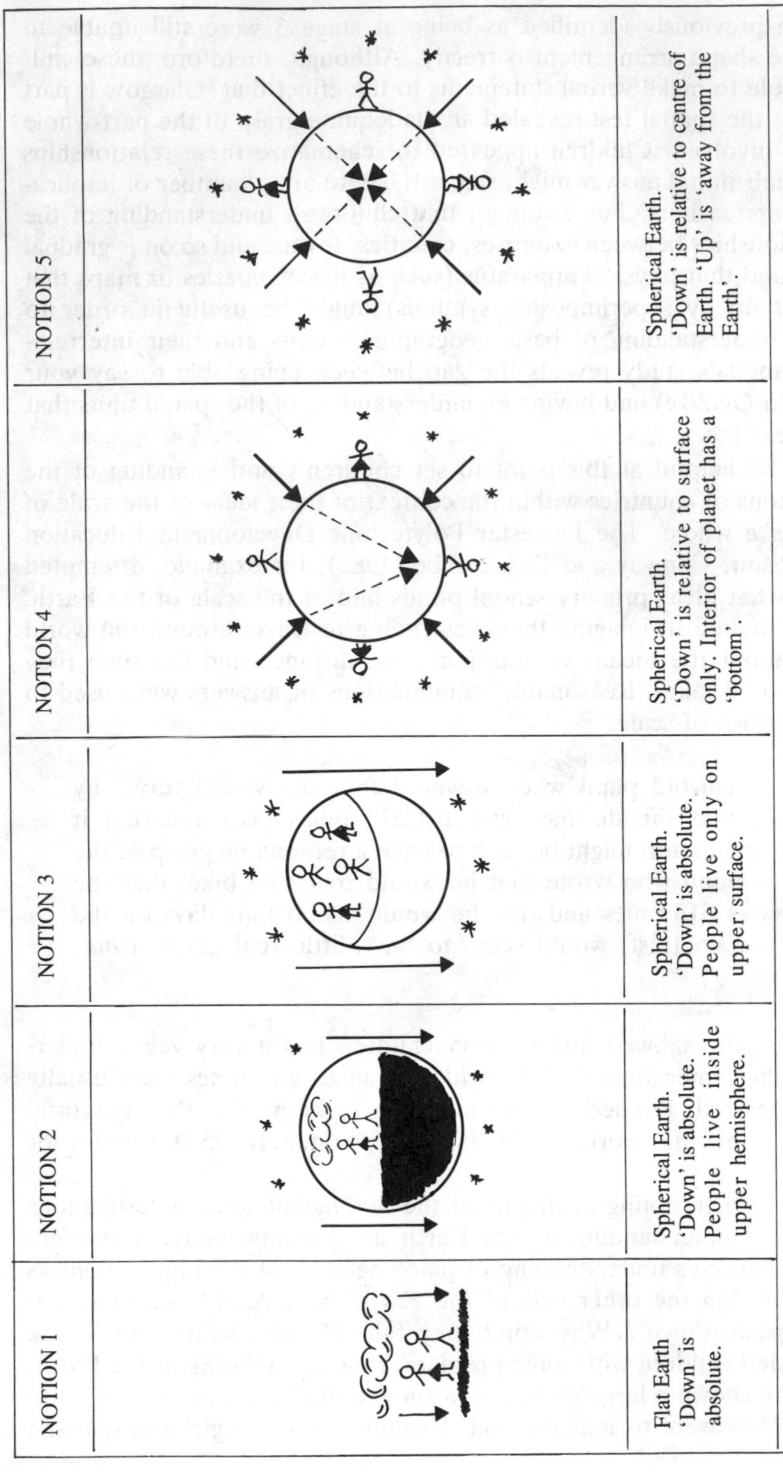

NOTION 1	NOTION 2	NOTION 3	NOTION 4	NOTION 5
Flat Earth 'Down' is absolute.	Spherical Earth. 'Down' is absolute. People live inside upper hemisphere.	Spherical Earth. 'Down' is absolute. People live only on upper surface.	Spherical Earth. 'Down' is relative to surface only. Interior of planet has a 'bottom'.	Spherical Earth. 'Down' is relative to centre of Earth. 'Up' is 'away from the Earth'.

Figure 2.2: Children's conception of the Earth as a cosmic body (after Nussbaum and Novak, 1976, Nussbaum, 1979 and 1985)

was standing on the surface of the Earth. (Young children find this in itself a difficult proposition. It is extremely common for children to 'stand' dolls on the Southern hemisphere so that they are attached by their heads, as this is the only way they can be imagined to be 'the right way up'.) Nussbaum and Novak went on, however, to pose a number of problems: 'Suppose this girl dropped a stone. Which way would it fall?'. The question was repeated for several parts of the Earth's surface — in both hemispheres — to see if children understood the idea of 'down' in relation to the Earth. 'Now suppose the girl is holding a glass of water. What happens to the liquid in the glass if she is standing here... Does something different happen if she is standing here...?' Further questions asked the children to consider what would happen to a ball dropped into an imaginary hole that went right through the centre of the Earth. 'Does the ball go right through the Earth and out of the other side or does it stop in the middle?' Children's notions about the nature of the Earth in space, whether 'down' is seen as being absolute or only definable in relation to the Earth, and their understanding of the effect of gravity, can be summarized in diagram form as shown in figure 2.2 (see also Nussbaum, 1979 and 1985). Although they can *state* that the Earth is round, like a ball, many children appear not to *believe* this. Probing questions reveal that they believe instead the Earth to be flat (notion 1). There is considerable confusion in their minds between the satellite pictures they see of a round Earth and their own experience of its flatness. The roundness of the Earth is taken by some to be just the 'curves of the roads' or the 'shape of the mountains'. Other children appear to believe that there are two Earths — the flat one they live on and the round one that astronauts photograph. Some children believe that the Earth is round, but not spherical. A ship could sail all round the Earth on some ocean which surrounds it. In all these versions, the sky is viewed as horizontal and 'down' is always represented as parallel no matter where you are on the surface of the Earth.

In notion 2 children believe that the Earth is a huge ball made up of two hemispheres. People live *inside* this ball on the flat planar surface of the lower hemisphere. The sky is the inside surface of the upper hemisphere. Outside the hemisphere is 'space'.

In notion 3 there is thought to be unlimited space *around* the Earth but it is still possible to 'fall off' it. Objects thrown upwards from the surface will only fall towards the ground from the 'top' of the Earth. Objects thrown away from the Earth in the 'lower' hemisphere will continue to fall away from the Earth. 'Up' and 'down' are still not defined therefore by reference to the Earth itself but to a more universal sense of 'right way upness' of which the Earth itself is part. According to this notion, it is only possible for people to live on the surface of the 'top' hemisphere of the Earth.

Children holding notion 4 appear to believe that the Earth is round and understand that objects will fall towards the Earth because of gravity. However, when questioned about the behaviour of a ball dropped into an imaginary hole passing through the centre of the Earth, there is some confusion. The interior of the planet is thought to have a 'bottom' even though 'down' directions on the surface are always towards the ground.

In notion 5, the properties of direction and the nature of the Earth and space are conceived as compatible with scientific conceptions. A ball dropped through an imaginary hole through the Earth will stop in the centre. 'Down' is therefore the direction of the centre of the Earth.

Nussbaum concluded that children needed to be made aware of the elements of the notions they themselves had about the nature of the Earth in space, however naive. It is suggested here that greater use of globes in teaching about distant places would enable teachers to confront children with their 'cognitive disequilibrium' provoking 'accommodation' as their ideas changed. It may be that children in the southern hemisphere have fewer difficulties accepting scientific notions of the Earth's gravity since they are clearly 'the right way up' from personal experience, although they seem to be 'upside down' on the model globe.

Attainment target 16 of the National Curriculum in science deals with the development of pupils' knowledge and understanding of 'the relative positions and movement of the Earth, moon, sun and solar system within the universe'. By level 2, pupils are to know 'that we live on a large, spherical, self-contained planet, called Earth'. Understanding that 'gravity acts towards the centre of every astronomical body' is not expected until level 7 however, because of the conceptual difficulties in this topic described by Nussbaum. Teachers making use of a globe in helping children to locate places in the wider world may find it helpful however to bear in mind these possible notions of the Earth in space.

As far as the Earth's surface is concerned, children *are* aware of landscape and landforms, but only insofar as it serves their own purposes, and is within the experience of (principally) their leisure activities (Birkenhauer, 1984). Studies based on photographs (Bayliss and Renwick, 1966) and local experience (Bishop and Foulsham, 1973) indicate that children tend to see the detailed foreground rather than the broad sweep of landscape or townscape behind. In a Bishop and Foulsham's study of children's perceptions of Harwich, it was found that although the most striking feature in the town centre was the lighthouse, children's drawings and maps ignored it, the nearest reference being to the public conveniences at the foot of it.

Piaget also examined children's notions of the nature and origins of the surface of the Earth — of geomorphological features and meteorological phenomena. Children appear to progress from attitudes of *animism* whereby everything is considered to be alive to *artificialism* whereby everything is explained as being 'man-made'. This, according to Piaget (1929), may have much to do with children's early religious education. Children are taught that God created the Earth and everything in it and that He continues in some way to supervise this creation from Heaven.

There is nothing surprising in the child simply continuing to think along the same line and imagining in detail the manner of this creation and supposing that God secured the help of a band of skilled workmen (p. 352).

On the other hand, because children see much human activity around them (industry, civil engineering, etc.) it is not perhaps unreasonable for children to conclude — as some of them seem to — that nature itself *depends* on human activity.

Children's Developing Sense of Their own National Identity

I can say I love London. I can say I love England. I can't say I love my country, because I don't know what that means. (Guy Burgess, in Alan Bennett's *An Englishman Abroad*)

Level 1 of Attainment Target 2 in geography requires children to 'name the country in which they live'. But how do children develop an understanding of their own *nationality*? Exploring national concepts is a complex task, unlike the investigation of physical properties such as length or shape. What, after all, is the nature and content of the 'normal' adult sense of nationality? The concept of nationality is rather diffuse and few people question its nature in times of political stability. Bay (1965, quoted in Davies, 1968) differentiates between two types of national attachment in adults. One is oriented towards freedom and is based on a concern for one's fellow nationals. The other is orientated towards power and is based on a concern for national unity and strength. These two aspects of national attachment may be invoked by different 'triggers' — such as music in the case of the former and attack by other countries in the case of the latter. These two components of national feeling will vary in relative proportions in times of war and peace. The notion of nationalism is complex because attachment to a country rests on a number of possible 'objects' for which individuals can hold loyalty or affection — such as the landscape, state institutions, the national leader or some ideological concept. That is why 'being British' means different things to different people. There are also regional and ethnic loyalties which may be stronger than national ones (for example, being Armenian or Azerbaijani). There is too a significant cross cultural dimension to nationalistic feelings. Nationalism seems very largely to vary with (amongst other things) the size of the country and the wealth of its citizens. The bigger it is and the wealthier it is, the more loyal its citizens are to it. (Kelman, 1965) But these do not appear to be the only factors in loyalty to country:

Nothing brought the differential solubility of nationality to our notice like the Korean prisoner of war defections. It proved extraordinarily easier to strip Americans of their sense of nationality than it was Englishmen, Ghurkas or Turks. Many special reasons for the discrepancy have been advanced, but may it not still be the case that to be a Turk (say) is to be something a good deal richer and thicker than to be an American? Something less easily exchanged for membership of the international proletariat? (Davies, 1968)

Many children in school will be faced with the question of loyalty to two nationalities, for example children with strong and recent family connections with other countries. Learning a new, or a second, nationality may involve (for both parents and children) substantial shifts in values. This is an important area in which further clarification of the issues and processes involved are needed. Local and national crises such as the 'Honeyford affair', in which a Bradford headteacher provoked a *cause célèbre* following his publication of an article on multicultural education in the *Salisbury Review*, seem to revolve (at least partly) around notions such as what it is to be British (Halstead, 1988). Teacher sensitivity is vital here and perhaps the best way of dealing with the issue in the classroom is in the context of loyalty to a whole range of individuals, places and institutions.

In a massive UNESCO cross-cultural study (1959), Lambert and Klineberg examined children's conceptions of their own national group and of other nationalities. Twelve countries were involved: the USA, South Africa (Bantu children only), Brazil, English Canada, French Canada, France, Germany, Israel, Japan, Lebanon and Turkey. A total of 3300 children, aged 6, 10 and 14 were questioned. Their attitudes towards *other* nations will be dealt with later. Standardized interviews, conducted by investigators in each country started by asking: 'What are you?' In general, as might perhaps have been expected, children did not refer to themselves by nationality, but rather as 'a boy' or 'a person' or 'a child'. However, there were interesting cross-cultural differences. Japanese children for example *did* show a marked tendency to refer to themselves by national identity. German, Turkish and Lebanese children also made frequent references to their nationality. However, even though nationality was not uppermost in the thoughts of most children when they described themselves, they did generally have definite group views of the characteristics possessed by their own national group when asked about it. The American children saw Americans as being good, wealthy and free. The Brazilian children saw Brazilians as being good, intelligent, cultured, happy and unambitious. Turkish children viewed Turks as being good, peaceful, ambitious, religious, patriotic and clean.

In a later study, Jahoda (1973) also found that nationality generally featured low in children's 'self images'. Only 3 per cent of Scottish children described themselves *primarily* as Scottish. Indeed, only one child in the 6–7 age group understood the question 'What is your nationality?' as compared with one-third of the 7–8-year-olds and three-quarters of the 10–11-year-olds. The whole concept of 'nationality' was shown by Jahoda to be problematic for children and likely to be a source of error. Scottish children for example found it difficult to sort out nationality from accent, dialect and language (Jahoda, 1964).

It may of course be that there are particular problems in dealing with terms such as 'country' or 'nationality' within the British Isles:

> There are no countries in the world less known by the British than those selfsame British Islands. (George Borrow, *Lavengro*, Preface)

Dennis *et al* (1972) asked children to complete the sentence: 'Our country is called...'. Few of the youngest children (8–10) were unable to give their 'country' a name and with increasing age, children named tended to give the response : 'United Kingdom', 'Britain' or 'British Isles', rather than 'England'. However, even at the age of 14–17, 45 per cent of those interviewed were choosing the less inclusive category of England. There remains, of course, amongst adults, confusion about whether their 'country' is, for example, England or the United Kingdom. Consider, for example the complexity of the following statement which summarizes the position:

> The British Isles consists of two large islands (Great Britain and Ireland) and many smaller ones. The United Kingdom consists of the kingdoms of England and Scotland, the principality of Wales and the province of Northern Ireland. The Republic of Ireland is a separate country.

Confusion arises, not least because of the popular usage of the term 'country' to mean 'a land' as well as 'a sovereign, self governing state'. However, it is not much helped by careless cartography. The maps of the British Isles in the Geography statutory orders (see figures 1.3a and 1.3d) show the United Kingdom (a political entity) in the same typestyle as Ireland (a physical entity). I am not suggesting that primary school children get bogged down in this complexity, or that they memorize some statement such as the one above as though it were their address. (Certainly one wouldn't relish the prospect of teaching young children some of the greater complexity that exists, such as for example, that the Isle of Man is a 'self-governing dependency of the British Crown'...) But there is an issue to be faced here by teachers for the National Curriculum requires children to 'name the countries (sic) of the United Kingdom' (Gg/2/2a). I think the implication is that understanding the spatial relationships of the British Isles, including the spatial structure of their own address, is potentially difficult and may need revisiting several times during the primary phase, certainly beyond level 2.

I have, incidentally, found the definition: 'a country is a land with its own people and its own laws' to be helpful in answer to children's questions.

However, even though for many children at the age of 6–7 the concept of nation is still rudimentary and confused, a further cross-national study showed that, for children of the same age, 'there is already a highly crystal-lised and consensual *preference* in children for their own country' (Tajfel *et al*, 1970). In this study, children were given photographs of young men and asked to sort them on the basis of whether they liked them or not. In a later session they were told that only some of these men were of their own nationality. The children then had to identify which ones these were. In almost all cases children showed a tendency to assign better liked photographs to persons of their own nationality. Tajfel and his associates acknowledge that this is an ambiguous task but there was seen to be some consistency in the selection of photographs liked and the assigning of them to the childrens' own nationality, indicating that perhaps some shared gener-alized image of physical features develops in children.

The generally expressed preference by children for their own country does have some exceptions, however. Under certain conditions children do consistently devalue their own national ethnic group. This happens especial-ly where there are acute tensions between groups or where the minority or underprivileged group are 'visibly' different. In these circumstances children may express preference for the dominant group (Milner, 1970; Hawkhead, 1979). However, even in conditions of 'nil visibility' of ethnic differences, children can show lack of preference for their own nation indicating that they are sensitive to subtleties of prevailing social attitudes (Tajfel *et al*, 1970). Slater and Spicer (1980) in a ten nation survey found that South African, Singaporean and Jamaican students ranked their own country low in response to the question 'Where would you most like to live?'

How does this preference for one's own country change as children become older? In a Dutch study with children of 8–12, Jaspars (1965) demonstrated that children preferred the Netherlands to other countries at all ages and that the preference for the Netherlands increased with age. These findings were replicated and confirmed in an English study (Middle-ton, Tajfel and Johnson, 1970) and in the USA (Targ, 1970).

However, there may be some difference between children's developing preferences based on nationality and those based on skin colour. Studies in the multicultural literature appear to suggest that attachment to ones own group does not consistently increase as children become older. White chil-dren appear to distinctly prefer other whites to the age of 7 or 8 but then their preferences neutralize (Aboud, 1988).

There do seem to be some cross-cultural differences in the extent to which children form attitudes towards their own country. Pride in homeland for American children and adolescents for example, appears to be especially strong (Dennis *et al*, 1972). In a study of 12,000 American elementary school children, Hess and Torney (quoted in Remy, 1975) identified three stages in the development of national identity. Before the age of 7 children develop a strong attachment to their country in which symbols such as the flag and Statue of Liberty are prominent. In the second stage positive feelings about America are based on ideological and political content such as the right to vote and freedom. In the final stage preference for America is seen as being a considered choice after comparison with other countries. By contrast, Australian children appeared to be slower to adopt patriotic attitudes, not talking of collective values until the age of 12 or 13 (Knoche and Goldlust, 1966, quoted in Davies, 1968). They also often chose to have been born elsewhere. However, they grasped the concept 'foreigner' much sooner. This could well be because of the greater collective awareness of immigrant history. Perception of Australia as a remote island may also sharpen the distinction between Australian and foreigner which is blurred for, say, Swiss children who are surrounded on all sides by other countries and for whom the concept of nationality may be confused as a result of the overlap between countries and areas where different languages are spoken in central Europe.

National Symbols

The significance of the flag is strong in American children's identification with nationhood and is an important part of school morning ritual. An early study by Horowitz (1941) into the development of patriotism reported that although younger children preferred the Siamese merchant flag (showing a white elephant), there was an increase in American children's appreciation of the US flag from grade 1 to grade 10. A replication of this study (Lawson, 1963) showed children recognizing and claiming attachment to the flag at a very early age. Weinstein (1956) used the flag as the basis for a subtle and probing set of questions on American primary children's ideas about their own nationality and other countries. His interview schedule included questions such as:

Who made the first American flag? Why do you suppose they wanted to have a flag?

Do all countries have a flag? Which flag is best? Why?

If you went to another country to visit, could you fly the American flag there?

Suppose the *government* decided to change the American flag and had it made green and white with a red apple in the middle. Would the new flag be an American flag? Suppose all the *people* wanted a new flag and it was green and white with a red apple in the middle. Would it be an American flag?

On the basis of such questioning, Weinstein traced nine (!) steps in a model of the development of children's understanding.

1. (age 5/6) The child 'knows' (sic) the American flag but does not know that other flags, or even other countries, exist.
2. (age 5/6) The child makes statements such as 'Our country is good, others are bad'. At this stage other countries are recognized as having flags too. Flags are seen as 'belonging to' the people who live in a country, rather than *identifying* that country.
3. (age 7) Countries are now differentiated according to geographical areas. They are not 'good' or 'bad' but 'possess' people, objects and physical events. The purpose of the flag is to show ownership. People who are 'owned' by a country naturally prefer their own flag. The American flag is best though, compared to all other flags.
4. (age 7) The first ideas of government emerge. The government acts to administer the country and also has the power to alter the flag if it so wishes.
5. (age 8) The notion of a multiplicity of flags emerges — many countries have flags, but also states which are parts of those countries. The American flag (and that of the United Nations) are still best though.
6. (age 8) Children at this stage now accept the symbolism of the flag. A flag flying on public buildings shows that the government is present.
7. (age 9) Children have by now a clearer notion of what a country is — national identity is now no longer merely a matter of 'possession', it involves identification with a group, and the goals of that group. The notion appears of government as a body which conducts relations with other countries.
8. (age 10) Notion of abstract loyalty appears — loyalty to a set of goals and to a group holding those goals. The notion of reciprocity appears: 'If I lived in a different country, and I liked the way things were, I would probably think their flag best.'
'There might be people in some country who liked another country's flag better than their own.'
9. (age 10/11) At this stage children have an increased knowledge of rituals associated with the flag — such as the flag flying at half mast covering the coffins of servants of the state and its use in identifying claims to territory. This is the stage of fully developed concept of the flag and of national identity.

How valid is the choice of flags as a measure of national attitudes? They are certainly powerful symbols and are widely recognized. They have, for example been exploited in national marketing campaigns to 'buy British', such as 'fly the flag' (advertisement for British Airways). But it seems unlikely that such a study could be replicated outside the United States, as the ritual significance of the flag appears there to be especially prominent. In 1990, for example, a spate of flag burnings by protest groups prompted serious consideration of constitutional change making desecration of the flag an offence.

Nevertheless, Jahoda (1963) used a range of country symbols, including flags, in a further study of national identity in Scotland. Reactions to costumes, buildings, emblems and songs were explored. By age 10–11 most of the children he interviewed were able to correctly name the National Anthem and the Union Jack. Social class was apparently a significant factor in correct identification of such symbols. By age 8–9, about half of the 'middle class' children understood the significance of such symbols as 'standing for' the geographical areas concerned.

Music has been used to prompt children's thinking about people's attitudes to their homeland. Oomen-Welke (1988) used national anthems as a starting point for teaching about national values. In a multicultural primary school in Germany, she asked 9–10-year-old children to analyze the ideas present in a number of national anthems. The national anthems of Greece, Turkey, Yugoslavia and Romania were of particular interest to the children of her class, because of their own family histories. The content of these anthems was compared with a number of German national songs, including *Das Lied der Deutschen* of 1841 ('Deutschland, Deutschland, uber alles ...') and the national anthem of the former German Democratic Republic ('Auferstanden aus Ruinen und der Zukunft zugewandt ...'). Such content analysis produced tables of the number of mentions of concepts such as 'German', 'brotherhood', 'Fatherland', 'peace', 'freedom', 'enemies', 'happiness' and so on. The anthems therefore served as a vehicle for discussing these difficult and complex concepts relating to national identity and pride in homeland. Clearly this is potentially dangerous territory and needs to be handled with skill and care, but readers who want to develop classroom activities along these lines can do so with the help of: Shaw, M., Coleman, H. and Cartledge, T.M. (1960, 4th edn. 1975) *National Anthems of the World*, Poole, Blandford Press. This book gives the music, original words and translations of some 200 national anthems, as well as a list of national days. The anthems themselves, with their recurrent jingoistic and heroic themes of struggle for freedom, beauty of the natural landscape and confusion to enemies are worth examining for what they have collectively to say about nationality.

The research findings relating to children's understanding of their own national identity is summarised in table 2.1.

Knowledge About Distant Places is Related to Attitudes

Cognitive and affective aspects of understanding the wider social world are inseparable. Hewstone, Jaspars and Lalljea (1982) demonstrate this in a

Table 2.1

Generalized 'level of development'	Children are generally found to:
I (age 6–8)	have no understanding of part-whole relationships (for example, Glasgow-Scotland-Britain) prefer their own country but for no rational reason
II (age 7–9)	have imperfect understanding of part-whole relationships prefer their own country for family and 'immediate social' reasons
III (age 9–11)	understand part-whole relationships prefer their own country by reference to collective ideals recognize and understand the significance of national symbols

study of how pupils represent themselves in comparison with others. British public (i.e. private) school pupils and pupils from state maintained comprehensive schools were asked about what they saw as being their own attributes. The public school pupils defined themselves as 'hard working' whereas they were described by the comprehensive school pupils as 'swots'. Although notions of industriousness were clearly shared therefore these were suffused with different evaluative connotations. The words we use frequently betray the feelings we have and there are many examples of this in relation to people and places. For example: 'We live in houses, they live in huts', 'We use simple technology, theirs is primitive'.

We can examine the relationship between cognitive and affective aspects of international understanding at a wider scale. Is there, for example, any connection between children's expressed preference for a particular country and what they appear to know about it? Several studies suggest a U-shaped relationship, with children knowing most about those countries they liked and disliked most strongly and least about the countries they felt neutral towards (Grace and Neuhaus, 1952; Grace, 1954; Johnson, *et al*, 1970). The question of a *causal* relationship between knowing about and attitude towards is, however, much less clear. It may be that children base their attitudes to distant people and places on the knowledge they have of them. Children who receive 'positive' information about countries might develop positive attitudes towards those countries. On the other hand, if the attitude is learned first, this might predispose the child to acquire only that information that confirms the attitudes that are already held. It seems likely that children do in fact follow the second sequence : the attitude comes first (Johnson, 1966; Johnson *et al*, 1970; Stillwell and Spencer, 1974).

Some doubt has been cast on the U-shaped relationship between knowledge and attitudes by Stillwell and Spencer (1974) who suggest instead a linear relationship with children knowing most about those countries they liked and least about the countries they disliked. To be fair, the original

'U-shaped' graphs drawn by Grace and Neuhaus are so shallow as to be perhaps properly described as saucer-shaped. But how stable are children's expressed preferences? Do they change when they learn (for example in school) more about distant places? One possible expectation is that there would be a shift towards greater liking for all countries. But this appears not to happen. When they exposed children to large classroom displays of information about India, Germany, USA and Russia, there was a significant shift by children towards liking Germany *more* but also a corresponding shift towards liking India *less*. Stillwell and Spencer speculate that the children's initial dislike of Germany was based on negative word association rather than any substantive information. Pictures on the wall display revealed that Germany was much like Britain and so a shift towards liking occurred. Pictures of India, by contrast, stressed differences in landscape, people and human activity and thus a shift from neutrality to dislike occurred. If this reasoning is correct, there are considerable implications for teachers regarding the presentation of information about distant places to children. Visual material may need to be carefully mediated by the teacher so that unfamiliar images are described in positive terms and with reference to the children's own experience.

It is also important to remember that in the primary school we are dealing as much with attitude *formation* as attitude *change*. Before learning about other countries many children are neither positively or negatively disposed towards those countries. They simply haven't thought much about them at all and don't have any clearly developed view.

Children's Attitudes to Distant People and Places

What is the nature of children's attitudes towards distant people and places? Are there patterns in the stability of preferences as they become older? Is there a point in children's development when they are likely to be more receptive to teaching for international understanding?

There is a large literature on national stereotypes and intergroup attitudes held by adults (see, for example, Isaacs, 1958), but relatively little is known about the nature and development of such attitudes in children.

First, a brief note about research methodology. Many investigations, in the way they put questions to subjects, have presented choices that legitimate unfavourable attitudes. Grace and Neuhaus (1952), for example, attempt to access their subjects' 'like' and 'dislike' of nations by asking them to complete sentences such as:

I feel much more hostile and aggressive toward, and would rather go to war against ----- than -----.

Children who may possess no hostile or aggressive reactions to any other nations are thereby prompted to express such feelings by the nature of the test itself. The same is true, but to a lesser extent, when children are asked which countries (and peoples) they like and dislike. The mature response being sought in many cases is something along the lines:

> You can't like or dislike any one nationality, you find good and bad people everywhere.

But asking for liked and disliked nations forces the respondent into a difficult and undesirable dichotomy. Further work on more rigorous forms of experimental design in this area would be welcome.

There is some evidence that children prefer countries that they perceive as being most like their own (Jaspars *et al*, 1983; Stillwell and Spencer, 1974).

This matches the findings of much of the literature in social psychology showing how we tend to consider other people as belonging to the same category as ourselves but do not often perceive ourselves as belonging to the same category as others. 'They' are like us but 'we' are not like them. (Codol, 1986).

It also relates to earlier work on interpersonal relations (Heider, 1958; Byrne, 1971 — quoted in Stillwell and Spencer) where people perceived as being most like oneself are preferred.

Even so, there are large intercultural differences in this regard as well as differences in the ages at which children are able to perceive 'like us' and 'not like us' (Lambert and Klineberg, 1967). Typically, younger children rely on observable features (such as physical features, clothing, etc.) to categorize others as different, whereas older children make judgments on the basis of personalities, habits, religion or politics.

This is commensurate of course with the increasing sophistication of children's thinking about people in general. A 5-year-old, for example, will claim friendship solely on the basis of who he/she is playing with at that particular moment or who has a desirable toy. With increasing age the child is able to discriminate between the personal qualities of others (Selman, 1980; Youniss, 1980).

But as well as expressing preferences for countries on the basis of perceived similarity to their own, children are also able to choose on the basis of whether places are seen as being desirable places in which to live. Many of the children in the UNESCO survey (Lambert and Klineberg, 1967) chose certain countries as being desirable in this respect because (unlike home) they were, for example, wealthy. This was the case for the Bantu and Brazilian children in the study.

As we would expect, it seems too that with age children's preferences for countries become more and more differentiated. That is to say, there is a greater range of strength of preferences as children demonstrate a larger repertoire of evaluative distinctions (Jaspars *et al*, 1983). What begins with very young children as a simple list of likes and dislikes becomes progressively more differentiated into more complex categories: strongly liked, weakly liked, indifferent towards, etc. Preferences of children at about the age of 6 or 7 for distant places appear to be primarily based on the appeal of the unusual or picturesque. Choices about 'liking' or 'disliking' are based on word association and randomly gathered information. Past wars often seem to have formed the basis for dislikes. Preferences at this age are fleeting. Later, at the age of about 8 or 9, preferences become more stable and are based on stereotyped views of the places concerned. Preferences are also increasingly based on *people* rather than *place* as children become older (Jahoda, 1962).

There seems to be strong cross-national evidence from the UNESCO study that children are most inquisitive and friendly towards foreign peoples and most likely to see them as similar at the age of about 10, than at either age 6 or age 14. Persistence of favourable views towards other people and places into adolescence seems to be dependent, to some degree, on learning at this stage. In one of the few longitudinal studies of children's attitudes to foreigners, Carnie (1971) tested children in four schools in the English Midlands during their development from age 8 to age 12. His tests revealed a steady rise in favourable attitudes throughout the junior years. 'The downward curve in international and interracial goodwill appears to begin when various factors come into play during adolescence' (Carnie, 1972). One of these factors, according to Carnie, is the gradual adoption by children during adolescence of the prevailing adult stereotypes of foreigners, replacing the freer, more individual views held in childhood.

But what about the ability of children to understand that people in other countries also have systems of attitudes and preferences? Middleton, Tajfel and Johnson (1970) devised an ingenious experiment to examine reciprocity. It was based on a simulation of a 'rescue' from a desert island. A model of the desert island was presented to the children together with dolls representing England and nationalities that the child had indicated liking for, neutrality towards and disliking for in an earlier test. The dolls were identical except for a label around each one's neck indicating nationality. Four toy boats were then shown to the child, each one 'captained' by a person from the countries in question. There were many dolls from each country on the island but the captains could only carry away four persons in each boat. Which dolls would captains from each nationality choose to save? The children were then asked what *their* choice would be if they themselves were a boat captain. The experimenters wanted to discover whether children's attitudes towards different nations would influence the behaviour they attributed to people who came from those countries. Would captains from liked nations be seen to behave as 'fairer' or more like the children themselves than captains from disliked nations? Younger children found it easy to understand that people from 'liked' countries would prefer their own nationals. With increasing age it was seen that people from disliked and neutral countries would also demonstrate that preference. Older children attributed their own system of preferences for countries to other people. Nationals from countries that *were* liked were seen to behave more fairly than nationals of countries that were disliked. Reciprocity therefore was not attained equally with respect to all nations. It was shown clearly that children's preferences influence their ability to adopt different points of view. This finding puts an important limitation on the general outline of development put forward by Piaget and Weil, with which this chapter opened.

Cognitive and affective aspects of understanding of nationality and of distant people and places appear to be intimately related to each other. At this point, a further summary table may help to review the development of children's evaluative ideas about distant people and places (see table 2.2):

Table 2.2

Generalized 'level of development'	Children generally found to:
I (age 6–8)	select 'favourite countries' on the basis of exotic features stress differences between themselves and foreigners deny that they themselves could become foreigners
II (age 7–9)	select 'favourite countries' on the basis of stereotypes have an imperfect understanding of the concept 'foreigner'
III (age 9–10)	accept more similarities between themselves and other peoples are increasingly able to see the point of view of other peoples understand that foreigners are people out of their own country

Society and Economy

The identification by the National Curriculum Council of 'education for economic and industrial understanding' as a cross-curricular theme has led to a revival of research interest in children's understanding of social and economic concepts (see especially, Ross, 1990). Many of these concepts, such as value, exchange, commodity, work, ownership, profit etc. are the building blocks of understanding the activities of people in places — both near and far. Almost all the work in this area has been within the framework of Piaget-type developmental stage theory and can be illustrated by understanding of the concepts of money and exchange.

In a study of 195 British primary school children, Furth (1980) examined children's understanding of the 'world of grown-ups', i.e. the societal world of community life with its institutions, customs, rules, services and products, roles and symbols. Furth, like so many others, identified stages in children's thinking about such matters. Four such stages were identified and these may be illustrated with reference to children's understanding of the function and operation of money:

Stage I
Money is freely available in society. Money transactions are simple exchanges without any precise meaning. The way people obtain money is primarily through receiving 'change' in such transactions.

Stage II
Money is given in exchange for goods. Children understand the notion of 'change' but not what the shopkeeper does with the money received.

Stage III
It is understood that the shopkeeper also needs to buy goods (in order to sell them) and that these purchases are related to the receipts from sales. However, the notion of profit is misunderstood, and often muddled with notions of greed.

Stage IV
Children understand that shopkeepers buy for less and sell for more. This provides for running expenses and the shopkeeper's income.

Further illustrations of children's understanding of the social world are provided by Hutchings (1990). Children aged 4 to 12 for example, were asked why they thought some people were poor. For many primary children, poor people are those whose money has been stolen, or who have not received enough from banks and shops, or who have spent what they had too quickly. It is worth bearing these studies in mind when considering children's likely understanding of poverty in economically developing countries.

A detailed survey of children's understanding of the social and economic world is out of place here but good summaries of the development of a number of interrelated concepts are to be found in Burris (1983), Hutchings, (1990), Schug (1990) and Linton (1990). Burris (1983, quoted in Holroyd, 1990) identifies a number of broad similarities in children's thinking across a number of specific concepts in the socioeconomic area. These are, for example, an inability to distinguish natural and social phenomena and a tendency to see social order as an external constraint rather than established through mutual agreement. Extrapolating from these general findings to children's understanding of distant people and places we might tentatively suggest therefore that children might find difficulty in distinguishing, say, natural features of the landscape from 'man-made' features. Perhaps too that a particular way of life in a distant part of the world is seen as given, rather than a response to environmental and other conditions and, as such, susceptible to change.

Holroyd (1990) has summarized a number of studies examining social and economic concepts and points out that many of them conclude that children achieve varying 'levels' of understanding, across a range of concepts. There also appear to be substantial cross-cultural differences. Children in some countries and cultures appear to understand in a more sophisticated way, the notion of, for example, 'profit' than others. Allowing for experimental differences, Holroyd concludes that children do not pass through 'universal' stages of development. The evidence all seems to show that experience, rather than maturation, is the major factor in children's understanding of socioeconomic ideas.

International Relations and War

As well as investigations into children's understanding of their own country and others there have also been parallel studies of the understanding children have of international relations and the concepts of war and peace. At a fairly early age, children seem to begin to develop orientations towards international politics. For example, from about the age of 9, American children have been shown to have some notion of international institutions and processes, be able to make simple evaluations of them and be able to suggest courses of action for their foreign ministers (Targ, 1970).

The model for much research into children's children's thinking about war, and in particular, nuclear war was set by Escalona in 1963. She asked 350 children, aged 4–18 to: 'Think of the world in ten years time. In what respect will it differ from the world of today?' More than 70 per cent of the children referred to the threat of nuclear war and seemed pessimistic about the prospects for the future. There has been follow-up research of this type in a number of countries (for example, Schwebel, 1982, in the USA; Cooper, 1965 and Targ, 1970, in the UK; and Richter, 1982 in Germany).

It appears that children develop, but subsequently lose, strong feelings against war at about the age of 10. Children of about 6 and 14 show the greatest hostility towards other nations, whilst there appears to be a point of maximum 'friendliness' towards other nations at about the age of 10 (Tolley, 1973). This peak of receptivity is supported by Carnie (1971).

Cooper (1965) interviewed English children from 7 to 16 years of age, using a schedule which included open-ended questions on verbal associations to the words 'war' and 'peace', the definition of war and the justification for war.

By the age of 7 or 8, most children appeared to have a fairly well-defined idea of what war and peace are. Word associations for the youngest children centred on military hardware. The 'exciting' weapons, ships, aeroplanes etc. were, with increasing age displaced by more negative notions of fighting, killing and dying. 'Peace' as a concept prompted far fewer responses than war and was generally perceived by children to be a period of respite, a state of 'non-war' and inactivity rather than a positive condition in itself which resulted from vigorous human interaction. Cooper suggests that, up to the age of about 11, children (boys in particular) have substantial experience of playground aggression and that they use these experiences to understand the nature of international warfare. Early definitions of war are as a 'big fight' and the same rules apply as to playground encounters. This view seems to be supported elsewhere (Webley and Cutts, 1985). When asked 'When is a war won?', younger children gave concrete answers mentioning for example the idea that the number of dead are counted up like in a game. Playground encounters also help to define young children's views on the inevitability of war. Wars are unlikely if each party is aware of the other's strength. Peace is the 'normal' condition but it can be disturbed by 'bullies' or by ignorance of the rules. Children also seem to develop more accurate ideas about international institutions and processes when these resemble their own experiences (Targ, 1970). Advice-giving and bargaining as international behaviours are well understood by children from their own peer group encounters. However, once past the age of about 11, children are more cynical or realistic about the nature of people and grow to recognize motivations such as greed and desire for power as being instinctive in humans. By this age, war seems to them to be more 'natural', even 'necessary' and people must work hard to keep their feelings in check in order to prevent wars occurring. War, amongst older children is seen as being bad but legal and military alliances as aggressive but good. According to Targ (1970), children increasingly develop a concept of international reality that justifies war, military policies and nationalism. Older children too appear to be far more pessimistic about their chances of survival in the event of a nuclear war.

Wars themselves prompt investigations into the perception of war. In response to the Vietnam War, Tolley (1973) conducted a large scale questionnaire survey on war amongst American children. After examining responses to the questions on attitudes to war Tolley was able to illustrate two polar types of American children holding, respectively, outspoken militaristic views and avowed pacifist views.

> The child most likely to cherish military values would be an eighth grade white boy. He would belong to a low income group, attend a military academy and probably worship at a Catholic or major Protestant church. A child possessing characteristics most associated with pacifism would be a black girl of about 10 in the fifth grade. Her family would be Quaker, well-to-do and she should attend a Friends' school. (p. 56)

An interesting feature of Tolley's work is that he compares children's reactions to war as an abstract concept in general with their knowledge and attitudes towards the Vietnam War in particular. A great variety of quality and quantity of information about the Vietnam War was held by American children. The variables accounting for the greatest differences between children were shown to be age followed economic status. Gender and access to media sources were less significant but contributed more than military parentage, school or the political views of parents.

Children's perception of war has also been investigated through an examination of the pictures children draw of war and peace. (Vriens, 1984, quoted in Dickhoff, 1987) Children were asked to make two drawings, one of peace and one of war. These were then analyzed according to their content and there was a follow-up interview with each child. The perceptions of peace and war of boys and girls seemed to be different. Girls rejected war from the age of 6 and had positive pro-peace attitudes at the age of 9. Boys, by contrast, talked and drew about war with enthusiasm between the ages of 6 and 10. War was depicted in their drawings as 'an heroic adventure, a spectacular game with planes in nose dive, explosions, secret missions, etc.' (Dickhoff, 1987, p. 40).

For many of the children surveyed by Davies (1987) the fear of nuclear war was a reality for a significant minority by the time they reached the end of primary education. Davies suggests that children's anxieties are not alleviated by the strategies most commonly used by adults to deal with nuclear issues, i.e. to ignore them or answer questions in an unplanned, ad hoc way. Children may sense that this is an area that adults themselves avoid discussing and this avoidance may add to children's fears. Children form their conception of social reality from what they see adults do. Their anxieties about the future may be alleviated if the adults with whom they have contact make it clear to them that it is possible for countries to resolve their conflicts in a peaceful way (Escalona, 1982).

The above, and other investigations into children's understanding of war and peace have a number of implications for teachers: (Alvik, 1968):

* Children frequently think about war, which gives parents and teachers opportunities for discussion.
* Discussion about war does not seem to provoke anxiety amongst children.
* Children have much concrete knowledge about war which they have gained from media but need help, through discussion with adults, in decoding issues.
* More could be done to inform children that war is a conflict between groups with incompatible values and that peace is a state which must be actively maintained.

Some Factors Influencing the Development of International Understanding

From all the studies above, it is possible to identify a number of factors that consistently appear to underlie children's understanding of distant people and places. These are: social class, gender and the children's own nationality.

'Class' differences in the way children think about their own country and others, are reported in the literature as being conspicuous and consistent. It has to be said, however, that the identification and definition of children's social 'class' is invariably crude in the earlier studies previously described. Often we are told only that children came from a 'middle class' school or a 'working class' school. Children variously defined as 'middle class' appear to give responses typical of older children — generally in the order of two years older (Middleton *et al*, 1970; Jahoda, 1962; Johnson *et al*, 1970). It seems reasonable to assume that this is related to home experiences such as the availability of books and illustrations, travel experience, opportunities for discussion and so on. Specifically, 'middle class' children are able to name more foreign countries than 'working class' children. They also appear to understand the concept of a 'foreign country' in a more or less conventional way, whereas 'working class' children, in both their naming and descriptions of places stress the exotic and picturesque (Jahoda, 1962).

Social class was also a significant factor in the age at which children achieved understanding of geographical relationships. Most 'middle class' children attained Jahoda's highest 'geographical stage' (i.e. they were able to demonstrate a correct understanding of the spatial relations of Glasgow-Scotland-Britain) by the age of 10–11. 'Working class' children lagged noticeably behind.

The children of 'middle class' homes were more likely to express liking for other countries than those from working class backgrounds (Lambert and Klineberg, 1967) Preferences for *particular* countries, on the other hand appear to be largely unaffected by social background.

Socioeconomic status appears to have a considerable effect on children's ability to understand both concrete and abstract aspects of war. 'Middle class' parents often acted as 'decipherers' of new bulletins and attempted to give their children a wider perspective on world events through discussion (Alvik, 1968). Ethnicity appears also to have some affect on children's attitudes to war. Tolley (1973) indicates that black American children seem significantly more opposed to war than white children. This relates to contemporary studies showing that black people more consistently opposed US involvement in the Vietnam War.

Although social class appears to be a factor therefore in the way children's international understanding develops, lack of clarity about what precisely is being measured throws doubts on the validity of the claims made.

Gender may also be a factor in children's international understanding. Boys seem to score more highly in tests of place knowledge (Morrissey, 1984; Johnson, Middleton and Tajfel, 1970) and there is the slight suggestion that boys have a more mature concept of nationality than girls. (Middleton, Tajfel and Johnson, 1970).

There seems too to be some differences in the preferences of boys and girls for particular countries. Girls appear to prefer Japan whereas there appears to exist a strong negative preference for Germany among boys (Stillwell and Spencer, 1974). The former preference may be related to the distinctive images of traditional Japanese women's clothing and hairstyles and the latter negative preference may be related to reading of war comics by boys (Johnson 1966).

Boys seem to be socialized into a 'will to defend country' much more than girls (Rosell, 1968) but this effect decreases with age. Girls seem to think more about the *consequences* of war than boys, and may therefore have a more negative view of it.

On the other hand, boys found war to be more complicated, morally and emotionally. They had to accommodate its sensational and attractive aspects as well as finding it bad and rejectable. Boys, as might be expected, show more interest in joining the armed forces when they leave school (Tolley, 1973).

Children's own nationality appears to be a further factor in the way they construe international relationships. Some attention has already been paid above to the preference by some nationalities for other more powerful or wealthy countries. Nationality concepts appear to be more developed among children from countries such as the United States, where the issue of nationality itself is more salient (Lambert and Klineberg, 1967; Middleton, Tajfel and Johnson, 1970).

Preference for one's own or for other nations appears to be linked to the majority or minority status of one's own group. The UNESCO survey found that children from some countries seemed to view the world as being populated more by peoples who were dissimilar to themselves than similar. Children in some societies seem to come to view themselves as culturally distinctive or isolated.

Summary and Conclusions

Some of the more important points raised by this chapter are summarized below:

1 Young children come to understand the 'nesting' relationships of geographical units (for example, locality, region, country, continent) very slowly and may not fully appreciate these relationships, even if they are able to make correct statements about them.
2 'Knowledge about' and 'attitudes towards' other countries are closely and complexly related.
3 Children's preferences for, and dislikes of, particular peoples and places are based first on their own idiosyncratic reasons and then on the shared views of their widening social contacts.

4 Young children appear to prefer their own country and prefer it increasingly with age.
5 Young children like other countries they perceive as being most like their own.
6 Children develop a greater range of likes and dislikes as they become older.
7 'Likes' and 'dislikes' for countries affect children's readiness to understand that others may act or feel as they do.
8 Attitudes to distant people and places are formed at least at the same time and probably before knowledge is gained about those places.

This chapter has traced a number of lines of research evidence that bear closely on the development of international understanding in children. The evidence is fairly strong on developmental stages but rather weak on the effect that teaching and experience can have on children's understanding of the relevant concepts.

Chapter 3

Images, Stereotypes and Prejudice

> All images are shaped by the way they are seen, a matter of setting,
> timing, angle, lighting, distance. Images carried about by some
> people for a whole lifetime may have been fixed by a single ex-
> posure, dating perhaps from an experience deep in the past. Or else
> they may emerge from a whole collection of pictures that a man
> takes with his mind over the years and which come out looking
> much the same because his mind's setting is fixed, like a fixed-focus
> box camera. This aperture is set by the totality of what a man is.
> (Isaacs, 1958)

The last chapter examined some conceptual frameworks for understanding
the development of children's knowledge and feelings about people and
places but gave little idea of the extent and variety of their mental geography. This chapter attempts to give a richer flavour of the construals that
children have into the wider world and identifies what appear to be some
consensus views of particular places. In attempting to understand these
images, we need to consider the issues of stereotyping and prejudice. This
involves us in a consideration of that alternative model of childhood thinking — that of the child as a processor of incoming information about the
world. But first, using the analogy of a voyage of exploration and discovery,
we need to map out the extent of the young child's 'known world'.

Discovery of the 'Known World'

What first interests young children about countries, according to Piaget
(1929), is the *name*. A large number of children interviewed by him defined
a country as a 'piece of land with a name'. Let's assume, for the time being,
that being able to name a country constitutes 'knowing' it. Clearly, there are
weaknesses in this definition. Children may have more or less accurate
information about particular countries which may or may not be related to
their ability to name those places. Nevertheless, the ability of children to

name countries has the considerable merit of being relatively easy to explore with relatively little ambiguity. Some extensive comparative data is, incidentally, also available for children at about the age of 13 (Saveland, 1983; Morrissey, 1984).

We can begin with the nursery. What is the extent of the known world of 3 and 4-year-olds? One exploratory study (Lambert and Wiegand, 1990) attempted to find out which countries were known by a sample of eighty children from a Yorkshire nursery. There are formidable problems of collecting such data. A large chart was kept, on which was recorded all the statements which children made in response to stimuli presented to them about distant places. A number of devices were used to prompt the children's talk. For example a 'magic carpet' game was played with the children in which they could go anywhere they wanted. Names of the places mentioned by children were recorded. Children were also shown dolls, models and pictures and these sometimes prompted the children to mention specific places by name. Despite the problems of data collection, and allowing for an immense variety of response (including quite often of course, no response at all) the very earliest definition of the 'wider world' known by, say, 4-year-olds might seem to be:

Spain, France, Africa, America and Australia

This 'world' is, of course, greatly confused in very young children's minds with other, much nearer locations, together with, for example, theme parks such as Kinderland and Disneyland — the suffix '— land' adding, one might suspect, to the confusion. Nevertheless, the specific countries above do seem to be prominent early on in the child's developing awareness of the rest of the world.

A larger study (Wiegand, 1991c) involved 222 children from four Yorkshire primary schools. Seven and 11-year-olds from each school were asked to write down the names of all the countries they knew. Spelling was unimportant and they were to include places if they were not sure whether they 'counted' as foreign countries. Seven-year-old children were generally able to name five or six countries but frequently showed that they were not sure of the definition of a 'foreign' country. The constituent parts of the United Kingdom were often given as foreign countries at this age (but disregarded by the 11-year-olds). Fantasy lands, both real (for example, Disneyland, Legoland, Flamingoland) and imagined (for example, Paradise, Never-never Land) were often included together with a few particular major world cities (New York, Los Angeles and Paris). Eleven-year-old children were able to name, on average, fifteen countries, and some could name more than thirty. Places listed sequentially on paper were often grouped into spatial/cultural patterns, for example, a typical listing at this age, (indicating perhaps some awareness of similarity between adjacent countries on the list) might be:

France, Spain, Italy; America, Canada; China, Japan; Australia, New Zealand.

These findings are similar to those quoted by Jahoda (1962) and the Leicester Polytechnic project on development education in the primary school (Allison, Conway and Denscombe, 1982).

The places known by at least 20 per cent of the whole sample of children ages 7 and 11 were mapped as shown in figure 3.1. At age 7 only the larger land masses are known. ('America' is here mapped as the USA). 'Africa' is known by approximately half the children but very few know any of its constituent countries. France and Spain, 'Russia', the Indian subcontinent, China and Australia make up the rest of the known world. By age 11, most of Western Europe is known, together with the larger countries of the Middle East. Previously-known countries are now frequently paired: 'America' with Canada, Australia with New Zealand, China with Japan. Boys especially now make mention of Argentina and Brazil (perhaps because of football connections) and some African countries are known (most notably Egypt, South Africa and Zimbabwe). The prominence of South Africa may perhaps be explained by persistent news coverage or the repetition of the word 'Africa' in the name of the republic. 'Egypt' features largely in early Bible stories and the pyramids and pharaohs seem to have some appeal to young children. But why Zimbabwe? Further questioning revealed two principal reasons for this country being known by so many — 'we just like the name'. As one of 'those faraway places with strange sounding names', Zimbabwe seemed to be unrivalled. Children just liked *saying* it. The second reason for its prominence seemed to be that Liverpool F.C.'s goalkeeper was born there! There remain, however, some striking gaps in the knowledge of 11-year-olds. Few of the countries of South-east Asia or South and Central America are known. This may perhaps be partially explained by bias in the media presentation of world news (see, for example, Goodey, 1974). However, it is remarkable that so few of the countries in Eastern Europe were known by the children considering the investigation was undertaken in early 1990, just after widespread reporting of major political changes in almost every Eastern European country. Neither did any of the children mention Lebanon or Israel, both of which were rarely out of the news in the period immediately preceding the study.

I was also reminded sharply that events which have shaped my own mental map of the world (for example, the Vietnam War and the South Atlantic War) were over by the time the children in this sample were born and there were no mentions by the children at all of Vietnam (c.f. Tolley, 1973) and very few of the Falkland Islands (c.f. Overjordet, 1984). There were also surprisingly few references to Ethiopia or the Sudan (c.f. van der Gaag and Nash, 1987).

However, although figure 3.1 shows the known world of all the 222 children questioned, there are significant differences between each of the four schools that made up the sample. The schools themselves varied on a number of dimensions.

Remote Estate Primary School is situated on a local authority housing estate four miles from a small coastal resort. The school is in an educational priority area and its teachers report a high unemployment rate and low incomes amongst the families in the catchment. Children rarely travel beyond the estate and few have been abroad. Those that have, travelled almost exclusively on package holidays, mostly to Spain.

Leafy Fringe Primary School serves the wealthy professional and business commuter belt of a major city. Travel experiences amongst these children is extensive, some having been on package holidays to Kenya and the Caribbean. Half of the children here have been to Spain and 16 per cent to the USA. These children also have much experience of independent, 'non-package' travel. More than half of the children, for example, have been to France in the family car and caravan.

Milltown Primary School serves part of the West Yorkshire conurbation. Almost all of its pupils come from families with strong Indian or Pakistani connections. Many children are bilingual, speaking Punjabi or Gujerati at home. Their own travel experience is often extensive. One-third of the sample of pupils at this school have been to India or Pakistan, for perhaps six to twelve weeks. These children generally stay with relatives and may attend school with cousins whilst they are there.

Small Town Primary has a mixed catchment with a fair spread of incomes and occupations amongst its children's parents. Children here have a variety of travel experiences, mostly to Western Europe. The travel of children at this school reflects closely the pattern of adult travel for Britain as a whole (outlined in *Market Intelligence*, 1984, *Business Monitor: Overseas Travel and Tourism (MA6)*, 1987). Figure 3.2 shows the differences between the known world of 11-year-olds at each of the four schools. There are differences in both the total number of countries known by the children in each school and the extent to which each child shares in that group knowledge. The world map of children at Remote Estate Primary School is the most restricted. Children here know only half the countries known by children at Small Town and Leafy Fringe. The world is poorly known beyond Western Europe. Australia, 'Africa' (rather than its constituent countries) and 'America' are as prominent as parts of Western Europe but there is little definition of the world beyond. Children from Leafy Fringe and Small Town have the most extensive world knowledge. Western Europe is well known, particularly by the Leafy Fringe children who know it more through touring than from a single package location. (These were the only children to mention Luxembourg, Liechtenstein and Monaco.) By contrast, Milltown children reveal a widespread knowledge of the Indian subcontinent and of the Middle East and Africa. This knowledge is often greater than that of Western Europe (to which few of these children had travelled).

The 'known world' as defined above was principally based on country

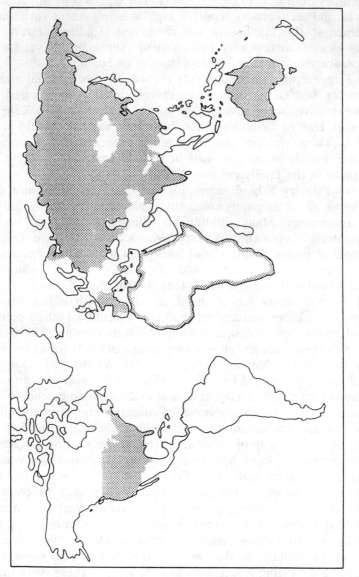

Figure 3.1: The 'known world' of (a) children aged 7

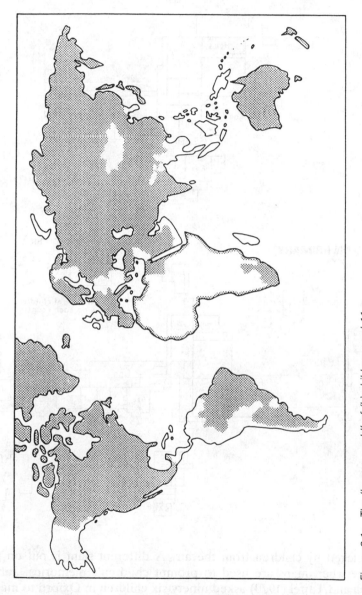

Figure 3.1: The 'known world' of (b) children aged 11

Source: Wiegand (1991c)

Figure 3.2: *The 'known world' of children from four Yorkshire schools. (The area of each country is drawn proportional to the number of children 'knowing' it)*

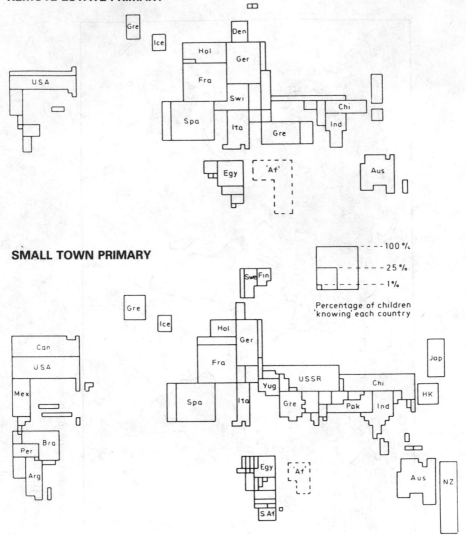

names plucked by children from the air. A different slant is put on global knowledge when maps are used to prompt children's memories. Johnson, Middleton and Tajfel (1970) asked ninety-six children in Oxford to mark the positions of England and nine foreign countries (Australia, China, France, Germany, India, Italy, Japan, Russia and USA) on a world map. All foreign countries marked correctly would have achieved a score of 9. The actual mean scores recorded were: 0.8 (age 7); 3.9 (age 9) and 5.1 (age 11).

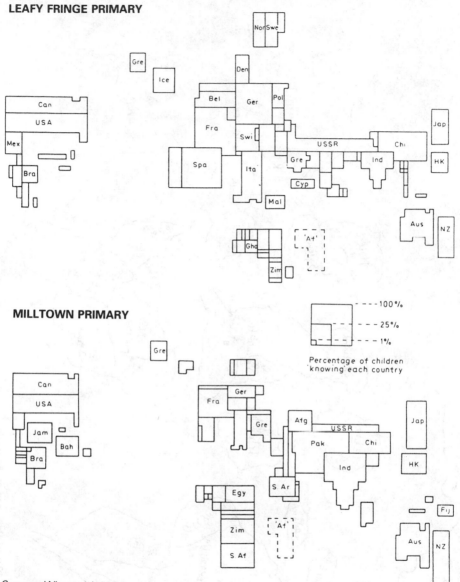

LEAFY FRINGE PRIMARY

MILLTOWN PRIMARY

Percentage of children 'knowing' each country

Source: Wiegand (1991c)

Readers may like to compare these scores with the results of their class tests after the implementation of the locational knowledge requirements of the National Curriculum!

Noticeable gaps in world knowledge (for example, unknown Eastern Europe) seem to persist through to secondary schooling. A study of 11–12-year-old boys in Manchester showed high scores on a map test of Europe for the correct identification of Western European countries, especially France,

73

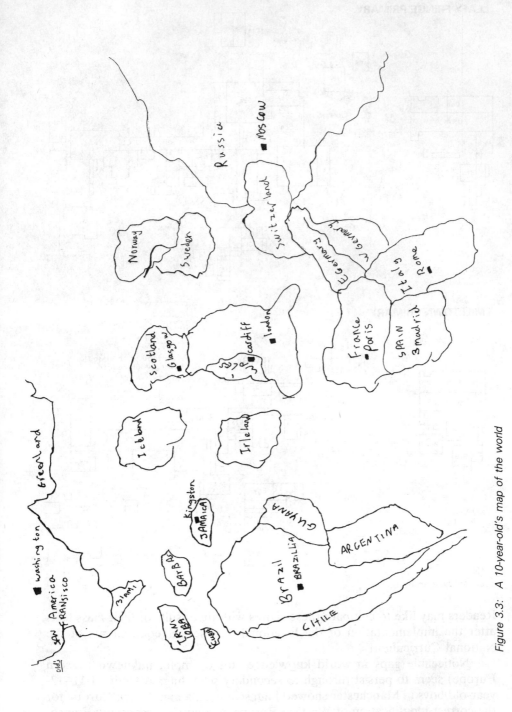

Figure 3.3: A 10-year-old's map of the world

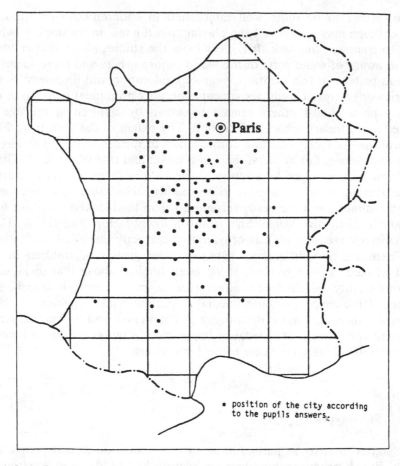

Figure 3.4: Pupils' attempts to locate Paris on a map of France

Source: Nebel, 1984

Italy, Spain and Russia but very low scores for Eastern Europe, particularly Hungary, Albania, Bulgaria and Romania (Watkins and Williams, 1982).

Although there have been many studies of children's freehand sketch maps of their local environment (for example, Catling, 1979), there have been few examining children's ability to draw a sketch map of the world. Yet it is clear that some children are fascinated by the world map and display an astonishing ability to recall the shapes and names of countries. Figure 3.3 was drawn by a 10-year-old from memory, in about ten minutes. In a study with a rather different focus, Nebel (1984) asked German primary and secondary children to mark the position of Paris on a map of France (see figure 3.4). The misleading notion of Paris being 'in the centre of

France' seems to be quite well established in children's minds although many children may well have been playing 'pin the tail on the donkey' when asked to complete this task. It is clear from the studies above that children become aware of some parts of the world before others and there seems to be some pattern in this mental voyage of exploration and discovery. Some countries or groups of countries appear especially prominent early on in the primary phase whilst others remain unknown by children at the age of transfer to secondary school and beyond. The extent of the known world at different ages is surely due to a constellation of factors including children's media experience, family links, their own travel and that of relatives. Other significant factors might be country shape — the 'boot' of Italy and the square Iberian peninsula appear to be readily memorable. Countries with distinct outlines are more easily recognized than land-locked countries with no clear or distinctive shape. Size is also a likely factor. The USSR, USA and Australia are high on lists of countries correctly identified.

There are also differences between some groups of children in the extent of their 'known worlds'. It has been implicit above that social class and the quality of children's direct (for example, through travel) and indirect (for example, through media) experiences are significant. These factors are discussed more thoroughly in chapters 4 and 5. The extent of some children's world knowledge is impressive, whereas the limited global awareness of others gives some cause for concern.

Stereotypes

As a 'starter' activity as part of an in-service course on distant people and places, British primary school teachers were asked to 'draw an Australian'. Figure 3.5 is typical of the drawings received and I acknowledge the effort of this unknown artist with thanks! It is clear from such exercises that powerful shared images exist about a number of nationalities in particular. Such images are frequently benign and may often be affectionate. They are perpetuated in a number of ways, not least by the tourist industry, for example:

> (Italians) move with a natural grace, they are insufferably good looking and until a diet of pasta, oil and ice cream takes its toll in middle age they are the sort of shape that Italian clothes fit. They seem to know instinctively what looks good and take care about how they look apparently more than anything else. They love to make a display of themselves and, better still their children and the spirit of peacock nation finds what we imagine to be its full expression in the evening promenade (passegiata) when the entire population goes public. (Morgan, 1987)

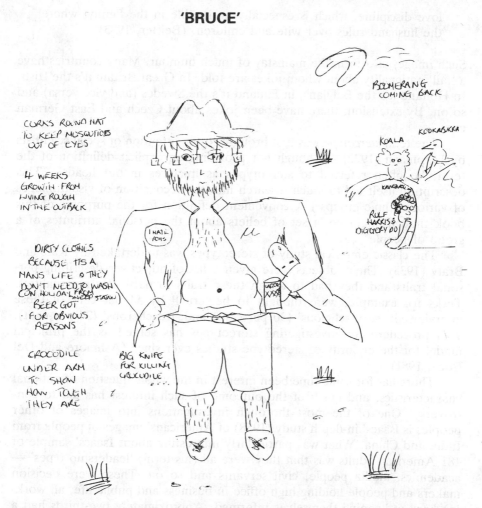

Figure 3.5: An English primary school teacher's image of Australians

Images such as these may also be shared internationally and may be found at all levels of education. Here is a summary of American college students' responses to a questionnaire on Germany:

> The country has one river, the blue Rhine, surrounded by vineyards and old castles. There are two cities: Munich and Berlin; and many snow-covered mountains with old picturesque farmhouses inhabited by ruddy cheeked people in quaint colourful regional costumes. The national beverage is beer, which is used to wash down *Sauerkraut*, *Sauerbraten* and *Knackwurst*. Germans are rugged, love to work, manufacture *Volkswagen* and *Lederhosen*. They are without humour, stodgy and conservative. Germans are perfectionists and

love discipline, which is especially noticeable in the family, where
the husband rules over wife and children. (Beitter, 1983)

Such images also form the mainstay of much humour. Many countries have
a 'fall' nationality about whom jokes are told. In Great Britain it's the Irish.
In Holland it's the Belgians, in Finland it's the Swedes (and vice versa) and
so on. By extension, there have been jokes about Czech and East German
cars.

The term *stereotype* was first brought to the attention of social scientists
by Lippmann (1922). Although not providing an explicit definition of the
term, he often referred to stereotypes as 'pictures in our heads'. (This
description itself led to much research into the recognition of visual images
of various ethnic groups.) A convenient definition for the purposes of this
book though might be 'a set of beliefs about the personal attributes of a
group of people'.

The classic empirical study of stereotypes was undertaken by Katz and
Braly (1933). Their subjects were given a list of adjectives describing per-
sonal traits and they had to assign these traits to particular nationalities.
Turks for example, were thought to be 'cruel' by 54 per cent of those
interviewed, 'very religious' (30 per cent) and 'treacherous' (24 per cent).
This procedure for investigating stereotypes has served as the principal
model for the majority of stereotype studies ever since (Ashmore and Del
Boca, 1981).

There has for some time been interest in the whole question of national
characteristics, and much of the outcome of such interest has led to con-
troversy. One of the most thorough investigations into images of other
peoples is Isaacs' in-depth study (1958) of Americans' images of people from
India and China. What was particularly interesting about Isaacs' sample of
181 American adults was that they were all (his term) 'leadership types' —
academics, media people, civil servants and so on. These were decision
makers and people holding high office in business and public life, all working hard at keeping themselves informed. Approximately two-thirds had a
substantial involvement in Asian affairs as part of their professional life.
Nevertheless, Isaacs' sample held between them a great many biases concerning Chinese and Indians. Fifty-four per cent expressed negative views
towards Indians whereas 70 per cent expressed positive views of the
Chinese. The Chinese stood highest in the esteem of those who had had
most contact with them and lowest in the esteem of those who had had least
contact, but Indians scored highest from those who knew them least.
Although the responses of Isaacs' sample were given on an individual basis,
there were a significant number of 'common holdings' — i.e. views shared
by the majority of the sample about the characteristics of Chinese and
Indians. To some extent the views of the sample towards these peoples
could be attributed to contemporary political events, but that is not the
whole story. Why is it, asks Isaacs, that some people see the same character-

istic differently? Why do some people describe Indians as talkative whereas others describe them as articulate?

One of the more difficult aspects of stereotypes is that, although they cannot always be legitimated, they may contain a 'grain of truth'. But how do we deal with the question of what is real and what is false? None of Isaacs' respondents held images that were pure fantasy. Each represented the 'truth' of someone's perception. Unfortunately, there is no template against which we can check the accuracy of the images people hold. Generalization is a normal device for learning but some generalizations can be checked every day for relevance and validity against reality. But in dealing with characteristics of peoples there is no such test and we are allowed free rein thereby to people our private geographies with caricatures.

It may be helpful at this point to define some terms and processes (following Leyens and Codol, 1988) relating to social cognition — that is, the way in which we make sense of the mass of incoming information about (amongst other things) 'national characteristics'.

We receive information about people and places *directly* by our own travel experiences and *indirectly* by, for example, the media, travel brochures and hearing about other people's holidays. This massive inflow of information is processed by a complex set of mental activities involving perception, memory, language and so on. These processing activities are termed *cognition*. From cognition comes knowledge. Knowledge allows us to react to new information and so cognition plays an important function in enabling us to act in our environment. However, our ability to process the huge quantities of information we receive is limited. We therefore develop strategies to reduce the amount of processing that is required. These strategies can distort the intake of information by, for example, selecting or simplifying it. Once information has been received it has to be sorted so that it can be related to previous learning. New experiences of distant people and places such as pictures, meetings or hearsay are compared therefore with our previous experiences. This is done through a process of *categorization* whereby the new objects of perception are put together with previous ones having similar characteristics. Each grouping like this is called a *category*. Categories vary in complexity. We have, for example, a much more complicated, and more acutely differentiated, conception of our own country than of a little known distant one. Categories are not independent of each other because they comprise pieces of data each with multiple properties. We use our previous experience to *generalize* about the characteristics of objects. This generalization process affects the subsequent information we choose to receive about them and how we integrate that information with existing knowledge. Neither are categories neutral. We value some characteristics of incoming information more than others and this valuing determines aspects of our behaviour.

How is this view of the mind as a processor of information related to the creation of stereotypes? According to Tajfel (1969), stereotypes are a special type of generalization derived from the cognitive process of categorization described above. (This analysis owes much to the work of Gordon Allport whose lengthy but immensely readable book (1954) is highly recommended.)

Stereotyping has four functions (Tajfel, 1981).

1 A cognitive function, which allows us, in the manner already described above, to make sense of a mass of incoming information. In this function, stereotypes are merely generalizations like any other and are not necessarily any more or less inaccurate, biased or faulty. However, it does seem to be the case that when presented with information on a continuous scale we have the tendency to group it into discrete classes. This has the effect of minimizing the differences *within* classes and exaggerating the differences *between* classes. Take height for instance. People appear to have the tendency to group other people into classes (such as 'tall', 'medium' and 'short'), based on the continuous variable, height. Once having made this classification, all those in, say, the 'tall' category are judged to be *substantially* taller than those in the 'medium' category.

2 A value preserving function. Categorizing physical attributes tends not to involve values. Categorizing people's personal characteristics usually does. Data on personal characteristics is also more ambiguous, subject to hearsay and rumour and much less easily verifiable than physical data. We also appear to be readily able to supply our own information on personal characteristics to form a more complete impression of others (Asch, 1946). Changing or dismantling physical categories does not involve any adjustments to our value system, but moving people between personal or social categories once they have been assigned to one involves a reconsideration of values. This may be threatening. A stable set of stereotypes may therefore be comforting because we have an emotional investment in it. Much more contradictory evidence is needed to dislodge these social categories once they are established and so categories built on evaluative information tend to be more permanent.

3 An ideologizing function. Stereotypes seem to have been created in the past to explain complex and stressful social events, particularly those involving gross actions against minority groups. The massive and widespread witch hunts in Europe in the sixteenth and seventeenth centuries are just such an example (Thomas, 1971). The ills of society are by this means attributed to a group.

4 A positive differentiation function. Stereotypes are persistent not only because of the durability of categories but because they serve an important function for those holding them. People identify themselves as members of a category and it becomes a useful defence

mechanism to be able to allocate others to categories too. Stereotypes thus help create a 'positive difference' between one's own group and others. Once people are classified into ingroup and outgroup, ingroup favouritism and outgroup discrimination tends to result. The distinctiveness and self-esteem of ones own group is reinforced and enhanced in this way.

The function of stereotypes is therefore more than just to introduce order and simplicity into the mass of social information received. This cognitive function alone is fairly benign. But the 'personal' and 'social' categories that may be created through this process are usually fairly durable and it may be difficult to dislodge them even in the face of contradictory evidence. For this reason it is often an easier processing task to bend the evidence to fit the existing mental categories. Stereotypes tend to dispose people 'to think in rigid categories' (Adorno *et al*, 1950, p. 228). Once stereotypes are set up they act as a means of sorting individuals. Persons may be identified as members of a category and will be assigned all the characteristics of that category. Stereotyping leads to the homogenization and depersonalization of individuals. They become perceived only in terms of their shared category characteristics and not their own unique and idiosyncratic personalities.

How do stereotypes emerge and change in childhood? According to Lambert and Klineberg (1967), the stereotyping process appears not much in evidence among 6-year-olds but becomes very apparent in the early teen years. Their evidence seems to suggest that the process of establishing the concept of their own nationality produces in children 'an exaggerated and caricatured view of one's own nation and people'. In other words the first signs of stereotyped thinking appear in relation to one's *own* nationality rather than in others. At the age of 6, children were making generalizations about their own people at the same time as they were describing foreign people in objective, factual terms. Foreign stereotyping did not start until the age of about 10.

Most research into stereotypes has considered the attitude of subjects to very large groups — men, women, Jewish people, black people etc. For adult subjects, these categories may be too broad to identify the true nature of subjects' attitudes towards them (Hamilton, 1981). We would know more about the nature of stereotypes if we were able to break down the members of stereotyped groups into subordinate classes. However, children are less likely to be able to differentiate such subordinate classes and so it seems likely that studies of children's stereotypes will be stuck at the superordinate level. Although there have been investigations into stereotypes for at least fifty years, there is much still to explore. The literature for example assumes that all stereotypes function in the same way, regardless of the objects of stereotyping. The principles are held to be the same whether the stereotypes are of Italians, Muslims or women drivers. Also, the fact that biases in our information processing can cause stereotypes does not imply that this is the sole cause of stereotypes. Motivation and social learning all probably contribute to their formation (Hamilton and Trolier, 1986).

Prejudice

Since the 1930s, stereotypes have been mostly linked to negative attitudes and prejudice. Indeed, Katz and Braly (1933), virtually equated stereotypes and prejudice: 'Racial prejudice is thus a generalized set of stereotypes of a high degree of consistency which includes emotional responses to race names, a belief in typical characteristics associated with race names, and evaluation of such traits' (pp. 191–2).

Prejudice is the holding of derogatory attitudes about members of a social group. It includes racism, sexism and jingoism. Aboud (1988) is more specific: 'prejudice refers to an *organized* predisposition to respond in an unfavourable manner toward people from an ethnic group *because* of their ethnic affiliation' (p. 4, my emphasis).

Aboud also draws a distinction between stereotypes and prejudice: 'Stereotypes are rigid, overgeneralized beliefs about the attributes of ethnic group members, whereas prejudice is a negative attitude' (p. 5). Clearly, the two are difficult to separate if the stereotypical attribute being applied is evaluative and negative (for example, 'Mexicans are lazy') than merely descriptive (for example, 'French people eat snails'). But note that in the case of these examples, children's perspectives may differ from those of adults. Eating something that seems unpleasant may have much more impact on a child (although the information was only descriptive) than information that is also evaluative.

It may be helpful at this point to clarify the meaning of the term 'race'. There is a link in many people's minds between skin colour and the use of the term 'race'. However, this vague concept is of doubtful use and has little scientific basis. Genetic differences between people which account for skin, eyes and hair colour are superficial and do not reflect any important biological differences between people. *Racism*, on the other hand, *is* real. It consists of behaviour and practices which result in the disadvantage of some ethnic groups. Racial prejudice consists of negative feelings and opinions about whole groups of people.

Where does prejudice originate? One view is that prejudice is a reflection of the different values attributed to groups in society. People are products of society and therefore adopt attitudes about the relative power and status of other social groups. Children adopt the attitudes of their parents. This explains why weaker groups are more generally singled out for prejudicial treatment but doesn't explain why some individuals are more prejudiced than others or account for changes in the level of prejudice shown by children at different ages. Tajfel (1987) suggests that we may behave in two ways at the same time. Firstly as *individuals* interacting with other individuals. In this type of behaviour we bring into play the whole range of our idiosyncratic characteristics and respond to others on the basis of our individual experiences. But we also behave as members of a group. This involves us in engaging in the principal characteristic that provides the definition of group membership. In the latter case we act the role of group member and adopt the prevailing group attitudes accordingly.

Group behaviour generally reflects the group interest (Sherif, 1966). If groups perceive their interests to lie in cooperation with other groups then inter-group tolerance and friendship will develop. But if groups are in competition, then hostile attitudes and perhaps behaviour are desirable because they sharpen and energize competitiveness. This view was illustrated by Sherif in studies relating to American boys' summer camps (Sherif *et al*, 1961). Sherif demonstrated that the attitudes of 'normal, healthy boys' to others could be altered by the circumstances in which they were placed. When competitive situations were set up the boys responded by being aggressive towards the opposing groups. When cooperative situations were arranged, the boys worked collaboratively and harmoniously. Membership of a group and the real or imagined conflict with other groups can produce distinctive social behaviour. Golding illustrates the same principle in the novel *The Lord of the Flies*.

How do racial attitudes develop in children? Goodman (1964) proposed a simple three stage sequence. First, children became able to differentiate between one racial group and another (the racial *awareness* phase). Second, rudimentary feelings about different racial groups emerged (the racial *orientation* phase), followed by the racial *attitude* phase in which stable attitudes were maintained by stereotyped notions. A similar, but more detailed series of stages has been suggested by Katz (1976).

Aboud (1988) explains the development of prejudice as two overlapping sequences (table 3.1). Some of these features bear close similarity to Piaget's account of development (see p. 54 and p. 58). The first sequence relates to children's development from early affective learning to skilled cognition. The second sequence relates to the focus of children's attention. According to Aboud, prejudice is reduced when children reach stage 3 of this sequence, i.e. at about the age of 8–10.

Can Teaching Overcome the Effects of Stereotypes and Prejudice?

One of the difficulties faced by teachers is that the processes which create stereotypes are useful to children; they help them to formulate concepts and make sense of a complex world. The problem for teachers is to circumvent the process in some instances of its operation and not in others. What sorts of strategy might help?

Providing children with more detailed information about the groups for whom they hold stereotypes is likely to result in their perception of more

Table 3.1:   The development of prejudice (after Aboud, 1988)

Development of cognitive skill	Focus of attention
1 Children are dominated by their feelings. Their attitudes are determined by their emotions.	1 Children are egocentric. They only see the world from their own point of view.
2 Children notice similarities and dissimilarities between others. This determines prejudice, with similar people being liked.	2 Children are preoccupied by groups and only see individuals as members of groups.
3 Children understand individual qualities and categories, that ethnicity is permanent and are able to reciprocate.	3 People are judged for their individual qualities and not for those of the groups to which they may belong.

and more subgroups within the larger category. The global stereotype is thereby fragmented into a number of smaller subgroupings. These subgroupings may still be broad generalizations, but they are likely to be less sweeping and therefore less subject to gross overgeneralization. Dealing with attitudes, however, is not so simple. For example, meeting individuals from groups about which one is prejudiced does not necessarily reduce the prejudice felt. We sometimes reason that the individual whom we have met is just not typical of all the others.

An alternative approach is to deliberately attempt to change one or more of the attributes on which the stereotype is based. The presentation of a broader range of occupations, appearance, lifestyles, etc. of the target group muddies the categories and encourages the child to use other cues as the basis for categorization. This approach to changing the stereotypes held by children may be gradual or sudden. In the former case it depends on the steady 'dripping' of more and more varied instances of lifestyles of particular peoples. As part of a topic on 'Germany' for example, a teacher may choose to select 'My day at school' from the perspective of a child whose parents are Turkish. The inclusion of a minority perspective forces the category 'German' to be widened or split. This approach can however, be complemented by presenting pupils with stark, disconforming instances which confront their existing beliefs directly (Rothbart, 1981). I have frequently played a locational guessing game with children (and teachers on in-service courses) using colour transparencies of different parts of the world. An aerial photograph of Johannesburg (skyscrapers, motorways, etc.) is shown to the group. 'Where is this?' Few participants can guess the correct continent, let alone the city. Games like this are a useful challenge by confronting the pictures in our heads with the pictures of reality.

There are disappointingly few studies of the effects of teaching on the reduction of stereotyping (but see Dunn, 1988). Not the least of the problems is the methodology of measuring the images that children hold about people and places.

Gaining Access to Images of People and Places

There have been a number of methodological approaches to finding out the images held about distant people and places and a good overall survey has been provided by Spicer (1984). *Attitude surveys*, for example, have included formal attitude inventories (Gough *et al*, 1950; Graham, 1951) and projective sentence completion tests (Knight and Rice, 1984).

Multiple item tests (Williams, Best and Boswell, 1975; Katz and Zalk, 1978) and continuous rating scales (Genesee, Tucker and Lambert, 1978; Verna, 1981) have been used to assess race prejudice in children. The latter allow the child to place members of ethnic groups on a continuum indicating the degree of liking. For example, Aboud and Mitchell (1977) asked children to place photos of peers from several different ethnic groups along a board, closer to themselves if they liked the person and progressively further away if they didn't.

The *preference studies* of Gould and White (1974) have already been described in chapter 1, in the context of the residential preferences of British school leavers. The same technique was extended by Gillmor (1974) for Irish school leavers and has been used by Hicks and Beyer (1968) for images of Africa and by Slater and Spicer (1980) for preferences of other countries. However, preference studies such as these can really only be used for older children or adults as younger children do not yet have enough knowledge from which to make informed choices. Nevertheless, when primary age children have been asked to express their preferences, they have preferred countries nearer home than those further away. German primary school children indicated most liking for the neighbouring countries of France, Switzerland, Holland and Great Britain. Least liked were Iceland, Ireland, Portugal and Norway (Nebel, 1984). There have also been early studies examining preferences for different ethnic groups using dolls. Clark and Clark (1947) used a forced choice question format asking children to choose whether they would like to play with a black or white doll.

Written test responses have principally been 'word association' tests. These have played a major role in studies of images because they are cheap and can quickly generate large quantities of data. However, the strongly collaborative nature of much contemporary primary classroom activity can make the collection of *individual* responses in a class context somewhat difficult. They are, of course, highly dependent on the writing competence of the respondent. Studies of free association to picture or word (for example, country name) stimuli include Haddon (1960), Gould (1973) and Whiteford (1984). A questionnaire format has been adopted by Robinson and Heffner (1968), and Pocock (1976). Diaries have been used by Pocock (1972) and Spencer and Lloyd (1974) for children's local, urban experience but I do not know of any studies that use diaries for children's overseas travel, although this would perhaps be a fruitful area of investigation (see chapter 5).

Free recall maps and pictures have been very widely used in the study of construals of the local, (especially urban) environment (Lynch, 1960) but some studies have made use of maps of more remote places (Wolforth, Popescu and Belanger, 1984) and of the world as a whole (Overjordet, 1984). Drawing pictures of distant people and places are a useful alternative to written responses where children's language skills are less developed (Bar-Gal, 1984; Nebel, 1984) especially when they are boosted by oral questioning ('tell me what you are drawing now') (Maurer and Baxter, 1972).

Oral interviews have already been discussed in the context of Piaget's early work. They can involve the interviewee in free association or more structured responses. Much hinges on the quality of the interaction between the interviewer and the interviewee and the method used of recording the interview. Very young children may be shy and reluctant to discuss their feelings with a stranger, especially in the presence of a tape recorder.

With many of these techniques there are considerable problems of data interpretation. Consider for example this extract from a child's writing about a picture showing a farmer in Zimbabwe:

> This man lives in Zimbabwe. He is very poor and has got no proper
> clothes. He only wears a rag around his waist.

Both language and concepts need exploring here. What is 'poverty'? How can it be compared with poverty which is more easily recognizable to children living in the UK? What are 'proper' clothes? Are the old shorts I might wear for summer gardening, 'rags'? Does he wear few clothes because he's poor or because it's hot? The nature of children's evaluative images must be seen in the light of their language development.

Children's Images and Stereotypes

What images do primary school children have of distant people and places and how do these images change over time? As part of the Yorkshire study described earlier, nursery children were prompted by a variety of stimuli, including pictures, dolls and models, to talk about distant places they had heard about (Lambert and Wiegand, 1990). For them, 'Spain' was a beach, hotel, sea, sun and sand. Only two children had been to Spain but these images were strong in the minds of all those who recognized the country name. 'Australia' prompted two images, one of the beach and sun, the other of kangaroos, crocodiles and koalas. The image of the Statue of Liberty was strong in the minds of children who knew about America.

The nursery children also showed that they were able to recognize and talk about a number of 'environments'. These form a set of discrete land-scapes each with their own set of associations. They were derived from conversations with more than 100 children. For example, children were shown a picture of Inuit (Eskimo) children in a village in Northern Canada.

Teacher: Tell me what you can see in this picture.
Child: It's Snowland.
Teacher: Do you know where Snowland is?
Child: It's the North Pole.
Teacher: Go on!
Child: Father Christmas has got some reindeers.

Clusters of ideas contributed by the children when they were shown pictures were collected and the following set of environments were defined, each with the characteristics shown below. These clusters form perhaps the first 'natural regions' which children become aware of.

'desert island': beach, palm trees, blue sea, hot sun, pirates, Robinson Crusoe
'jungle': trees, monkeys, parrots, snakes, lions, tigers, hot, Tarzan
'bibleland': grass, sheep, goats, camels, shepherds, Jesus,
'Sahel': sand, starving, black people
'North Pole': snow, igloo, 'Eskimo', Father Christmas, reindeer, penguins
'Costa': beach, sea, hot sun, hotels, pool, holidays

Some indication of the widening perception of places between the ages of 7 and 11 may be gained from table 3.2. Twenty-five children of each age group were asked to 'write (or draw) all the ideas that come into your head when you think of ... Australia'. The table shows the number of mentions of particular pieces of information and reveal an increased number and range of responses by age 11. Figure 3.6 also shows two fairly typical drawings of the same subject from children at age 7 and 11. The example quoted here is obviously based on responses from a limited number of pupils but teachers attending inservice courses at the same time reported virtually identical results when asked to replicate the test with their own classes. What 7-year-olds principally know about Australia is that it is hot, dry and has kangaroos. The power of TV soap operas from Australia (for example, *Neighbours* and *Home and Away*) is immediately noticeable by age 11, and may account for the predominant surf and skateboard images. There is also an increase in geographically accurate information intermingled with crude stereotypes. The latter are quite likely reinforced by at least two series of popular humorous TV advertisements for brands of Australian lager. These exploit the stereotyped images of male Australians by invoking references to flying doctors, sheilas, crocodiles, sheep shearing, etc. As in a cartoon drawing the scene has to be set quickly so that the joke can be appreciated and the cliché is thus a useful device. But the extent to which children see

Table 3.2

AUSTRALIA

Total word association responses from twenty-five 7-year-olds

hot/sunny/warm	20	big	1
dry	8	skyscrapers	1
kangaroos	7	tigers (sic)	1
good/nice	3	elephants (sic)	1
reference to TV programmes	2	wallabies	1
koalas	2	accent	1
crocodiles	2	bush	1
sea/ocean	2	spiders	1
T-shirts	1	noisy	1

Total word association responses from twenty-five 11-year-olds

reference to TV programmes	32	Ayers Rock	2
kangaroos	18	sea/ocean	2
hot/sunny	17	near Japan/Singapore/New Zealand	2
koalas	11	crocodiles	2
other side of world/down under	11	sharks	2
cities named	9	skate boards	2
Jason Donovan/Kylie Minogue	8	bicentennial celebrations	2
surf/surf boards	8	Captain Cook	1
beaches	7	flies	1
bush/outback	6	possums	1
accent	6	spiders	1
Sydney opera house/harbour bridge	6	snakes	1
sport	5	Rolf Harris	1
aborigines	5	lager	1
deserts/dry/dusty	5	time difference	1
boomerangs	4	forest	1
money/dollars	4	island	1
dingoes	4	sheep	1
wallabies	3	didgeridoos	1
reference to a relative	3		

---

the boundary between joke and reality is not always clear. Most of the facts listed here as 'known' by children stress *distinctiveness* — of lifestyle, animals and climate. Animals appear to be a powerful feature of children's images of distant places.

If this exercise is repeated for a number of different countries, several observations may be made about the responses. Firstly, if 'single mentions' are ignored, a remarkable degree of image uniformity is apparent in the minds of the children. Places are characterized by a very narrow range of associations. This appears to be true not just for young children. Whiteford, for example (1984), used a word association test with college students in which each student had to best characterize each of fifteen places in three words. There was virtually unanimous agreement on:

China	rice, highly populated, communism
Japan	mountains, highly populated, sophisticated industry
South Africa	hot, racism, diamonds

7-year-old

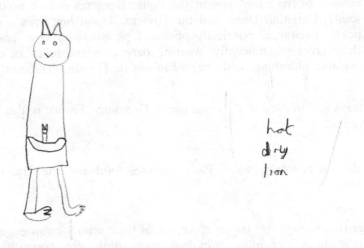

hot
dry
lion

11-year-old

Figure 3.6: Drawings of 'Australia' by a 7-year-old and an 11-year-old

Secondly, some images are for children especially salient and many appear to have a 'logo' or emblem function in that the one image represents the whole country. This emblem might be an animal (for example, kangaroo) or a building (for example, windmill), or food (e.g. frogs' legs). There also appears (in Europe at least) to be a reasonable degree of uniformity in the images held by children from different countries. France, for example, for English children:

consists of the Eiffel Tower, the Folies Bergeres (which no-one can spell), Christian Dior, and the Riviera. Upon her lives a race of fickle, excitable, politically obsessed people who dine and wine themselves magnificently, wearing berets, in the midst of unmentionable plumbing; and over all looms de Gaulle. (Haddon, 1960)

Whereas for children of the same age in Germany, France is also linked with terms such as:

the Eiffel tower, wine, Paris, cheese, food and the sea. (Nebel, 1984)

Older (i.e. secondary) pupils make use of their school knowledge to include terms such as Versailles, Napoleon, revolution, etc. Nevertheless, these older pupils retain the hackneyed associations of bread, wine and cheese.

Secondary pupils in Europe also appear to share attitudes towards particular countries. A few years before the reunification of Germany, a large scale cross-national study reported a striking mental demarcation of Europe into a 'liked' tourist west and a 'disliked' political east. Across the four countries in which the study was undertaken (UK, West Germany, Denmark and The Netherlands) there was a marked similarity between clusters of countries on both sides of the 'west/east divide' about which pupils had much, accurate information and those which were not mentioned at all or about which little was known. Poland, the (then) Democratic Republic of Germany and the USSR, for example, were referred to frequently but Czechoslovakia, Bulgaria and Romania hardly appeared (Williams, Bülmann, Hahn and van Westrhenen, 1984). In a related study of the perceptions of Danish pupils to other European countries, Biilmann indicated that some stereotypes are extremely firm. The Netherlands, for example is associated to a high degree with Amsterdam, The Hague, dykes, low land, vegetable and flower gardening, land reclamation, dairy farming and windmills (Bülmann and Williams, 1984).

It is not clear to what extent images change over time. Jahoda (1962) summarizes the 'chromium plate and candyfloss' images of America among primary school children:

AGE 6/7
all/some are black
different speech and clothes
warm climate
cowboys, Indians and 'stars'

AGE 8/9
big cars, skyscrapers, rich
different accents, some black, fancy clothes
big size and large population
climate
cowboys, Indians and film stars

AGE 10/11
big cars, skyscrapers, nice shops, wide roads
different accents, clothes, manners, some black people
climate
film stars, singers, actors
big size and large population

Twenty years later, how have these images changed? The reader is invited to compare these images with those of a convenient sample of pupils! Better still, to guess in advance which images will be uppermost in children's minds at different ages. Are cowboys and Indians as prominent today? To what extent have they been replaced by police dramas or a current soap opera? American holidays (generally to Florida) are now within reach for the lucky few and first hand experience is now able to test the television images.

However, some places seem to evoke for children a persistently negative and ill-informed response. Most noticeable of all is that of Africa, and in view of the National Curriculum requirement that children should study a locality in an economically developing country it is worth reviewing the evidence for what they know and feel about that continent as a whole. Of all the images of distant places in children's (and adults') minds, those of Africa remain the most distorted and pervasive. Reference has already been made to the widely held view of African homogeneity.

The darkest thing about Africa has always been our ignorance of it. (Kimble, 1951, quoted in Porter, 1987)

Consider the racism and arrogance of the term 'darkest Africa'. Dark to whom? The great empires of western Africa? Timbuctoo had a higher form of government, law and, some claim, religion in 1400, than Paris. (Bunge, 1965)

Africa south of the Sahara ... is a hot, primitive land where wild beasts prowl the steaming jungles stalking and being stalked by black savages armed only with spears and poison darts ... a strange land of huts and drums and mystery. (Hicks and Beyer, 1968)

Major misconceptions among *secondary* school pupils abound. For example that most of Africa south of the Sahara is covered by jungles rather than grasslands, that large wild animals would be more likely to be found deep in the jungles rather than in parks and game reserves and that when European explorers first visited Africa they found no towns or cities, only small villages of huts, rather than strong kingdoms. Over a period of thirty years, Porter (1987) invited his students at the University of Minnesota taking an introductory course in Africa to write the names of African countries on an outline map on the first day of the course. He reports a great decline over this period in the ability of students to name countries or locate them correctly. <u>Images on the other hand, remain strikingly persistent.</u> Jungles, <u>animals, poverty, hunger, diamonds, mud huts feature highly.</u> *Tarzan* and *Daktari* have much to answer for in the formation of these images.

Primary children in Britain appear also to have these associations. The overwhelming perception of Africa is negative, of 'Africa starving' or 'Africa primitive' (Jungkunz and Thomas, 1986). A first-year primary class were asked what images came to mind when the word 'Africa' was mentioned. They came up with the following list:

> deserts
> trees
> foodsacks
> sand
> Band Aid
> Ethiopians
> poverty
> hungry
> no houses
> sun
> heat
> suffering
> crying
> hospitals
> food
> fields
> insects
> vultures

(Oxfam, 1986, quoted in van der Gaag and Nash, 1987)

Similar images were present in the minds of primary children in Leeds in 1989:

> (after listening to music) 'It sounded like tap dancing but it couldn't have been because they don't have any pavements'. (8 years)

> 'They have mud houses, made of straw at the tops, like you see on Tarzan.' (8 years)

(Teacher) 'Do you think you'd like to live in a house like that?'

'I wouldn't like to live in mud'.

The 'mud hut' label appears to be so strong in fact that children persist with it even in the face of contradictory photographic evidence (Graham and Lynn, 1989). It is reassuring that such images decline during the years of secondary schooling. Hibberd (1983) for example shows how in a word-association test, 'mud huts' was mentioned by almost 40 per cent of 12-year-olds, but this had decreased to 7 per cent for 15-year-olds. 'Witch doctors' decreased from 16 per cent to none. It is not clear of course whether the change in the 'knee-jerk' reaction is accompanied by any increase in positive attitude.

Africa is almost always referred to as one entity, a 'country' rather than a continent. It appears broadly homogeneous rather than varied. There is very little knowledge of the names of any of the countries that comprise it. The notion of 'Africa' as synonymous with 'Ethiopia' appears to have been widespread in the 1980s (Dunn, 1988; Jungkunz and Thomas, 1986). The identification of Africa with famine may occur very early. Here are two nursery children responding to a picture of (apparently happy and healthy) black African children herding cattle:

generalisation African children don't have any food. Their mummies and daddies don't give it to them. They don't like to be fat. That's why they don't get any food.

Well, they're from Africa and they don't have any food for the babies. They're starving.

When other children were confronted with this idea it seemed clear that the message from home of 'eat up your dinner because there are African children who are starving' had already taken a firm hold in their minds.

Other children from the same ('white') nursery demonstrated a fairly strong negative reaction to the children in this picture. Race prejudice among nursery children has been noted elsewhere. Jeffcoate (1977) for example noted that when white nursery children were shown pictures of black people by their teacher they talked about them in a 'neutral' way but when the same pictures were left for the children to discuss informally in the presence of hidden tape recorders they seemed to use racially offensive language.

However, Africa also seems to be liked by many young children because of the appeal of the unusual and the exotic (Jahoda, 1962).

'They've got lions, tigers, elephants and polar bears (sic)'. (age 7)
(p. 94)

93

Summary and Conclusions

There is some pattern to the young child's developing image of the world. This pattern is expressed in both the countries known and what is known about them. Some countries, such as Spain, France, China and 'America' are known early on in childhood. The global 'mental map' expands throughout the primary phase but by the age of 11 there are still some large (and predictable) gaps in children's world locational knowledge.

Some countries rapidly become associated with 'emblem' images. These images are generally of fairly long standing and are perpetuated by the media and often exploited by the advertising industry (in promoting the country itself for tourism as well as its products). Amusing and exotic details are often particularly well known to children (such as frogs' legs or corks dangling from hats). But animals too are especially interesting to them and attract much attention.

There is a fairly high degree of consensus in the nature of the images of certain countries amongst children and this is often shared by children in a number of other countries.

Many children seem to have been taught that some particular groups of foreign people are especially *different* from themselves and it seems likely that the same peoples have been used universally to illustrate contrasts in ways of life, even though that contrast may no longer exist. Some images are stable and enduring, but others are subject to topicality.

Nevertheless, children are *interested* in people from other parts of the world. More interested in *people* than *places*. The message here is important. Traditional approaches to the teaching of geography would have looked at the physical characteristics of place and then considered how these would affect lifestyle. This process needs to be reversed. First describe how people live, then look for the underlying factors that help to account for that particular way of life (Haddon, 1966).

Environmental stereotypes and preferences can be considered as pre-Copernican in that the world revolves and observations are structured around the observer. The further away the environment and the more unlike his or her own, the more children are likely to see it in terms of stereotypes. Goodey's (1973) model (see p. 6) is useful because it differentiates between two sorts of experience in relation to far places. One is pro-active which relies on the child's direct experience of place through, for example, visits abroad. The other is vicarious or 'second-hand' experience which may come, for example, from television and books. Clearly the nature of the directness or 'immediacy' of the experience obtained in each of these ways could be disputed. A child might go on holiday to Spain and notice very little, but be gripped by a television programme on the Arctic. Nevertheless this broad distinction is used as the basis for the next two chapters which consider the *sources* of children's images of distant places.

Chapter 4

Long Distance Information

As cold waters to a thirsty soul, so is good news from a far country.
(*Proverbs*, XXVII, 25)

The sources of children's images of far places are many and various. They hear about visits made by friends and relatives, they watch the Eurovision song contest, they read 'Made in Taiwan' labels on toys, they collect stamps, they eat from the local takeaway restaurant, follow the World Cup, see films, listen to music.

They use many products which are associated strongly in their minds with their place of origin:

They have the best stuff in Japan, like cars and bikes and tellys. (9-year-old boy)

I tried chopsticks. We got a Chinese carryout and my Mum brought some chopsticks and a special little Chinese bowl and I tried but I couldn't get anything in my mouth. I could get the chicken in but not the peas. (7-year-old girl)

This chapter is concerned with children's *indirect* experiences of places — mostly far places. One of the weaknesses of the developmental and social psychology approaches outlined in the last two chapters is that they both focus firmly on the *individual* and neglect the social and cultural contexts of the transmission of information. However, the effect of separate information sources are difficult to study because they are difficult to isolate from each other.

I shall examine below three sources of children's so-called *indirect* experience of far places: books, comics and television, trying to explore, with the help of some specific examples, the representation of people and places through these media and the ways in which this representation may be biased.

Research into Children's Books

Much of the research dealing with the treatment of people and places in children's books has focused on bias. There have been a number of broad surveys of bias or distortion in the presentation of the world to children, most of them separating fiction from non-fiction, and the same distinction is made below (see Zimet, 1976; Dixon, 1977; Stinton, 1979; Preiswerk, 1980; Klein, 1985). Different countries have different traditions of investigation in this field. Research into bias in children's books in the United States, for example began, to grow in the wake of the Black Civil Liberties movement and focused primarily on social studies text books for use in schools. Work in the United Kingdom on the other hand has principally been concerned with children's literature and reading materials. Elsewhere in Europe, the work of the Georg Eckert Institute for schoolbook research in Braunschweig, Germany, has been notable, dealing with a full range of educational materials across all subjects. This institution, and the Information and Documentation Centre for the Geography of the Netherlands, has carried out much international research into textbooks and their revision. Case studies of such work and reports on international conferences examining the treatment of other countries in school books may be found in Marchant (1967), Boden (1977), Meijer and Hillers (1981) and Meijer (1991). (The journal of the Georg Eckert Institute for International Textbook Research in Braunschweig is worth consulting in this context. Many of the articles are in English.) Although much of this work is oriented towards secondary teaching materials rather than primary, many of the organizing principles as well as the methodology for book scrutiny are the same. The objectives of such book research are not always clearly defined however. David Wright (1983), for example, claims that international textbook research has stagnated into an unnecessarily pedantic correction of *facts* and that not enough attention has been paid to the role of textbooks in enhancing *understanding* between peoples.

Both fiction and non-fiction for children (including textbooks and information books) have been criticized for their racism and ethnocentrism.

Ethnocentricism was first defined in 1906 by Sumner as 'a view of things in which one's own group is the centre of everything, and all others are scaled and rated with reference to it... Each group nourishes its own pride and vanity, boasts itself superior, exalts its own divinities and looks with contempt on outsiders' (p. 52). It is different from racism in that there is no necessary belief that there is a biological foundation to the feelings expressed of cultural superiority. The term 'ethnocentricism' has also been widened, especially in connection with geography teaching materials, to 'Eurocentricism' whereby the world is evaluated according to European norms.

Racism and Ethnocentricism in Children's Fiction

Racism in children's literature has traditionally been fairly comprehensive in its targets. The author W.E. Johns' fixation on race, for example, is quite extraordinary. His hero Biggles habitually confronts German 'stinkers', 'cunning' Orientals and African 'savages'. But of all the racist images, most attention has probably been paid in children's literature to the treatment of black people. A number of discrete stereotypes have been recognized in American children's literature (see Broderick, 1973; Banfield, in Preiswerk, 1980). One such stereotype is the representation of the black person as a 'contented slave', unable to survive without the discipline and structure of slavery itself. Contented slaves accepted their position with good grace. They were stupid but loyal, and proud to belong to white people of quality. Related to this image is a further one — that of the 'comic black'. This figure appears in the form of story-telling plantation negroes or lovable eye-rolling servants called Mammy. This 'plantation' tradition of American literature is most recognizable in Harriet Beecher Stowe's *Uncle Tom's Cabin*, Edgar Allen Poe's *The Gold Bug*, Joel Chandler Harris' *Tales of Uncle Remus* and Theodore Taylor's *The Cay*.

There is also a strong British colonial tradition of the 'inferior black' in children's literature (Kuya, in Preiswerk, 1980; Dixon, 1977). Prominent exemplars of this stereotype are to be found in Defoe's *Robinson Crusoe*, Marryat's *Masterman Ready*, Ballantyne's *Martin Rattler* and *Coral Island* and various books by Rider Haggard, Rudyard Kipling, Thomas Hughes and G.A. Henty. These books are, however, little read today, at least not in their original version. But their biases have survived in modern favourites. Of these, Roald Dahl's *Charlie and the Chocolate Factory* has been discussed by Bouchard (1979), Hugh Lofting's *Dr. Dolittle* by Suhl (1979), P.L. Travers' *Mary Poppins* by Schwartz (1979) and *Pippi Longstocking* by Reeder (1979). Dixon (1977) has discussed the use of black figures, most notably in the form of golliwogs, in Enid Blyton's stories (see also Rae, 1982). The publishers and authors of these books have made revisions following such criticism and (cynics say) an increased awareness of racism by the book-buying public. The 'Oompa-Loompas', for example, (the factory labour force of *Charlie and the Chocolate Factory*), are no longer from Africa and no longer black.

Children's literature dealing with foreign countries often does so in an historical setting. The images created about distant places are, therefore, dated and may frequently mislead children about the realities of the contemporary world. The treatment in fiction (and non-fiction too) of Native Americans is a good example of such frequent misunderstanding. Happily, since the publication of Dee Brown's *Bury My Heart at Wounded Knee* which gives the 'Indians' version' of the history of the American West there has been a wider appreciation of the distortions of 'savagery' in the 'cowboys and Indians' genre of stories and films. The practice of scalping, for example, was not general, the operation was not fatal, warriors' honours were not measured by the number of scalps and scalping was, in any case, a direct result of encouragement in the shape of scalp bounties offered by the colonial and more recent governments. The typical example of the Indian as 'noble savage' in fiction is to be found in the *Leatherstocking Tales* of James Fennimore Cooper. Accurate representations of the contemporary lifestyles of Native Americans are largely absent from children's literature. Children also, both in the United States itself and overseas, have little impression of the great diversity of Indian life and culture (Napier, 1970, quoted in Zimet, 1976). The only picture in their minds is that of the Plains Indians. The images from the cowboy films remain prominent: 'prairie, horses, buffalo, tepees, chieftains, feather head-dress, medicine man, cowboys, extermination by the white man' (Becker, 1976). Neither are these images restricted to *English* literature. Lutz (1980) has evaluated the racist content and ideological function of German children's books about Native Americans. German writers have, naturally, borrowed heavily from previous English language interpretations of the history of the West.

Foreigners in children's literature (like foreigners in films), are often given contrived and stilted language to represent 'foreign' speech, and writers often reveal little knowledge of the culture of those groups they are writing about. For example Puerto Ricans in American fiction have often been given Italian names, not Spanish (see Zimet, 1976).

Faraway Fiction: Some Suggestions

There is disappointingly little good contemporary fiction for primary age children which is set in other countries. There are, of course, numerous collections of *folk tales*, each with their own distinctive identification with a particular place. Sometimes those places are imaginary and these 'countries of the mind' (Townsend, 1987) such as Ursula le Guin's *Earthsea*, Tolkein's *Middle Earth* and C.S. Lewis' *Narnia* can be important vehicles for children's exploration and discovery of the characteristics of place. The value and importance of folk tales to children's development has been fully argued elsewhere (Cook, 1976; Bettelheim, 1977) and I shall accept the case as proven. What follows are a few recommendations for collections that represent a range of countries and varying traditions. Floella Benjamin's *Why the Agouti has No Tail and Other Stories* (Hutchinson, 1984) has stories from the Caribbean, Africa, India and China, whilst the Federation of Children's Book Groups has *Stories Round the World* (Hodder, 1990). The latter all have a strong geographical or cultural background and the compilation, produced for International Literacy Year was 'tested by children' before the final selection was made. For older children Marcus Crouch's *The Whole World Storybook* (OUP, 1983) has, as the title suggests, tales from all over the world. Other traditional story collections include Kathleen Arnott's

African Myths and Legends (OUP, 1978) and Rani Singh's *The Indian Storybook* (Heinemann, 1984). There are also a number of useful reference books for teachers who wish to know more about mythology and legends in other parts of the world. The *New Larousse Encyclopedia of Mythology* (Hamlyn, 1968) has chapters on Indian, Chinese, Oceanic, Celtic and African mythology. *Legends of the World*, edited by Richard Cavendish (Orbis, 1982) has chapters on India, Malaysia, Africa, Australia and the Pacific Islands and *Funk and Wagnell's Standard Dictionary of Folklore, Mythology and Legend* (New English Library, 1972) has summaries of stories arranged by both subject and area.

A good starting point for stories from other parts of the world would be Anansi, the half man — half spider of the Afro-Caribbean tradition who uses trickery to outwit larger and more powerful creatures, particularly the fierce but rather stupid tiger. Read about him in (amongst other collections) *Listen to this Story* by Grace Hallworth (Methuen, 1977) or *Anansi the Spider Man* by Philip Sherlock (Macmillan, 1956). Another good starting point would be the Dreamtime legends of the Australian aborigines. Earth, landscape, sky, stars, animals and people were all made in the Dreamtime. Spirits of the unborn live there and the souls of the dead return there. Several books by Patricia Wrightson deal with the Dreamtime. Try the anthology *Beneath the Sun* (Collins, 1972).

However, folk tales, although greatly enriching children's literary experience do not offer images of *modern* life. Indeed I think there is a real danger that the *only* stories children may read or hear about other parts of the world are myths, legends, fairy tales and fables. What is needed are more stories which just happen to be set in other countries and thereby offer real contexts for action and feeling. It is also important that children read and hear stories that are *contemporary*. Excellent though they are, Meinert de Jong's *The Wheel on the School* and Erich Kaestner's *Emil and the Detectives* do not allow us to see The Netherlands and Germany as they are *today*. I suggest below a number of examples of good children's fiction set in other countries. It represents a personal and partial selection rather than a comprehensive list. I have grouped them into two very broad categories; that is, as considered appropriate for reading with children at Key Stages 1 and 2. Further suggestions for stories that are set in other lands are listed in Anthea Raddan's annotated fiction list *Exploring Cultural Diversity* from the School Library Association (1985) and (in two volumes) *Guide to Children's Books for a Multicultural Society*, compiled by J. Elkins, edited by P. Triggs and published by *Books for Keeps*, 1985 (for ages 8–12) and 1986 (for ages 0–7). These two volumes are, now, sadly out of print but *Books for Keeps* has commissioned a new, one volume combined edition which is likely to be available in 1992. Reading lists including recommended fiction and anthologies for children about the Caribbean, India, Bangladesh and Pakistan, are available from the Commission for Racial Equality (see appendix for address). African and Australian stories are reviewed in separate chapters in

Dorothy Atkinson's *The Children's Bookroom* (Trentham Books, 1989).

For reading to younger children some of my favourite stories are by Jill Tomlinson. They deal with young animals growing up in contrasting environments. In *Penguin's Progress* (Methuen, 1975; Magnet, 1979), Otto is a penguin chick who lives 'on his father's feet at the bottom of the world'. Pongo (*The Gorilla who Wanted to Grow Up*; Methuen, 1977, Mammoth, 1990) is a young gorilla who lives in the mountains of Africa and Pim (*The Aardvark Who Wasn't Sure*, Methuen, 1973, Mammoth, 1989) is an aardvark from the African veldt. In each of these stories we learn (together with the young animal) what it means to grow up in a specific climate and landscape. Otto the penguin chick, for example, learns that you have to huddle up with the other penguins to keep warm when there is a blizzard, that the edge of the ice cap breaks up in summer and that although seals aren't a danger, you have to watch out for skuas.

Rosemary Friedman's *Aristide* (Hutchinson, 1966; Dragon, 1987), by contrast, is about a French boy who visits England — accidentally. He is on holiday at Le Touquet with his grandmother when he falls asleep on his inflatable mattress and floats across the Channel. His reception by a gang of English boys allows a gentle exploration of language and culture differences. These are developed further in a sequel *Aristide in Paris* (Dragon, 1987), when one of the friends Aristide has made in England pays a return visit to France. Similarities and differences feature strongly in the books and both deal with issues such as fighting, bullying and name-calling. The children frequently argue about whether this or that is better in France or England and there is plenty of scope for class discussion during and after the story.

Similarities and differences are also shown visually in Nigel Gray and Philippe Dupasquier's *A Country Far Away* (Anderson, 1988; Picture Puffin, 1990). This is a full colour book with two parallel picture strips and text which accompanies both sets of pictures. One strip illustrates life in 'Africa', the other life in Britain. The text is simple ('we went swimming', 'we went shopping') and, apart from some reservations about the generality of 'Africa', I think the book does much to demonstrate the common interests of children everywhere. Africa is also treated (again, rather unspecifically) in Alexander McCall Smith's *Akimbo and the Elephants* (Mammoth, 1990). This story focuses on the important issues of environmental conservation and ivory poaching and presents them both in an understandable way.

There are a number of picture books for young children set in the West Indies. Errol Lloyd's *Nini at Carnival* (Bodley Head, 1978) is a Caribbean 'Cinderella' story about a little girl who has no costume to wear at the carnival. Karl Craig's *Emanuel Goes to Market* (OUP, 1970) and John Agard's *Dig Away Two-Hole Tim* (Bodley Head, 1981) are also worth looking out for. Helen Cowcher's *Rain Forest* (Picture Corgi, 1989) is another picture book with strong artwork illustrations of rain forest life that many children would find exciting.

Ruskin Bond's *Flames in the Forest* (Julia Macrae Books, 1981; Young Puffin, 1988) describes a forest fire in rural India. Romi has to cycle seven miles home from school through the forest. His route is blocked by fire but he eventually struggles through a river with his bicycle to avoid the flames. *Ghost Trouble* by the same author (Blackbird, 1989) is about pranks from the pret (ghost) who lived in the peepal tree until grandfather had to chop it down. There are many books by Ruskin Bond set in India and I can recommend them. *Nanda in India* (by Terry Furchgott, Deutsch, 1983) is also worth reading. Not only does it have the interesting approach of describing the country through the eyes of a young boy returning to school from a visit to his grandparents in India but it concentrates on the scenery of the country rather than poverty which is stressed by many books.

As for poems, I can recommend the two anthologies from many cultures collected by Morag Styles and published by Cambridge University Press as *I Like That Stuff* (1985) and *You'll Love This Stuff* (1986). Each has a glossary of Caribbean dialect words used in some of the poems. I also like the West Indian voices that come through the poems in *I din do nuttin* by John Agard (Bodley Head, 1983; Magnet, 1984). Several of these poems are in West Indian creole, whereas Rastafari language is used (also with a glossary) in the picture book with large text, *Niyabinghi*, by Khadijah Frischauer (Salaam Books, 1987) The title refers to a gathering of Rastafari held on special days to celebrate events in their history. The problems and challenges of reading dialect material such as this with children have been described in some detail by Edwards (1983).

For older children there is, as you might expect, a larger range of fiction set in far places. A good introduction to the theme could be found in Jamila Gavin's *The Magic Orange Tree* (Magnet, 1987). This consists of stories about city children whose families come from far away and the children grow up surrounded by memories of distant places.

Earthquake, by Ruskin Bond (Julia Macrae Books, 1984; Walker Books, 1989) describes the effect of a natural hazard on a small community. This takes place at a specific location — Shillong, in the Cherrapunji Hills of North-east India. The location is helpful as it enables the place to be pinpointed on an atlas map and further information may therefore be obtained about it. The story could easily be used as a starting point for a project on India, particularly as there is quite a lot of incidental information provided about schools, houses and food. *Avalanche* by A. Rutgers van der Loeff (University of London Press, 1957; Puffin, 1959) for older children also has specific locations, this time in the Alps. The international dimension to this story is enhanced as it concerns a skiing party from a Pestalozzi Children's Village. Although historical, the same author's *Children on the Oregon Trail* (Puffin, 1963), also has a specific location — the trail from Fort Laramie to Oregon and California which could be identified and developed with the help of an atlas. Andrew Salkey's *Hurricane* (Puffin, 1977) is another natural disaster book, this time set in Jamaica. Other good

Jamaican stories are to be found in *A Thief in the Village and Other Stories* (by J. Berry, Puffin, 1987). Gustos is nearly killed in a hurricane, Nenna and her brother patrol the coconut plantation against intruders, Becky longs for a bicycle and Fanso longs to find his father who walked out thirteen years ago. A further collection of West Indian stories is Clare Cherrington's *Sunshine Island, Moonshine Baby* (Young Lions, 1985) and poems and stories about Trinidad and Tobago are found in E.P. Springer's *Godchild* (Karia Press, 1988).

One of the most powerful books of all for 7–11-year-olds is Beverley Naidoo's *Journey to Jo'burg* (Longman, 1985; Young Lions, 1987). Frightened that their baby sister will die, Naledi and her younger brother Tiro make the 300 km journey to Johannesburg to find their mother who works there as a maid. Readers are spared few of the realities of apartheid — the pass laws, life in the townships, racism and malnutrition. Poverty in Soweto is contrasted with the comfortable wealth of their mother's employer. But this most moving story is also about love and freedom. It is told with clarity and directness. Ian Strachan's *Journey of a Thousand Miles* (Methuen, 1984) is also a most moving story about a contemporary issue. It is a young boy's account of the escape of a group of Vietnamese boat people. The complete text may be too demanding for top primary but parts are certainly worth using.

Another good 'journey' book, this time set in America, is Cynthia Voigt's *Homecoming* (Fontana, 1984). A family of four children set off in search of relatives who might take them in after their mentally unstable mother has abandoned them in a car park. Again, the location is real (Bridgeport, Connecticut), and therefore locatable in an atlas.

Landscape and environment are important themes in *Storm Boy* by Colin Thiele (BBC, 1978). The boy and his lonely father leave city life and with the help of an aboriginal friend, the boy becomes attuned to the animal world.

Finally, also set in Australia but in an entirely different type of book, is Osmar White's *The Super-Roo of Mungalongaloo* (Puffin, 1978). Super-Roo is the Head Animal at the wonderful Willawallawalla Waterhole at the foot of the purple and pink Mungalongaloo Mountains. One of his jobs is to keep out human polluters and foreign animals. So when the intrepid explorer Dr. Alastair Angus Archibald McGurk M.D. sets out with his pedigree camel Cathie Khan from Afghanistan on an epic quest of discovery he finds that the dreaded Deadibone Desert of Australia holds secrets even more amazing than he could have imagined. The book is full of hats with dangling corks and sporran jokes. It's harmlessly funny and in my view well worth considering as an introduction to the whole issue of jokes about other nationalities and of raising awareness of stereotypes.

Racism and Ethnocentrism in Children's Non-fiction

Textbooks provide more than just information for their readers. Consciously or unconsciously all the partners in the publishing process (author, editor, artist, picture researcher, designer) convey their attitudes to the reader, often on issues not directly related to the subject of the book. There is a particular danger in the production of materials for *young* readers because of the degree of simplification necessary when writing for children. This act of simplification is not a value-free process. Selections and generalizations are made which may give partial or stereotyped views of the world. Such selection may be a deliberate attempt to prejudice the reader (probably quite rare) or the result of poor quality research and writing by the author (probably much less rare). It is likely also that authors and publishers avoid controversial issues in the interests of a quieter life and thereby create an impression of a world more comfortable than we 'really' know it to be.

One view of textbooks is that they are instruments of imperialism and colonialism (Falcon, 1980). According to this analysis, the dominant group is seen as needing to develop among their own young people those ideological beliefs which give legitimation to power. From an early age, therefore, the written word is used to reinforce the notion that the dominating group has a right to lead and exploit other, inferior, groups.

The treatment of black people in children's non-fiction has at times been little better than that in fiction. Becker (1973) claims that the large number of children's books in Germany about the work of Alfred Schweitzer exhibit considerable bias in that they show Schweitzer as helping his black 'children' because they are unable to help themselves. Similarly, Aborigines have fared badly in Australian children's books (Lippman, 1980 in Preiswerk, 1980). When visible (and they have often been omitted altogether from Australian history and literature, especially in books for younger children), they have been shown to be unreliable, timid, wild and uncivilized. Black South Africans too are frequently referred to in texts, not as 'people', but as 'apple pickers' or 'workers'. By this means they are regarded not as people but only as service agents for whites (Klein, 1985).

Many non-fiction books appear to confuse the concepts of culture, civilization and race. There is the underlying assumption that some peoples are 'closer to nature' while others have evolved to the stage of 'culture' and some have arrived at a stage of 'civilization' and that all this is related in some way to their being of superior stock (Preiswerk, 1980).

Several surveys of geography textbooks in the United Kingdom indicate that such books are highly likely to contain images of the 'third world' that are ethnocentric and that these images often develop from a colonial perspective (i.e. in the terms adopted by the Brandt report, a 'Northern' view of the 'South'). Hicks (nd) examined twenty textbooks that dealt with the 'third world' or global issues in general. Such issues were often seen only as 'problems', unrelated to their social, economic and cultural contexts.

Neither was the reader's own experience connected to the issue in question, with the result that the issues appeared to become depoliticized and devalued. Causes of Third World poverty were neglected and underdevelopment usually seen to be a state of affairs in which people 'just happened to find themselves'. There was no mention of the explanation of underdevelopment as an historical process arising from the unequal relationship between rich and poor countries and that this process still continues today. Rather, there was the assumption that the poorer countries of the world needed to 'catch up' with the richer ones. This assumption can often be identified in the text by the use of the word 'still', for example: 'they are still farmers'.

The entire process of development is frequently seen only from the perspective of Western Europe and North America. 'Development' itself tends only to be equated with *economic* growth. Critical questioning of this view or discussion of development as also being the development of human beings rather than of countries tends not to be encouraged. According to Hicks, a representative sample of textbooks commonly in use in the UK in the 1970s was giving the following clear messages to readers:

1 The main problem today is the Third World.
2 Third World poverty is due to a combination of chance and inbuilt obstacles.
3 Follow the example of the 'North' and take-off to development will occur.
4 There are too many people in the Third World.
5 Peasant farmers need educating and everyone needs help from the North.
6 Colonialism is nothing to do with geography.
7 Minority groups are backward and need help.
8 Multi-ethnic Britain is a figment of the imagination. (Hicks, 1988, p. 29)

Ethnocentricism can be clearly seen when books imply that 'we' were responsible for 'their' development. This may be detected in a common treatment of countries in children's reference books where the article or information *begins* with the country being identified as a former colony. The implication is that this was the 'starting point' in its history or development. The same effect is seen when countries are described as being 'discovered' by white Europeans. Some good reference books avoid this. The *New Oxford Children's Encyclopedia*, for example (OUP, 1991) attempts to describe countries from a contemporary perspective and *concludes* each entry where appropriate with a 'flashback' section on its history.

Many non-fiction books for children present the values of Europe as universal. Anyone who doesn't behave like us must be funny or inferior. Any country not espousing these values is seen to be 'backward' in its evolution. This is sometimes emphasized by an attempt to help the young reader by making a direct comparison in the form of a transfer of concepts to his or her own culture, for example: 'They're in our stone age' (see Preiswerk, 1980, for other examples).

David Wright has been a persistent textbook-watcher in the United Kingdom for at least fifteen years, often focusing attention on particular texts to demonstrate ethnocentricity (Wright, 1979 and 1985). One popular text for 11-year-olds, for example, makes no reference to black people in its chapters on Australia, yet deals in some detail with immigration. Differences between West Africans and 'us' are emphasized through an exercise whereby pupils have to use a photograph in the book to make a drawing of a man's head, 'adding labels to indicate those features which are distinctive'. This seems to be an attempt to illustrate and emphasize racial differences rather than similarities between peoples and appears more likely to give white readers the impression that they are 'normal' and that others are 'funny' (Wright, 1982).

However, notwithstanding the issues of bias described above, writers of non-fiction for young children are faced with a number of quite fundamental problems. They wish to portray the world's variety. They know that children are generally more interested in people than place. By necessity they are restricted to a relatively small selection of simple and clear images. And in so doing, if they are not very careful, run the not inconsiderable risk of recreating stereotypes. It is usually much easier to see stereotypes in the books and teaching materials of a previous generation. The images of 'Little People in other Lands' in the flashcards used to teach the alphabet in the mid-nineteenth century (figure 4.1) did at least have the merit of introducing *very* young children to far peoples — for which I argued for in chapter 3. But the image of, for example, 'Ohio', has been pervasive and some school materials have an incredibly long shelf life. When I started teaching in 1969, for example, my first class of 9-year-olds had been issued with *Work in other Lands* as a geography text:

> The darkies who grow the cotton in the 'Cotton States' of Tennessee, Alabama and Georgia, are happy people with very few cares. When the cotton is sold the darkies have a great feast, and there is a killing of hogs, and a great making of corn meal bread. On Saturday some of the negroes drive to the nearest town, with their wives and children in the cart. In the town there are ice cream and bananas for the children, shoes for everyone and then cheese, maize, flour, coffee, sugar and tinned meat to take home. (Walter, 1934, p. 18)

A more effective approach than the description of distant people from an 'outsider's' point of view is the personal story line. This is the story of Mr. Santos, who lives in the arid North-eastern shoulder of Brazil, taken from *Oxford New Geography: A Course for Juniors, 3* by Gordon Elliott (OUP, 1980, pp. 62–3). The story is presented in cartoon strip format (the first two frames are illustrated in figure 4.2).

Figure 4.1: 'Little people in other lands': Nineteenth century alphabet flashcards from the Leeds University Museum of the History of Education

1 Last year the rains did not come. I lost all my crops.
2 My family were hungry. I had no money. I went to my landlord to borrow money for food.
3 He lent me a sack of beans. But they lasted for only a month.
4 After that we went hungry. One of my children died because I could not afford to call the doctor.

Figure 4.2: The story of Mr Santos (from Oxford New Geography: A Course for Junior 3 by G. Elliott, OUP, 1980)

5   I went to the city of Recife to look for work. Later my family joined me.
6   We built a house of cardboard and old sacks. That was all we could find.
7   I could not get work. There were hundreds like me.
8   After three months my little son looked like a skeleton.
9   Each day he went to the city to beg for food.
10 He often asked me why some people could afford to throw food away.
11 What answer could I give him? How could he understand ...
12 That when you are poor, no one seems to care if you live or die?

The story is accompanied by simple, clear resources describing the unreliability of rainfall in this part of South America and contrasting the way of life of the Santos family with the Lima family who are much better off. Rural to urban migration, land tenure, self-help housing and disparities of wealth are all complex and sensitive issues, difficult to describe in a few words, but it seems to me that this author has made an honest attempt to present the issues simply and clearly in a form that teacher and children could discuss.

Developing Teaching Materials

Much of the literature of research into teaching materials deals with issues such as the characteristics of textbooks (for example, their readability and analyses of their contents) or the criteria used in their selection. Little attention has so far been paid to the process of how teaching materials are *created*. Yet this is a fruitful area for consideration. Greater accuracy may be achieved, together with a clearer indication of what images are being transmitted, if we are able to identify stages in the production process and points at which critical decisions are made. Meijer's (1983) 'schoolbook realization' model (figure 4.3) provides a framework by which we can examine how a book comes to be written and produced. We can use this framework as a way of looking at books dealing with distant people and places. Critical points at which bias may distort images of far places can be identified in the development process. It is hoped that the following discussion will raise dilemmas which need to be faced by teachers and authors when introducing places to children. Understanding more about how teaching materials are produced helps in the selection of those materials and in the creation of supplementary resources and activities for the classroom.

In Meijer's model there are six stages in the realization process of a schoolbook, identified by numbers on the diagram.

Working from a European perspective, Meijer highlights the early role in the realization process of 'educational authorities' (for example,

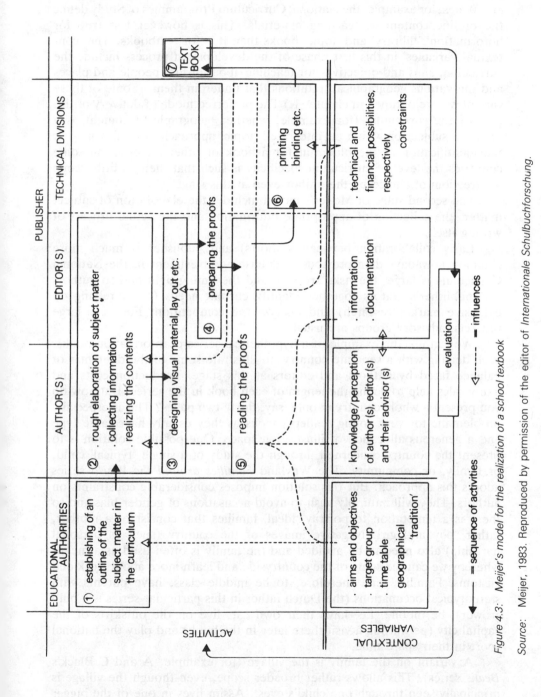

Figure 4.3: Meijer's model for the realization of a school texbook

Source: Meijer, 1983. Reproduced by permission of the editor of *Internationale Schulbuchforschung.*

ministries of education) in prescribing the content of curricula. In England
and Wales, for example, the National Curriculum Programmes of Study define
the outline content of teaching materials. This is however less true for
'information', 'library' and 'topic' books than it is for textbooks. The 'contextual variables' in this first phase of the development process include the
curriculum aims and objectives for teaching about distant people and places
and the various geographical traditions that underpin them. (Some of these
variables were outlined in chapter 1.) The preferred mode of delivery of this
part of the curriculum (for example, whether 'geography' is taught as a
separate subject or within an integrated 'topic' approach) will also help in
the identification of the blueprint for a book or other material. In some
countries the level of curriculum specificity is such that there is little scope
for freedom of choice by the author even at this stage.

The second stage of Meijer's model includes the elaboration of subject
matter, the collection of appropriate information and the actual process of
writing itself.

Early collaboration between author(s) and publisher is much more
common nowadays than previously. Publishing investment in the National
Curriculum is large, the risks are high and the timing tight and so authors
and publisher's editors together identify current needs (often relying on
extensive market research) and analyze the competition. For very large
projects, advisory groups are usual.

We can use the example of a hypothetical series of information books,
each dealing with a separate country, to illustrate some of the dilemmas of
balance faced by authors and editors at this stage. Production costs and
likely sales help to define the length of each book in the series. But how do
you present a whole country in only, say, thirty-two pages? This is especially
problematic for very young readers' books as they usually have large type
and a generous allocation of illustration space. One possible solution is to
present the country concerned through the study of a single 'typical' child,
or family, or community. The Wayland *Families around the World* series
adopts this approach. But this solution imposes considerable constraints on
authors. They will naturally wish to avoid accusations of gender bias and so
there is a temptation to portray 'ideal' families that consist of a mother,
father, boy and girl. Negative images of the country (such as personal
hardship) also need to be avoided and the family is often used as a means
whereby we can see some of the countryside and learn more about work and
customs. Families tend therefore, to be middle class, have parents with
stereotypical occupations (the Dutch father in this particular series is a bulb
grower), be mobile, i.e. have their own car, live on the outskirts of the
capital city (permitting a visit there later in the book) and play the national
sport in their spare time.

A variant on the family is the village (for example, A and C Black's
Beans series). This allows rather broader scope, even though the village is
principally seen through one child's eyes: 'Assim lives in one of the bigger

houses in the village . . .' (*Pakistani Village*, p. 5), but there are others, and these are seen in illustrations. Similarly, Assim has friends whose parents have occupations that are different from those of his own. The village setting allows the rhythm of life to be described — season and harvest — but there is still a tendency towards the ideal. The village tends to be located near enough to a large town to enable the 'plot' to include a trip there so as to make the point that not all of Pakistan is rural.

An alternative to the one family/one child/one village approach is adopted in the Wayland *My Country* series in which up to 30 separate characters from the title country present a brief (approximately 150 word) autobiography, reflecting the variety of lifestyles to be found in that country.

My name is Knud and I'm a pig farmer.

I'm Kaspar and I'm looking for a job.

This approach allows the introduction of a good range of economic activity, life style and age groups and allows for the treatment of minorities. The depth of each 'mini autobiography' is, however, necessarily limited. We learn little of the real life of each person depicted. But these books are for young children. For older readers, the *We Live In* . . . series by the same publisher has more depth — about 500 words per character and the issues presented by each inhabitant are correspondingly more demanding. Longer hours for less money, according to a Paris taxi driver, lack of faith among the young according to a French Catholic priest and small-scale bakers being threatened by the increase in sales of mass-produced, inferior bread. The presentation of these viewpoints is powerful because we learn something of the people who are putting forward their views but they are nevertheless seen as *individual* points of view. Individualized experiences make it easy for children to identify with the nature of the problem but at the same time, (for older readers especially), the individualization process helps to trivialize the issue to being an individual one only and not a problem of national concern. Unemployment is an example.

It is not my intention to appear critical of any of these resources. On the contrary, I think they are, on the whole, very good. But each approach adopted has inherent weaknesses and needs to be complemented with further, additional material. There is a fundamental conflict of width versus breadth therefore at the planning stage of such a country-based series of books.

The factual content of a book at the next stage of the realization process is, at least partly, determined by the author(s)' own knowledge and perceptions. The choice of case studies and exemplars are defined by his/her own range of experiences and interests. Inevitably, these are patchy and so gaps have to be filled. This means the author has to rely on secondary information sources. But information is not uniformly available for all parts of the world. We have already seen (in chapter 1) that media information may be biased. There exist similar distortions in the availability of good case study material around the world. Primary school materials generally need highly *localized* information, relating to *specific* families, workers, homes, schools, small communities. To obtain this needs a wide range of personal contacts and often implies first hand field collection of material. Language problems hinder the collection of authentic resources at the local level. It may be necessary, therefore, to rely on material from governmental and commercial sources which may contain quite explicit biases or be presented at a level of bland generality. The cost and time of obtaining information may also be a significant factor. Contrary to popular belief, schoolbook writers do not receive royalties on a par with Harold Robbins or Jeffrey Archer, and whilst some may manage the occasional exotic holiday, the collection of authentic, detailed case study material is immensely time consuming.

Once information *is* collected it has to be selected and simplified. These processes are responsible for much of the distortion about far places. But how best to represent a country in a very brief space is problematic. It is difficult to avoid cliché, (although it is worth noting that what is cliché for adults is not necessarily so for children). And how is the 'distinctiveness' of place to be achieved? Much working life is routinely the same for children and families everywhere. 'Identity' in some senses may therefore depend on images that are a little removed from everyday experience. In foreign books, Britain is 'recognized' through, for example, Beefeaters and Scottish pipers, yet few children in Britain may have seen these figures for real. Writers of information books want to put children in touch with the familiar symbols of particular countries (for example, Dutch windmills, cheeses, clogs and tulips) but at the same time they want to present an authentic image of place that may in fact be disappointingly familiar to the reader. It is, after all, both a disappointment and a comfort to know that the same brand of cornflakes you eat grace the breakfast table of the foreign child you are reading about.

Kantor *et al* (1983) has outlined some of the tensions faced by authors in the actual process of writing for children. Authors know that when they write for young children they have to use short, simple sentences. But this may make the meaning of relationships more vague. They also try to use known, vernacular words, but this often blurs meaning. If they omit less important detail the young reader is left to make his/her own inferences and if explanation is condensed in order to use space effectively then the reader faces conceptual overload and the information presented will not be fully processed.

Authors face a minefield of language problems when presenting distant places. Pejorative terms (such as 'huts' and 'tribes'), although probably in widespread use by the readers, need to be avoided. Specialized vocabulary is a further difficulty. 'Grassland' does not quite mean the same as 'savanna', and may cause some confusion with meadows or football fields. But 'tidal wave' does mean the same as *tsunami* and is probably a preferable term to use in the primary school. It often helps to give a foreign, exotic flavour to the writing if foreign language words are used, and children do like their sounds. But for weak readers there may be a considerable loss of under-standing. Perera (1988) quotes the following foreign words from just eight pages of a book written for junior age children: *frigorificos, gauchos, lur, machetes, padi, polder, puesteros, rajah, sheik* and *vik*.

Descriptive words for countryside and landscape (such as 'rolling hills') can also be problematic. It's also necessary to avoid 'non-statements' such as: 'Kenya is rich in history' or 'the people lead a traditional lifestyle'. An author may want to stress that a place has great attractiveness but what does 'beautiful' scenery mean? Who is to say?

Writing for young children needs to be lively and much liveliness is indeed achieved in the '*My Holiday In* ...' series (published by Corgi). These are self-completion holiday workbooks intended to be based on the reader's own holiday experiences.

The part of Spain we are staying in is called ...

The countryside around is hilly/mountainous/flat as a pancake.

I have seen: Spanish dancers/bull fighters/people playing pelota with their funny (sic) rackets. (Mostyn, L. (1987) *My Holiday in Spain*, Corgi)

But liveliness is dangerous stuff and needs careful handling.

The conventions of information presentation in books about distant places often give rise to confusion (Perera, 1988). Consider for example, the following statements:

Snow from the Swiss mountains feeds some of Europe's major waterways, such as the Rhine (Rhein).

Belgium was a founder member of the European Community (EC).

Mont Blanc is the highest point in Western Europe at 4810 metres (15,781 feet)

Sri Lanka (Ceylon) is a fascinating island.

Disneyland is near Los Angeles (California).

The capital of Spain is Madrid (3,244,000).

Each statement (taken from books for junior age children) uses parentheses, but in each case the brackets are used for a different purpose. In some cases the brackets give alternative, equivalent information (for example, the foreign or former name for a place or feature, or the conversion of statistical information) whereas in others, extra information is provided (such as more accurate locational information — the name of the state — or a population statistic). These forms of presentation of geographical information are very common but children need to be able to decode them in order for these conventions to work.

Stage 3 of Meijer's model refers to visual aspects of the book. A number of people are involved at this stage.

The *design team* are responsible for the appearance and layout of the pages. The balance between the illustrations and the text has to be visually 'right' and illustrations and text have to 'work' together (Goldsmith, 1984). Children can be highly sensitive to the character of a book. The age of children shown in illustrations and the density of the text are critical factors in making the material seem accessible to the reader. Layout issues may also distort content. For example the author may have to supply another paragraph as there isn't enough text to complete a double page 'spread'. The number of illustrations may have to be reduced as there isn't enough room for them on the page. These design adjustments may cause imbalance in the book if the author has already carefully balanced the text and illustrations to show, for example, ethnic minorities according to some rational proportion. Some books are designed so that there is colour on every *other* spread, whereas others have full colour only in sections of the book. This may have implications for the sequential presentation of material. Some issues may by this means be systematically excluded from the more visually powerful colour sections.

Photographs in children's books evoke powerful and long lasting images of what places are like. They can help overcome common misconceptions (for example, that the steppes are not step-like). It seems reasonable to assume that the technical quality of the photograph will affect the strength or memorability of the image. Colour photographs are therefore probably more memorable than monochrome and large photographs more than small ones. Wide angle views may reveal 'geographic quality', a term used by Halverson (n.d.) for a 'well-balanced arrangement of items of the cultural and natural landscapes as a basis for working out geographic relationships' but for younger children, close-ups of people and places may illustrate better what it is like to 'be there'. Aerial views are often used in children's books, but although these show people and nature in a 'new perspective' (St. Joseph, 1966), such a perspective is generally unfamiliar to children. For young children, ground level views are probably best. However, there are constraints of time and cost in researching and commissioning artwork and photographs. A budget is allowed for photograph reproduction fees and search time. Often the types of photographs specified by the author are not available from picture agencies and are too expensive to commission.

Children do not see everything in a picture and their attention is not necessarily focused on what adults see. Children tend to approach photographs by looking at parts rather than the whole. Good illustrations of distant places therefore need *detail* — things happening in the foreground that capture the attention. It's also important in the preparation of learning materials to integrate photographs with text. Children need to be *taught* to look at photographs (Graham and Lynn, 1989) of distant places, and text can point them to search the picture for details. Few children perceive the broader patterns of landscape in photographs of unfamiliar places. Children like to 'imagine themselves into' what they see; there is a strong element of fantasizing about being there (Long, 1953 and 1961; Bayliss and Renwick, 1966). However, images of distant places used with children have to be used with care. To young children, pictures a few years out of date can appear to belong to quite another time and therefore be seen as indicating 'the olden days' and as a result are often associated with poverty.

Children's comprehension of photographs is not limited to the recognition of the content depicted. They are capable of understanding the medium itself in more depth and their perception of what is depicted may be enhanced by their own experience of taking photographs (Kose, 1985). There have been recent attempts to develop children's critical understanding of photography and other related media, especially television and film through the analysis and production of their own media artefacts (Bazalgette, 1989). Such *media education* addresses issues of how the media work, how they produce meanings, how they are organized and how audiences make sense of them. There are clear implications here for the study of distant places represented in media but the 'visual dimension' remains far less explored for geography than it does for history (see, for example, Unwin, 1981).

Cameras tell lies! And photographs have an undeserved reputation for objectivity and may be a source of bias (Wiegand, 1982). Such bias may be revealed in the sources of the photographs used in texts. Many photographs, for example, are available free from commercial or Government organizations which may well have vested interests that are reflected in the visual material they provide. Wright (1982) calculated that 84 per cent of the photographs of South Africa used in seven books on that country came from the South African Government Information Service and allied bodies. Publishers are naturally anxious to reduce production costs and there is a tendency therefore to rely on picture sources with lower reproduction fees.

Although guidelines on the production of non-racist, non-sexist materials are well established in publishing business, *artists* may be less familiar with these issues. They may, for example, only do part of their work for books or be responsible for only a few illustrations in any particular book and therefore not be aware of the total visual balance. Checking of art roughs is therefore an important stage in a book's progress. An example of how sex bias in illustrations can occur will illustrate this point. In a workbook to accompany an atlas (Wiegand, 1988) an exercise was devised which would enable children to identify the origin of placenames in the British

Isles. The exercise was to be illustrated by Anglo Saxon, Viking, Roman and Norman scenes. The artist (well known for accurate and well researched drawings of the period) produced a number of roughs. The balance of the composition of all four pieces of artwork was, however, felt to be such that men were given prominence in every picture. They were always in the foreground or placed more centrally than women or were seen in active roles whereas the women were generally shown in more passive ones. The balance would be better restored if some alteration could be made. The redrawn scene of a Roman villa shows the *woman* in a more dominant role (figure 4.4).

Reference has already been made above to the inherent problems a textbook writer faces in balancing detailed content with breadth of coverage. The same tensions occur in achieving visual balance. This can be illustrated by reference to stages in the preparation of the *Oxford Rainbow Atlas* (OUP, 1987). It was decided to illustrate each map page with images that gave children some view of what life is like in the part of the world shown on the adjacent map (figure 4.5). Some of the maps showed whole continents and so a considerable degree of simplification and selection was required. What sort of images should have been shown? As the atlas was intended for very young children it was thought that the pictures should relate to the reader's own experiences and be compatible with research findings on children's responses to illustrations. So, interiors and domestic scenes were chosen, together with photographs of children of the same age as the reader. Clearly, accuracy was to be important. 'Authentic' scenes had to be identified to avoid transmitting images that did not 'really' exist. Photographs were obviously best therefore. But finding good quality photographs of local, small-scale details that would appeal to children, proved impossible. The picture agencies are full of pictures of monuments, aerial views and so on but not of 'real' homes, schools and playgrounds. Even where photographs *were* found, they were not 'compatible' in a technical or design sense. Children are used to seeing good quality images and it defeats the object if the pictures are poor. Rather than have a jumble of unmatching photographs on each page, therefore, it was decided to commission an artist to create a montage of images from photographs supplied by the author. In this way, details of technically indifferent photographs could be used or features combined from several pictures to create a montage that was 'authentic' but also artistically pleasing. This also allowed much greater control over the balance of images throughout the book. But it was also thought to be an attractive idea to give photographs of children (aged approximately 8 or 9) who lived in the areas shown on the pages. Each page needed, therefore, to have balance in the view it gave of the group of countries or the continent to be illustrated but there also had to be a balance of scenes throughout the book to represent the variety of the world's environments, as well as achieve a balance between boys and girls illustrated and ethnic balance. Accurate information had to be given alongside each

Figure 4.4: *Alterations to the artist's rough drawing (above) give the woman more prominence in the picture than the man. (Artwork by Richard Hook)*

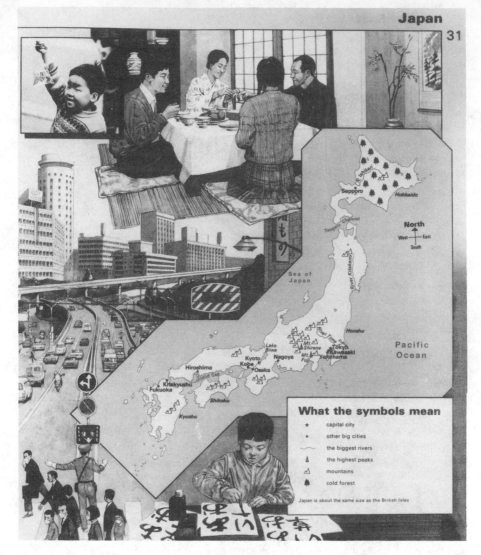

Figure 4.5: Illustrating life in distant places by assembling images on the page (from The Oxford Rainbow Atlas, OUP, 1987, p. 31)

map, showing what was most typical but at the same time avoiding the persistance of stereotypes. Note that 'Africa' was to be represented by a montage of some eight discrete scenes! There was space for only one child's photograph on the page for 'Australia'. Boy or girl? Black or white? The purpose of this case study is to illustrate the no-win situation for textbook authors. If you always show the 'average' situation, you miss out minorities. But if you show some minorities you obtain overall balance in your representation of the world but perhaps at the expense of a few parts of it. This dilemma points not just to careful selection of material on the part of the *author* (and insistence on being involved at all stages of the production of the book, such as amending artist's roughs and watching the development of the design) but also to a careful mediative role of the *teacher* to interpret the book's selectivity to the children.

These points on the balance and integration of the text layout and illustrations indicate strongly the need for close and frequent cooperation between editor, designer, author, picture researcher and artist.

The final stages of textbook realization involve technical aspects of production. The content has been established at this stage but production errors may still distort the final product. Delays in the production process may date the contents and statistical information is especially vulnerable, requiring careful checking at proof stage.

Final production is followed by reviews. Meijer's model helpfully includes a feedback loop which implies modification of later editions in the light of comments received. However, the high costs of revision may lead to books being updated very slowly with only superficial corrections being made.

The purpose of this section has been to indicate that it is not the author or editor alone who is responsible for possible misrepresentations of places in books. Production of an information book is an interdependent process with many people involved. More effective systems of quality control may need to be developed, but there is general agreement that the overall situation is better now than, say, thirty or forty years ago.

France — A Case Study of the Representation of a Country

Some of the points made above may be illustrated by comparing the treatment of France in a selection of children's books. (An earlier analysis of Holland along the same lines was made by Fisher, 1982.)

In *Pleasant Paths to Geography*, (no date, but approximately 1950s), Spink and Brady adopted a narrative form of presentation. Geography is taught through the adventures of Tom and Betty who visit various parts of Britain in turn. From a cliff on the South coast they look across to France. By a happy coincidence there is a French man staying at their hotel. Daddy allows them to talk to him that evening.

> 'Please Mr. Roget, what is that funny newspaper?' 'Ha, ha! You do not understand it Tom? That is because it is from my France, and its words are French words. In France we do not speak your language, you know. We speak our own French language. When my friends meet me, they do not say "Good day Mr. Roget", but "Bonjour Monsieur Roget".' All three laughed at this, and Mr. Roget gave

them other words, and made them say them after him. What fun it was. 'What a funny language to learn', said Tom. (Spink and Brady (n.d., p. 111)

Ethnocentrism is writ large in this text (everything French is 'funny'), but the literary 'style' (reminiscent of the worst reading schemes) raises issues of pedagogy. How was the book to have been used? 'Reading around the class' seems likely to have been the most obvious way of using the text. Clearly the presentation of information about other countries is not unrelated to the use the writer anticipates being made of it in the classroom. There is at least though in this book an honest attempt to make the information palatable by weaving it into a 'story', even though this story is contrived. The same basic information content (i.e. justification of interest in France through its proximity to the UK and the focus on the first most obvious difference — that of a language) is found in *Little Folk in Many Lands*, intended for 7-year-olds (figure 4.6).

1   This little boy and girl are playing in the sand. If you were there you could not make out what they are saying for they speak French. You might know they were French from the boy's dainty clothes.
2   They are too busy to look about them but if they did look up, they would see far off, across the blue water the white cliffs of England. The steamers take about an hour to cross over to France from our shores. So, we should be good friends with the French since they live so near us. (Lawrence, H. (n.d.), *Little Folk in Many Lands*, pp. 14–15)

A popular way of introducing countries to readers is the 'tour'. In this approach, the country is seen through an imaginary visit (often initially by air to enable the outline shape of the country to be noted as a preliminary to map and atlas work). This touristic approach is easy to understand and also has a quasi-story level of interest but countries are by this means generally presented not in their own right but through the eyes of the visitors themselves. What is worth noting on such a journey? What does the author bring to the attention of his/her young companion? A nice attempt at comparison of lifestyles is to be found in Finch's *The Children of Europe*:

We cannot help thinking how nice it would be if we had cafes in England, outside which people could sit as they do in France, sipping their coffee, drinking their wines or syrups, eating their meals, and chatting with their friends as they watch the people go by. Then we remember how fickle is British weather. Cafes are all very well in a bright, sunny land like France; but in England, where it may rain any day and every day, and where we rarely get much real summer, they would be impossible. (Finch (n.d.) p. 11)

Figure 4.6: Little Folk in Mary Lands: France

The making of friends on such an imaginary visit is a vehicle for speculation about reciprocity:

> We cannot help wondering how Jean and Marie will feel when they come back to England to stay with us. How will they get on with our beds and our meals? (*ibid*, p. 12)

The *imaginary* tour of children's books has now been replaced (at least in Western Europe) by the *real* tour because of increased travel possibilities. There has been a recent growth in real handbooks for the young traveller. Some of these combine information with great pace and jokiness. Adults may find some of these a little *de trop*.

> Madame Tussaud (wonder woman in wax). Make your own death mask: First find a severed head ... (Cunliffe and Usborne, 1985)

However, like the guidebooks of a century ago, it still seems necessary to the authors to describe the inhabitants:

> Parisians ... always shake hands with each other when they meet. This is a diplomatic preliminary. Before long they will be waving their arms about and shouting in rapid French. (*ibid*, p. 43)

> Parisians move fast and talk fast. They are impatient and quick witted. Parisians take some getting used to. (Kuttz and Unger-Hamilton 1984, p. 11)

The 'visit' approach is also used in the *Families around the World (Wayland)* series. We visit the Michel family in *A Family in France* (Jacobsen, P.O. and Kristensen, P.S., 1984). As noted above, a case study family has to present a positive image of the country and serve as an introduction to some of its most characteristic features. Perhaps the family is known personally to the authors. Mr. Michel is a champagne producer, Elizabeth Michel is a doctor. We learn something of their life and aspirations. As a family they are ideal. But it is clearly *adults* who are doing the visiting: on the way, 'we' stop at a bar, and 'we' receive after our visit to the Michels' house a present of two bottles of champagne. The whole visit is adult-centred and we learn little of children's perspectives.

There are also books which deal primarily with the landscape of France. In *A Journey Down the Seine* (Bolwell (1985) Wayland), there would seem to be considerable problems in the presentation of material for young readers without a great deal of human interest. The book has few pictures of people and rather too many of bridges and barges. Simplification and selection can lead to 'exchangeable' statements, with little real meaning:

> Normandy is very beautiful.

> Rouen has many old buildings.

Some of the difficulties of factual writing may further be illustrated by a comparison of the following openings of two books on France:

> France is an old and beautiful country in Western Europe. Its official name is the French Republic. Except for the Soviet Union, it is the largest country in Europe. Metropolitan France includes the rugged Mediterranean island of Corsica off the coast of Italy. France also has a number of overseas possessions, mostly small islands, in different parts of the world. (Norbrook, 1985)

> France's most popular festival is Bastille Day, which is held on 14 July. On 14 July 1789 the French won their freedom from the king. People buy flags to wave. There are parades, carnivals and dancing in the streets. (Rutland, 1980)

These two books are not in competition with each other as they are written for different age readers. Norbrook wants to introduce readers to the country as a whole, its location, position in world affairs, etc. But the first sentence is a problem in that it could apply to any country in Western Europe. It gives the reader no information worth having. What is an old country? Does old refer to the landscape or the existence of the present state? Who is to say whether a country is beautiful or not and is it all beautiful, or only parts of it? Examples of similar statements are:

France is a land of contrasting scenery. (p. 5)

The French are a complex mixture of peoples. (p. 8)

With the Pluckrose opening, by contrast, we have sense of 'being there' more immediately. A national occasion is a good opportunity to introduce national symbols such as flags. We are provided with information concisely in short simple sentences.

Inuit People — A Case Study of the Representation of a Way of Life

You made a picture of us in your minds, you whites, now you believe the picture. (Jonasee, an Inuk from Frobisher Bay, quoted in Forham, D. (1979) *Eskimos*, Macdonald Educational)

Eskimos no longer live in igloos (except perhaps for overnight hunting trips in winter). They live in small coastal villages with populations ranging from fifty to 1000. They aren't called Eskimos any more either, and unless you really want to use this rather derogatory Indian word meaning 'the eaters of raw flesh', you would do better to use their own word for themselves, *Inuit*, meaning simply, *the people*; one person is an Inuk and the language is Inuutituk. (Burpee, 1981, p. 113)

Despite increasing awareness of the contemporary lifestyle of most Inuit, these are a people who have been defined in children's books almost exclusively in terms of their past. *Lands of Ice and Snow* is an example:

Some of the people who live in the Arctic are called eskimos. They are used to the hard conditions in which they live. They wear thick clothes which are often made from the fur of animals that they have killed. Some Eskimos used to live in igloos, but not very many know how to build them now. Igloos are built from blocks of frozen snow. (Connell and Driscoll, 1977, p. 18)

Here, the authors *know* that the Inuit no longer live in igloos but the temptation to illustrate the page with an igloo is too strong to resist. Why is this? It could be because of a wish to provide the reader with what he/she expects to see. If this is the case then it is an inexcusable exercise in disinformation. More likely it is that neither the authors nor the artist have adequate reference material for modern Inuit homes and so fall back on a more widely available image.

A further example is seen in *Find Out About Eskimos* (Hughes, J. (1985) London, Hamish Hamilton). Not until page 30 of a 32-page book do we read: 'The old Eskimo life that we have seen in the last few pages has almost vanished.'

Many publishers have however worked hard to update their materials. *Eskimos: The Inuit of the Arctic* (Wayland, 1984) has been followed by *Inuit* (Wayland, 1989). The front cover illustration of the second edition now shows a hunter driving a Ski-doo instead of the earlier dogs and sledge. But a closer examination of the order of ideas in the later edition is instructive:

> The Inuit used to build snow houses called *igloos*. They trained dogs
> to pull sledges called *komatiks*. Nowadays the Inuit live in houses
> like the ones in this picture. They travel on sledges with motors
> called skidoos. (Smith, 1989, p. 7)

The problem for the writer is that the image of the igloo is so firmly embedded in the mind of the reader that it seems to be necessary to go along with this imagery before disabusing the reader of it. There is of course, a good case for identifying the subjects of the book with what is already in the readers' minds. It is a matter of saying 'You know those people who live in igloos? Well, they don't...' The same is true for the titles of books. Most books refer to 'Eskimos' in the title but give the term 'Inuit' in the text. And yet as long as authors do this these people continue to be defined by their past.

For contrast, compare the order of presentation of the following text from *Eskimo Boy*:

> Otto and his family have a wooden house in the centre of the
> village. It has two rooms — a small room they sleep in and a larger
> one they use as a living room and kitchen. They keep their house
> warm with a coal stove as there is no gas or electricity in their
> village.
>
> In the past the Polar eskimos did not have wooden houses.
> They used to live in small huts made of turf. The walls were lined
> with sealskin and they burnt seal oil lamps for warmth and light.
>
> None of the Eskimos in Siorapaluk live in igloos, but some-
> times when they are out hunting they build them as a shelter against
> a storm. (Alexander, 1979, p. 2)

These authors refute the idea of igloos at the very beginning of the book and there are no illustrations at all of igloos to accompany the text. The photographs are realistic and believable — a photograph of 'relaxing after a long day's hunting' shows the hunters looking genuinely exhausted, smoking, staring at their small primus stove, still wearing their waders, the tent floor littered with discarded tin mugs, and so on.

Presenting another lifestyle in a positive way can be a difficulty for a writer. Consider this description of a small settlement in Greenland:

> On one bank of the bay, there is a small Eskimo village. One of the houses belongs to Amsirk. Amsirk is the best hunter in the village. His house is surrounded by empty cans and bottles. This is a sure sign that its owner is prosperous. (Brewer F., trans. Benson, B. (1980) *Hunter in Greenland*, Cambridge, Cambridge University Press, p. 1)

Waste disposal is expensive in the Arctic because of high transportation costs. What would give a Residents' Association in South-east England some cause for complaint is shown here in a positive way. This particular book deals effectively with the reality of hunting. Although not too gruesome, the artwork illustration of a dead seal being dragged to a sledge does not spare us the bloody trail across the ice.

> It is dark when Amsirk gets home. His wife Inza helps him to drag the seal into the house. It is her job to skin the seal. She uses a special knife called the 'woman's knife'. As she works, her daughter Makra watches her carefully. Skinning a seal is a skilful job. (*ibid*, p. 3)

This description of Inza raises another issue in the description of distant peoples. Her work is described as skilled but she is defined only in relation to her husband. Sex bias is easier to combat in the reader's own society than in other societies. The author has a responsibility to present women in a positive way but how is the reality of a sexist society to be presented to the reader?

Ethnocentrism is especially stark when the physical attributes of people are described.

> (Eskimos) ... have wide faces and a brownish skin. Their eyes are narrow and slanting, their hair is very dark and straight ... (Newman, 1978, p. 6)

The least that can be said about this descriptive approach to physical features is that it is likely to emphasize physical *differences* rather than similarities.

For readers who wish to develop their own teaching materials on Inuit people there exists updated information in Creery (1982), Alexander (1988) and Pelly (1990). For further ideas on teaching about the Inuit see Harnett and Welch (1986) and Legge (1988).

Table 4.1:   Criteria for the evaluation of books dealing with distant people and places

Does the book exclusively endorse European values, lifestyles and concepts?

Are British or European lifestyles presented as either superior or as the 'highest level of development'?

Are groups of non-Europeans referred to as 'tribes'?

Are homes in other countries referred to as 'huts'?

Is the history of other countries presented as starting with their 'discovery' by Europeans?

Is the way of life of other cultures seen in a simplistic, naive way?

Are festivals and customs presented as being exotic?

Are there distortions or omissions in the treatment of the country's economy?

Is the description of other ways of life balanced, with positive instances?

Is the country described in its own terms, rather than being seen from an outsider's point of view?

Does the book challenge stereotypes directly?

Is it implied that poverty is the fault of the poor, or inevitable, or tolerable?

Will the self image of children whose families come from the places described be enhanced?

Do the illustrations of less economically developed countries portray people in active and dominant roles?

What experiences and insights does the author have which qualifies him or her to write the book?

Is the role of women in other cultures adequately presented?

Does the book contain terms which are offensive to some groups?

How recent is the book? Does it portray an accurate picture of life there *today*?

Checklists

A number of checklists have been devised for evaluating the racist and ethnocentric content of children's books (for example, Preiswerk, 1980; Stinton, 1979). Table 4.1 is adapted from some of these so as to be applicable to children's books dealing with distant people and places.

Atlases and Globes

There is little evidence in the research literature for what children learn about the world from atlases and globes but there *are* a large number of children's atlases available on the market. Sandford (1988) has provided a taxonomy of these. Other surveys and classifications include Gerber (1984) and Stoltman and Freye (1988). Junior atlases are especially variable in quality (Sandford, 1978) and some maps *are* clearly better than others (Noyes, 1979). Many children's atlases are more than just books of maps however — they may contain photographs or artwork or 'factfiles' of information about the countries shown.

HMI evidence for the extent of atlas and globe use in schools has presented a consistently disappointing picture over the last ten or twenty years. In one of the most recent surveys for example:

> Pupils achieved satisfactory or better standards in map work, including the use of atlases and globes in only a quarter of the schools. (HMI, 1989, p. 12)

Notwithstanding a disappointing school record, there is a large High Street sale of atlases. About three-quarters of 11-12-year-olds in a survey of 1600 British children were found to possess an atlas at home (Sandford, 1980).

Maps are a form of language and children need to master this language in order to maximize their access to the information stored in the map (Gerber, 1981a and 1981b). Learning to decode maps is a gradual process and depends on the ability of the individual to identify and understand the various components of the map and then to understand how those elements are integrated. There has only been limited research into children's competence in cartographic language (Bartz, 1965 in Gerber, 1981; Gerber, 1981a and 1981b; Sorrell, 1974) and virtually none into *young* children's cartographic fluency. Insights of this sort are obviously important and could be useful in improving map design but Petchenik (1983) has suggested that atlases produced *solely* on the evidence of children's understanding and level of attainment could produce a new generation of users with even lower competence, producing a downward spiral of expectation and performance.

All maps (and atlas maps in particular) have features that make decoding of them difficult. They are selective, they omit much detail, they simplify reality (for example, complex outline shapes are smoothed), as well as exaggerate (those details judged to be more important are emphasized). Generalization is fundamental to map-making. The smaller the scale of the map the greater is the amount of generalization. Generalization is also subjective; the cartographer has made decisions about what features of the real world to show on the map and what characteristics of those features to highlight. Towns, for example, may be described by their area, or their function, but it is usually population size that is selected as the information to be mapped. This level of abstraction may be beyond the child's grasp. Some towns, for example, will be omitted from small scale maps whilst others will be grouped into conurbations. But it is as important for the child to recognize what *isn't* shown on an atlas map as it is to recognize what *is*.

A number of points are made below (following, in part, Bartz, 1965) about aspects of map language of relevance to children's understanding of the world through atlases. The discussion is presented in order to identify good practice in atlas design for young children and to serve as background briefing for the selection and purchase of school atlases.

Projections

A globe is a true representation of the Earth and, provided it is large enough, will show all parts of the earth's surface in their correct positions, shapes and relative sizes. Because large globes are awkward to carry around, there have been some ingenious attempts at making inflatable and folding globes. But none of these has ever been entirely satisfactory and so the central problem for cartographers remains: how to represent the spherical surface of the earth on a flat piece of paper?

Map projections are ways of transferring the framework of meridians and parallels (lines of longitude and latitude) from a globe to the plane surface of a piece of paper. It is possible to create a framework of meridians and parallels so that the *area* of the land masses is correct, but this can only be done at the expense of their shape. It is also possible to reproduce the correct *shape* of the land masses, but, again, only at the expense of correct relative area. It is also, of course, possible to draw a map with both area and shape incorrect and in so doing, achieve a compromise that reduces the overall error. There are a number of common solutions to the problem that are widely reproduced in school atlases. Perhaps the most widely recognized projection is that by Mercator (figure 4.7a). Mercator was a Dutch geographer (1512–94) who devised a chart for seafarers on which every straight line was a line of constant compass bearing. The huge contemporary success of this map led to it being used for purposes for which it was never intended and until recently it was the most common representation of the world in school atlases. However, because users were not aware of its limitations for non-navigational uses it gave rise to many misapprehensions about the relative sizes of the world's main land masses. Distortion in high latitudes on this projection is gross. Greenland, for example, appears to be the same size as Africa. (In fact, their true relative sizes frequently come as a shock when comparison is made with a globe.) Recent attention has been given to the weaknesses of the Mercator projection by the various development agencies who have pointed out that the map gives messages to readers about the relative sizes (and, therefore, perhaps, importance) of the 'rich North' and 'poor South'. This map has also been used, quite wrongly, to show, for example, vegetation cover. When the map is used in this way the relative areas of, say, ice and tropical rain forest are completely distorted. To show those sorts of phenomena you need an *equal area projection*. There are many such projections that show correct relative areas of the land masses, but perhaps the best known of these by now is the Peters' projection (figure 4.7b). Although professional cartographers have pointed out that this projection is neither original nor unique, the map has gained a considerable amount of political acceptance. The distortion of shape in this projection however is severe. Africa appears to be twice as long as it is wide whereas in reality it is about as wide as it is long. According to one commentator, the land masses are 'reminiscent of wet, ragged, long winter underwear hung

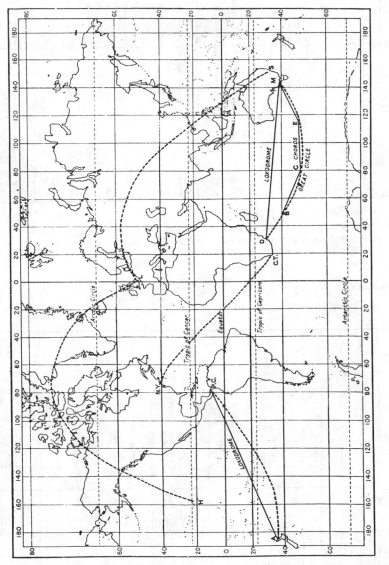

Figure 4.7a: Mercator's projection

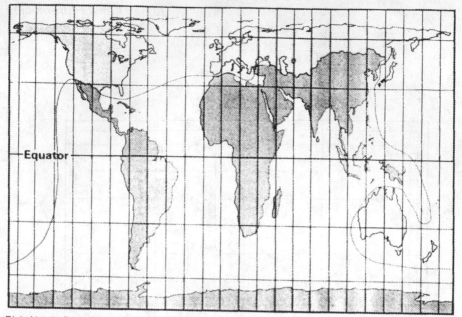

Rich North–Poor South. Peters' projection

Peters' projection is an equal area projection. The land masses are the correct size in relation to each other, but there is some distortion in shape. This projection has been used to emphasize the size of the poor countries of the South compared with the rich countries of the North.

—— Brandt Line   ▢ Rich North   ▣ Poor South

Figure 4.7b: Peters' projection

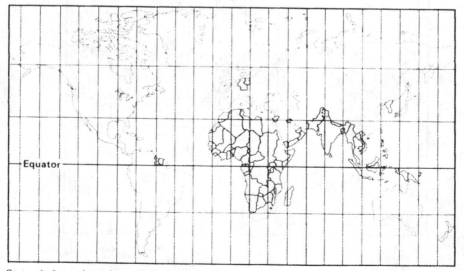

States independent since 1945. Gall's projection.

Gall's projection gives a reasonable compromise between accuracy of shape and area. A modified version is used in this atlas as a general purpose world map. This map shows states which have gained their independence since 1945.

▨ States independent since 1945.

Figure 4.7c: Modified Gall projection

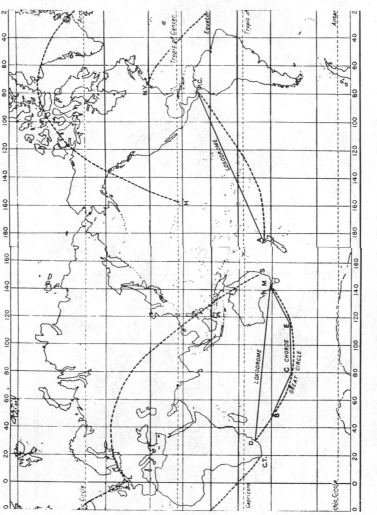

Figure 4.7d: Mercator's projection centred on the Pacific Ocean

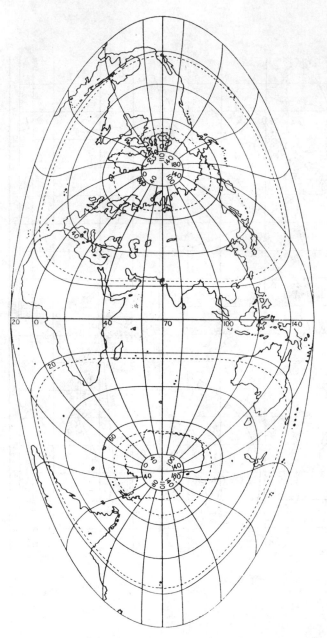

Figure 4.7e: Transverse Mollweide projection

out to dry on the Arctic circle' (Robinson, 1985, p. 104). In an article reviewing an atlas based entirely on the Peters' projection, King and Vujacovic (1989) ask whether this is 'a new era of cartography or a publisher's con trick'.

More satisfactory as a projection for general use would be the Eckert IV (as used in the Open University's *Third World Atlas*, compiled by Crow and Thomas, 1983), the Winkel Tripel (in Kidron and Segal's *New State of the World Atlas*, 1984) or a form of the Gall projection (for example as in the *New Oxford School Atlas*, OUP, 1990, see figure 4.7c). The latter is an example of the many projections which attempt to achieve a compromise so that they can be used for general purposes and is, in fact, the projection used by the NCC to represent the 'world to be known' of the National Curriculum.

However, these are not the only ways of representing the world. Conventional projections are often thought to be Eurocentric, precisely because Europe is usually shown in the top centre (dominant) position on the map. Splitting the world map through the Atlantic rather than the Pacific (figure 4.7d) gives a different perspective. The British Isles are now seen in a rather different relation to the rest of the world. They are now on the 'edge' of the page in a position rather similar to that usually occupied by New Zealand. And what if the poles were not covered in ice and thinly inhabited? Would a more common world map then be something like that shown in figure 4.7e? North America and the Soviet Union are closer together than is commonly supposed and transverse projections which 'wrap' the map around the world the other way' are helpful in highlighting this.

The point of this discussion of map projections is to emphasize that 'we' are not in the 'centre' of the world and that it is necessary to be confronted with alternative views if we are to correctly understand the spatial relationships between countries.

Symbols

Symbols cannot be understood without a legend (or 'key'). The legend on maps for young children needs to be placed prominently on each page as children's habits for searching for the legend are not well developed. The practice of using a standard legend (to be found on another page of the book) seems inappropriate for young children. It also seems reasonable to make symbols as 'memorable' as possible by making them resemble the features they represent. But caution is needed. The triangle symbol often adopted for a 'highest point' can be misleading. Not all 'highest points' or 'peaks' are peak-like — some may be quite flat and children easily confuse flat with low. This argues for careful explanation in preliminary pages, matching the symbols used with photographs of real exemplars. It's also important to clarify that some of the features shown on the atlas maps are invisible on the ground — country and administrative boundaries for example are not always evident. In fact, this whole issue of what maps show *and what they don't* needs to be clarified for children.

When selecting an atlas, look for legends that have meaningful headings. 'What the symbols mean' is preferable to 'key' or no heading at all. The same applies to map titles. 'Map to show roads and railways' is preferable to 'communications' (Sandford, 1985). Similarly, 'farms' and 'factories' as titles are preferable to 'agriculture' and 'industry'. For a further discussion of children's understanding of symbols and signs, the reader is referred to Gerber (1981).

Colour

Colours may be used on atlas maps for different purposes. Some colours indicate phenomena on a *nominal* scale — for example colours on political maps merely indicate where one country ends and another begins. Other colours represent phenomena on an *ordinal* scale — that is one colour represents 'more than' another colour. Land height layer colours are an example. Where colours represent environments there probably needs to be a picture of that environment forming part of the legend. Reference to land height colours needs to be in an understandable form (for example, 'mountains' is preferable to 'land over 1000 m').

Scale

Few children of primary age will readily appreciate the scale of small scale maps. Scale expressed as a representative fraction (for example, 1:44M) is not generally understood at all (Bartz, 1965). Graphic (linear) scales help but care needs to be taken in the way these are presented. A full textual explanation is desirable.

The use of comparitor maps which compare the map on the page with a small inset of a part of the world more familiar to the child, such as the home country, is a useful technique. But it assumes that the child *is* familiar with the size of his/her own country in some meaningful way — for example how long it would take to travel from one end of the country to the other.

Place names

Children are more aware of the names on the map than of anything else (Bartz, 1965). But place names are fickle. The same place may have several names in different languages. Compare for example: Venezia (Italian) with Venice (English), Venedig (German), Venetie (Dutch), Venecia (Spanish), Venetsia (Finnish), etc. Foreign language versions of place names usually reflect past historical or colonial associations, and are usually the result of mispronunciation. Not all of these find their way onto the map — for example 'wipers' for 'Ypres'. Given a number of alternative versions for the name of a place, which one does the cartographer choose? In Britain, the Permanent Committee on Geographical Names for Official Use makes recommendations for dealing with foreign place names in atlases. Local versions are generally thought to be preferable, because that's what the place is called by the people who live there and presumably they know best. However, if the locals use a different alphabet the name must be transliterated using the locally-preferred system (for example the Chinese-preferred pinyin system of turning Chinese sounds into the Roman alphabet gives Beijing, not Peking; Guangzhou, not Canton). Using local names throughout an atlas would reduce inconsistency and ethnocentrism, were it not for the fact that children live in an inconsistent and ethnocentric world. The place names *they* know are Moscow, not Moskva; Lisbon not Lisboa (Sandford, 1985). So decisions have to be made by the cartographer about when to use the local name, when to use the anglicized version and when to put both (assuming that there is space). These choices might depend on the age of the target readership.

As an exercise, consider the following selection based on the editors' judgment of what might be appropriate for an atlas targeted for 14–16-year-olds:

Dunkerque; Hannover [i.e. no anglicized version given]
Praha (Prague); München (Munich) [local name first]
Cairo (El Qahira); Alexandria (El Iskandariya) [anglicized version first]

Readers are invited to reflect on what constitutes the difference between each of these pairs of place names and to formulate their own preferred solution for these and other places using a selection of atlases. Would you use the same solution for an atlas aimed at 8–9-year-olds? If not, why not?

Anglicized names are usually used for large scale topographic features such as mountain ranges, especially where these spread across several countries. But most small scale topographic place names are only given in the local language and young map readers can find difficulty with the mass of unfamiliar words. With the aid of the glossary in a good atlas, knowing just a few foreign words can help. The map of Japan begins to make more sense when you see that the suffixes *-misaki* and *-wan* are, respectively, capes and bays in Japanese. Names in South East Asia begin to form a pattern when you know that *Muang* means city and *Kepulauan* means islands.

Type Style

Once the cartographer has decided what to call a place, she/he has to label it on the map. How readers scan maps and pick out the information they want from the background 'noise' of colours, symbols and other labels has only really been investigated relatively recently. Great attention is always paid by cartographers to the type style used to label different classes of feature. (Gerber, 1982). For example, topographic features are often in italics, except for peaks which are often in condensed type. Settlement names are usually shown in upper and lower case and administrative areas in capitals. The importance of places is shown by the size of the type and whether the type face is bold, medium or light. Pupils need to understand these rules in order to 'read' the map and teachers need to make the 'hidden language' of the map more explicit. Atlas maps are basically about 'far away places with strange-sounding names' and the unfamiliarity of place names means that pupils need all the help they can get in discriminating between the type styles on the maps. The search strategies children use when scanning maps have been investigated by Phillips, Noyes and Audley (1978) and Sandford (1980) and there have been some attempts to incorporate scanning practice into teaching materials associated with atlases (Wiegand, 1988).

The Treatment of Foreigners in Children's Comics

Comics are popular. Zimet (1976) estimated a weekly purchase by British children of twelve-and-a-half million comics and although more recent figures appear to be difficult to obtain, there is now a much wider range of comics available than ever before.

Early research on children's comics emphasized their possible effects on the personality of the growing child (Wolf and Fiske, 1949; Riley and Riley, 1955; Wertham, 1954). George Orwell, for example, wrote in 1939 that boys' papers both reflected and helped to preserve, a reactionary society supported by the press barons. The treatment of nationalities in comics received attention on both sides of the Atlantic in the early post-war years. In this connection, Berelson and Salter (1946) examined the treatment of Americans and others in popular magazine fiction in the United States and several publications of the Comics Campaign Council referred to the tendency of British comics to make non-British people (especially those who were dark skinned) the enemy or inferior characters in stories.

It was not until twenty years later, however, that sustained attention was focused on the stereotypes of foreigners in comics (Johnson, 1966). Johnson analyzed a sample of comics readily available in Oxford and in-dicated that they were a powerful source of nationality images. The most striking references of course came through a sample of British and Amer-ican war comics. These introduced a form of sanctioned death and violence to the young reader as well as much pejorative name calling of the enemy. Nearly all war stories at that time were concerned with the Second World War which suffered some distortions in its presentation. The heroes of the British war comics were (naturally enough) British, but with occasional references to Australians or New Zealanders. There was little reference however to Americans and allies were always portrayed as white. The 'enemy' was always German or Japanese and France, Belgium and Italy were seen as 'locations' for the war rather than nations involved in the conflict. War stories were the sole content of the specialist war comics studied by Johnson but such stories also featured prominently in 'boys'' comics and 'juvenile' comics. The portrayal of war became progressively more realistic in its depiction of violence.

How has the situation changed a further twenty years later?

Nursery comics have few references to other countries. Where they do, they tend to be benign and educational. Animals and vehicles possessing human characteristics occasionally visit other countries. This is generally in the context of holidays and the places visited are usually described in terms of a single attribute, for example, hot or cold. There are frequent references to the North Pole whenever a cold location is required for the story. 'Juvenile' comics (e.g. *Beano*, *Dandy* and *Beezer*) are still going strong. There are also generally few references to other nationalities in these comics today. However, when foreigners do appear they are subject to the same anarchic attacks as parents, teachers and other authority figures. In one story, Dennis the Menace is offered £1 million for his dog Gnasher by an Arab who is so wealthy that his purse has to be pulled behind him on a small trolley.

I find this joke funny. Not because it pokes fun at Arabs — it doesn't. The joke depends on a notion of wealth as bringing with it the problem of what to do with all that cash. To be effective, jokes need to be succinct. This requires that they are peopled by characters we can recognize quickly. 'Englishmen, Irishman, Scotsman' jokes only work because we think that we can recognize the distinctive dispositions of each of the characters in the story. We can predict how they will behave in the situation defined by the joke. These characters are as recognizable as well known joke settings ('a man goes to the doctor . . .') or formulae ('Knock, knock . . .'). It may be more helpful to concentrate on how we might explain these conventions to children, and how they are generally intended to be harmless and how in fact they usually are, rather than simply to criticize the popular portrayal of particular nationalities.

Nevertheless, it is clear that some portrayals of foreigners can be offensive. In fact, the publishers of the *Beano* chose to refuse a request to reprint here the cartoon described above in view of the outbreak of the Gulf War. On reflection I think they were right to do so. War isn't funny. Nevertheless, there are still war comics in existence, although fewer seem widely available nowadays. The theatres of war in comic books have been extended to take into account Vietnam and the Falklands. Each enemy nationality talks in a distinct patois. The Germans still say 'Achtung!', 'Himmel!' and talk about 'Engländer Schwein'. In one episode of 'Death Squad', a Russian soldier is referred to by the Germans as a 'stinking subhuman'. In a Vietnam story, 'these tough little gooks never know when they're beaten' and in 'Invasion!', defiant Tommy Baker and his pals are chased by Argentinian soldiers who shout 'Vamos!' and 'Rapido!'.

Some of the locations for the institutionalized characters of the juvenile comics have a basis in geographical reality. Little Plum (your redskin chum) inhabits a world of deserts, canyons and plains similar to that of Desperate Dan's Cactusville. It is not known how durable these place-images are for children or how they condition understanding of minority groups such as North American Indians. The latter are usually given the 'hostile savage' treatment although it is the African groups who generally come off worst (Laishley, 1972).

However, although specific place and nationality references in war comics appear to have been reduced, these have been replaced by fantasy and futuristic worlds and wars which are no less disturbing. An examination of the treatment of nationalities in computer game software would be timely.

Johnson (1966) also compared the preferred countries of war comic readers and those who did not read war comics. The differences were striking in that war comic readers exhibited a strong dislike of Germany and Japan and a strong preference for America, Australia and England. Careful to point out that the differences in preference need not have been *caused* by reading such material, Johnson nevertheless indicates that the differences between the two groups of children are large enough for it to be highly unlikely to be a chance difference. It was also found that war comic readers possessed *less* information about the countries they expressed dislike for than those for which they expressed liking. This indicates a sinister aspect of the war comic material: that they provide only a negative image of place, created in a vacuum of information. In an earlier piece of work which supports Johnson's findings, Bailyn (1959) reported that 11- and 12-year-old children who spent a great deal of time reading comics, watching the television or films were more likely to agree with statements such as: 'All people are either all good or all bad'. Greater exposure to comics appeared to dispose children towards dichotomous absolutes — all good or all bad.

Television

Television is undoubtedly the most important source of children's information about the wider world (Hartmann and Husband, 1974) and more than half of the 278 children surveyed by Jungkunz and Thomas (1986) said that television was their main source of information about a range of (less economically developed) distant places presented to them.

Children are very knowledgeable about television. They know, for example, with great accuracy, the scheduling of programmes. Children also watch a great deal of television. By the age of 6 *months* they may be in front of a television for one-and-a-half hours per day (Hollenbeck and Slaby, 1979) and this figure rises to between two and three hours during the years of primary education in Western Europe and North America where there are large numbers of television sets (c. 90–98 per cent) available in each home (Liebert and Sprafkin, 1988).

However, these are average figures and it is clear that some children will watch television for much longer than this. Indeed, Cullingford (1984) cites examples of children who watched television virtually from the moment they came home from school to the time they went to bed.

According to Cullingford, children show, from the age of 6, an over-whelming preference for *adult* programmes. Thrillers and serials seem especially popular. But preferences do not imply that children only watch the programmes they like. Neither do they 'see' everything that they watch. Children's visual attentiveness is not high (Yussen, 1974) and the way television is attended to is different from reading a book or listening to a teacher. They appear not to approach television as a way of learning any-thing. 'The pleasure lies in the atmosphere and in the fulfilment of the anticipation' (Cullingford, 1984, p. 21). But where, specifically, in this time-consuming occupation, do children's images of places come from?

The most 'obvious' source of information would seem to be the news and yet Cullingford claims that this is one of children's least favourite TV programmes. The presentation is too verbal, the subject matter bores them and the programme as a whole is too challenging. It is not entertainment. It is as though the news serves as a way of dividing up the evening's viewing. 'Only about 20 per cent of 9- and 10-year-olds could cite international news even in a vague way, such as 'space shuttles' or 'Russians in space' (*ibid*, p. 62). In this they are not much different from adults. Finnish research, for example, demonstrates that adults often remember little of the content of the news (Nordenstreng, 1972). The presentation of the material as a series of (often) unconnected items in a fairly unsystematic way may not help. Significant factors in being able to remember news items appear to be the 'concreteness' of the news item and the extent to which the audience are able to identify with the story. Repetition on a day-to-day basis, the amount of time given to the item in a programme, whether there is strong visual material associated with its presentation and the location of the item within the news programme also seem to be significant in the impact an item makes (Booth, 1970). Children are most interested in the news when there are local events reported but they are generally unable to discriminate between the significance of the relative importance of the items presented. Children appear to have little recollection of the news items that they have seen and may appear to be little affected by, for example, scenes of violence. In his study of children's understanding of war, Tolley (1973) notes that the gen-eration of children he worked with was the first to observe televised combat, but their response to documentary scenes of actual violence on news broad-casts was less than to a Western shoot-out. Certainly, the exposure of children to fictional violence does seem to have been large:

> Between the ages of 5 and 14 the average American child witnesses the violent destruction of 13,000 human beings on television...

One television station showed in one week, mostly in children's viewing time, 334 completed or attempted killings. (Guitar, quoted in Larsen, 1968)

Personalization of news items helps to make them memorable. Children *do* appear to follow the exploits and travels of members of the Royal Family. Repetition and reinforcement are clearly important in recollection of major media events. The Sahel famines are fixed in the minds of children because of the sheer overwhelming reinforcement of the message.

Children like advertisements (Cullingford, 1984; Singer and Singer, 1981). This liking though appears to bear little relationship to the products being advertised. Rather, liking is based on the characters in the advert (whether real or cartoons) and on repetition (Krugman, 1965). It may be, therefore, that advertisements using images of distant places are especially effective in establishing stereotypes. There are, for example, at the time of writing, a number of television commercials advertising brands of lager which employ humorous popular images of Australians.

Serials and soap operas seem perennially popular. Many of these are set in specific locations: *Coronation Street*, *EastEnders*, *Neighbours*, *Home and Away*, *Dallas*, *Falcon Crest*, *Knot's Landing*, *Black Forest Clinic*, etc. They appear to be watched avidly (even addictively) by children, several times a week (even several times a day as the midday episode can be video recorded) and they are scheduled at peak times. The distinction between entertainment and reality on television is blurred. The opening sequences show locational images which support the dramatizations which are generally of one social group. There has been little work on the impact of these soaps on children's images of Australia, America, Germany, etc. but it would be astonishing if they were not effective image-creators. The extent to which the locations in which the action takes place become associated with the prevailing ideology and sub-culture of the series itself and its characters has also yet to be fully explored.

There is a considerable body of research evidence on the effect of television on ethnic minority groups (Berry and Mitchell-Kernan, 1982). Some minority group children and low income children may be especially susceptible to the socializing influences of television. Although most of the research in this area has been into the portrayal of minorities in the home country there are lessons for the likely impact on children's images of distant peoples. The North American Indian, for example, is generally portrayed as being a Plains Indian, wearing beaded and fringed clothes and hunting buffalo. The great range of other Indian lifestyles are largely ignored.

Even when contemporary Indians are shown on television, the majority of programs about them tend to be of a documentary style. They may discuss life on a particular reservation, but most do not relay information about American Indians residing in urban areas, even though one half of the American Indian population currently resides in non-reservation settings. (Morris, 1982)

Many children will obtain their images of natural hazards through television and film. Disaster movies are a powerful source of information on natural hazards but this information is often flawed (Liverman and Sherman, 1985). Although the physical characteristics of earthquakes, floods, hurricanes, etc. are generally accurately represented, the human response to such hazards is not. Mass panic, for example is a frequently suggested response, as well as the implication that disaster victims are incapable and that crime is wide-spread. Films generally fail to show the real nature of personal injury, with victims receiving either minor cuts and bruises or being killed outright. Little attention tends to be given to warning systems or to recovery after the event. There is the strong implication in many such films that natural disasters are more likely to occur in the Western world, whereas in fact they predominate in the economically developing world.

Can film and television influence children's attitudes to places? Peterson and Thurstone's early (1933) study of films indicated that they can. Despite the use of naive research methodology, films such as *All Quiet on the Western Front* were found to influence attitudes to Germans after just one exposure to the film. Later studies have showed that television is able to improve attitudes towards ethnic groups. Bogatz and Ball for instance, (1971, quoted in Christenson and Roberts, 1983) showed how watching *Sesame Street* improved the attitudes of black children and white children to black and Hispanic children. One of the very few pieces of research aimed specifically at investigating how children's attitudes to other children in the world may be changed through film is Roberts' (1974) study of the television programme *The Earth's a Big Blue Marble*. This was an American series aimed at 10–12-year-olds which took its name from a photograph of the Earth as seen from space. It was a weekly, thirty minute programme in a magazine format including documentary style presentations and animated folk tales about aspects of children's lives in other parts of the world. Roberts and his students tested children (using semantic differential scales) before and after watching the programmes to see if there was any change in the way the viewers thought about children in other parts of the world. They found that after watching the programme there was a general increase in children's perceptions of the similarities among peoples and also an increase in the perception of the state of well-being of other children. There was an accompanying decrease in feelings of ethnocentrism. However, the programme appears to have been constructed deliberately to present the world in a positive light by portraying life in other lands as 'exciting, attractive, and often just plain fun' and it appears to have been highly successful in transmitting the idea that all people are fundamentally the same. Nevertheless, Roberts reflects on the implications of convincing children that people are similar:

Is it possible that in creating such a belief we might simultaneously create conditions under which a person who is perceived as different for any of a vast array of reasons might be more likely to be labelled as a deviant?, treated as a deviant? It is clear that different sub-cultural groups do differ in a wide variety of ways. And while it seems to us to be important that children recognize the fundamental differences among men (sic), it also seems to us to be important to teach children to recognize, accept and value differences. (*ibid*, p. 50)

Kemelfield (1972) evaluated the effects of schools television programmes about Pakistan on 9–12-year-olds. Generally these programmes seemed to be associated with a positive attitude change in the young viewers, except in an area with a high proportion of children whose own families had come from Pakistan. Non-Pakistani children in this school apparently became, after the programme, more sensitive to the possibility of a culture clash as a result of the information received. (This is not dissimilar to Stillwell and Spencer's (1974) findings quoted in chapter 2.)

It seems that white children who exhibit the most prejudice against black children are those who watch more violent programmes, which generally appear to show black people in negative ways, and fewer programmes (such as *Diff'rent Strokes*) which show black people in positive ways (Singer and Singer, 1983). This doesn't prove that television causes prejudice but it does suggest that some types of television programmes may encourage or discourage prejudicial attitudes. Notwithstanding this, television authorities in the United Kingdom continue to show old films which show Africans and American Indians as savages and Germans and Japanese as the enemy.

Tolley (1973) investigated the effect of the media on children's knowledge and views of the Vietnam war. The children interviewed stated that they learnt more about the war from television than from any other source and indeed those who watched the most television were found to hold more factual *information* about the war. But the *attitudes* of television viewers and non-viewers were quite similar. As we have noted before, factual understanding appears not to have much relationship with attitudes. Parental mediation of what is watched is a much more important variable in the formation of attitudes, especially for the children of 'middle class' homes.

The nature of the images children receive from television about distant people and places, is as yet, poorly understood. The complex mixture of visual and verbal clues and the way children attend to the medium creates a reaction that is different from the 'conscious'. It seems likely that repetition of some screen images of place will create a vague mood of place. The literature on imaging (for example, Horowitz, 1978; Paivio, 1971) suggests that familiar scenes can exert a powerful effect on thinking and that visual material is more easily retained than other information. But detecting the pictures of places in children's heads and examining the significance of those for international awareness and understanding is, as yet, some way off.

Tolley (1973) asked why schools contributed so little to children's understanding of an issue as important as the Vietnam war. It seems that most teachers appeared to believe that primary age children should be sheltered from such harsh realities and feared the backlash from parents regarding the outcome of discussions which might polarize the community and provoke objections. However, even very young children were exposed to much media information about the war. Tolley felt that teachers were abdicating their mediating role when children were being exposed to un-coordinated incidental vicarious experiences.

Two Examples of Media Images of Place — Ethiopia and the Falklands

News coverage of the 1984 Ethiopian famine and the 1982 South Atlantic War illustrate the power of the media to create strong images in children's minds.

The Ethiopian famine story broke on 23 October 1984, with Michael Buerk's now famous television report. Although there had been earlier reports (for example, by Buerk himself in July that year), the October footage was especially effective, not only because of the quality of the photography and reporting but also because of the generous seven minutes allocated to it in the BBC 6.00 p.m. news. Bumper European grain harvests described in the same news bulletin may also have added to the impact of the famine report (Harrison and Palmer, 1986; Shipman *et al*, 1986; Gill, 1986).

In 1985 the Food and Agriculture Organization of the United Nations established the cross-national *Images of Africa* project. This formed part of a study of the news media and the campaigns and information materials produced by non-government organizations in response to the African famine. The UK *Images of Africa* project team have described how news-paper reporting following the Ethiopian famine stressed Africa's problems and dependency. The lasting images in the public's mind were of hopeless-ness, powerlessness and conflict. Biblical images were reflected not only in the language used to describe the famine ('deliverance' , 'mercy') but also in the composition of the photographs which, being chiefly of mothers and children, echoed Madonna and Child religious art (van der Gaag and Nash, 1987). The Ethiopian story unfolded in a series of clearly identifiable stages. After an initial 'conscience stirring' phase, emotion was channelled into activity and the apportioning of blame. Later 'mercy missions' and the 'generosity of the West' were emphasized, followed by the Band Aid story.

On the whole, the picture presented was one of a people who had allowed themselves to fall into an apathetic state of despair and inevitability. There was no attempt to present a historical context to the famine and Ethiopians were given few chances to speak for themselves. (*ibid*, p. 35)

People in the West responded generously out of genuine humanitarian motives but the point which has been made repeatedly since the appeal is of the damaging images and impressions created by TV coverage. The general problem is that the media's superficial response to topical events has priority over the development of greater understanding over the longer term.

The most disturbing aspect of TV coverage of 'Band-Aid' for me was its negative portrayal of the relationship between the West and Africans — and this is very important because it determines how the West views Africans. Of all the pictures I have seen of 'Band Aid' and its 'subsidiaries', the one that sticks out in my mind is of Bob Geldof, KBE, looking like a latter day Lawrence of Arabia, walking in the desert with hundreds of black hands tugging at his robes — welcoming this white saviour in their midst. TV deals in imperialist stereotypes today, just as it did twenty-five years ago. The impression such an image left with me is: 'Africans starve to death — for whatever reason — and it is the West, this time in the guise of Bob Geldof, which comes to their rescue'. They are portrayed as passive and helpless, spectators to their own destiny — the West is the superior partner (Badawi, Z. (1988), in Twitchin, p. 135)

Perceptions of Africa by young people aged 13–18 were studied by the UK *Images of Africa* project team. The image of the begging bowl at this time was especially strong. Pupils' reaction to photographs was generally one of pity, even when the photographs presented were not necessarily of people in distress. When photographs were shown of happy, smiling people the response was that 'we must have helped them' (Grant, 1986). In the minds of many of the young people interviewed Bangladesh was thought to be near Africa, presumably because of the 'disaster' association. Maps of Africa drawn by those interviewed were labelled 'famine' and 'poverty' right across the continent. This response, of a whole continent in need of assistance, and of all Africans as victims, seems to have been widespread (Davis, 1985).

Three years later, primary school children in Leeds still carried the images of Ethiopia in their minds, reinforced, one supposes, by Live Aid, Comic Relief and their own fund raising.

I wouldn't like to go to Ethiopia because they starve. Quite a lot of boys are almost bald and they've got flies all over them. Their arms are very thin. (8 years)

They can't grow food and so they starve and that's why we send them money and rice and tins of stuff. (5 years)

In Ethiopia you have to go to wells to get water. It's not easy and Mrs. F. says its about from Heckmondwike to somewhere. And we tried to carry a bucket and half the class could hardly lift it. (6 years)

They just sit down in Africa and cry. (8 years)

On 2 April 1982 Argentinian troops invaded the Falkland Islands, a group of two main islands and about 100 smaller ones in the South Atlantic Ocean. Britain had occupied the islands since the 1830s after the expulsion of an Argentinian garrison. Argentina has since refused to recognize British sovereignty and has continued to refer to the islands by their old Spanish name — The Malvinas. A naval task force of 100 ships sailed 8000 miles to the South Atlantic to engage the Argentinian forces. More than 1000 men lost their lives. Argentina surrendered on 14 June 1982.

The impact of the South Atlantic War on the world image of children was not just confined to Argentina and Britain. In the seventh week of the conflict, after steady reporting of the war by newspapers and television, Norwegian children (aged 7–16) were given the task of drawing a world map from memory (Overjordet, 1984). Because of the difficulty of evaluating the world maps of the very youngest children, only the maps of those children over 10 were analyzed, but the Falklands figured prominently in the maps that were drawn. Sixty-two out of 141 children marked and named the Falkland Islands which were ranked eighteenth in order of frequency of reference of all 'countries', higher than the USA, Germany, the Netherlands and Argentina itself! Selected maps are illustrated in figure 4.8. The significance of this small investigation according to Overjordet is that world images are not stable, but greatly influenced by world events and their media coverage.

Figure 4.8:   Norwegian children's views of the world during the South Atlantic War

Figure 1 (7 years)

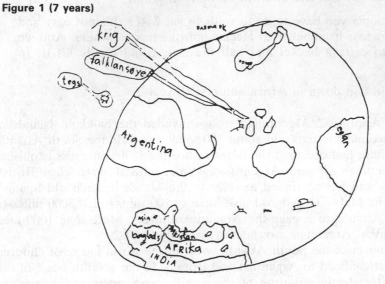

Figure 2 (9 years)

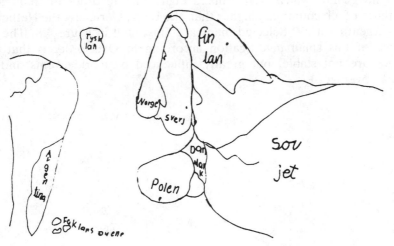

Figure 3 (10 years)

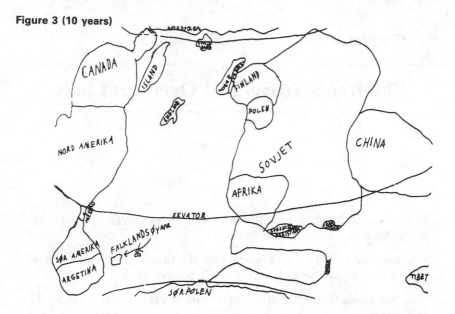

Figure 4 (11 years)

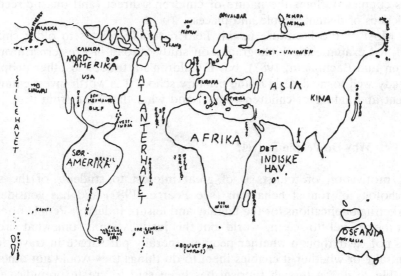

Source: Overjordet, 1984.

Chapter 5

Children's Travel and Overseas Links

'If we were in Moscow now it would still be all frozen up', he said, going down the steps beside her.

'I know', said Nellie. 'But when you do things at school in geography you know them, but you don't believe them.'

'No, you have to see them for yourself. It makes you want to do that.' (Penelope Fitzgerald, (1988), *The Beginning of Spring*, Collins)

This chapter outlines the nature of children's direct (and quasi-direct) experiences of distant people and places.

Most of the literature in this field naturally relates to older children (see, for example the bibliography on study abroad in Western Europe by Baron and Bachmann, 1987), but if children's attitudes to other peoples is already well formed early in the primary school it is worth investigating the extent and nature of children's travel and what they take from it.

Why Do People Travel?

The motivation of tourists is of great interest to students of the social psychology of tourist behaviour (see Pearce, 1982) and has considerable marketing implications for the holiday and leisure industry. People often say that they travel 'to see the world' but this justification is somewhat circular! It is not clear though whether people generally participate in travel for its own sake or whether it enables them to do things they would not otherwise be able to do. Although tourism has been said to create prejudice (most tourists can't stand other tourists!), travel is generally regarded as being 'good for you' and there is a long tradition of beneficial justifications for it.

In the seventeenth century, for example, travel was widely associated with an educative function. The 'Grand Tour' was a finishing school for Elizabethan courtiers, providing a mixture of world knowledge with a training in courtly manners, despite the later questioning of its value by those who noted with distaste the affectations of the returning young tourists (Hibbert, 1987). By the nineteenth century, travel was widely justified on health grounds as spas and seaside resorts grew in numbers and popularity. An increasing awareness of landscape aesthetics was coupled with the commercial development of areas of great natural beauty. The educational, health and aesthetic benefits of travel became available to all with the development of mass air transport, annual paid holidays and the consequent growth of the package tour industry.

The Contribution of Travel to International Understanding

The notion that travel can change attitudes is implicit in much tourist literature and there is a little evidence that travel can reduce ethnocentric and authoritarian attitudes (Smith, 1955 and 1957). However, deeply-rooted attitudes appear not to be much changed by the experience of travel and the methodological problems in separating the effect of travel from larger scale social and cultural influences are considerable. In any case, Pearce (1980) has indicated that the travel motivations of many tourists are predominantly relaxing, drinking and having a good time rather than meeting the local inhabitants or studying their culture.

Travel may have an influence on both the traveller(s) and on the host locality. Mings (1988), for example, reported some influence of tourism on international understanding as a result of American tourists visiting the island of Barbados. The Barbadian workers in contact with the tourists demonstrated some knowledge of the USA and some sympathy towards it but was not however significantly different from the attitudes of other Barbadians who are not in contact with tourists at all. Evans-Pritchard (1989) presents another view of local residents to visiting tourists. In this study, Pueblo and Navajo Indians were found not only to hold stereotypes of tourists but made a living by making and selling models of these white visitors! We know even less about *children's* responses to foreign visitors. One potentially fruitful area of enquiry might be to investigate children's attitudes to foreigners in areas which receive large numbers of tourists such as the South coast resorts in Britain or major cultural and tourist honeypots such as Oxford and Stratford.

Notwithstanding the limitations on the evidence, however, tourism *does* bring people closer together (at least physically) and the potential of the industry for promoting international understanding is large. In 1988 there were some 400 million tourists worldwide and the industry is one of the most consistent growth sectors in the world economy. Prospects for its continued growth are promising. Current forecasts for example indicate that international travel will double by the year 2000.

These millions of daily person-to-person encounters are potentially a powerful force for improved relations among the people and nations of the world; relations which emphasize a sharing and appreciation of cultures rather than a lack of trust bred by isolation. (D'Amore, 1988, p. 43)

Where do Children Travel?

No official statistics are available for British children's overseas travel experiences, (although the British Tourist Authority have plans to collect and publish figures on *unaccompanied* children), but some inferences may be made from the pattern of adult travel (see, for example, English Tourist Board, 1989). In the mid-1980s the British took about twice as many holidays abroad as they did in the previous decade (see table 5.1). Package tours represent a steady 50–55 per cent of these holiday visits, and the most popular destination for such tours continues to be Spain, including the Balearic Islands of Majorca, Minorca and Ibiza. However, British holidaymakers are increasingly travelling to a wider range of destinations, with France, Greece and Portugal gaining an increasing share of the foreign holiday market (see table 5.2). The most popular destination for *independent* holiday travellers is France (the destination of approximately half the independent tourists), followed by Spain.

Obviously, these overall figures conceal wide variations in the frequency and destination of holiday travel. Some indication of this range may be obtained by considering the travel experiences of Y5 and Y6 (age 9–11) children from four Yorkshire schools (Wiegand, 1991). Mill Town Primary serves part of the West Yorkshire conurbation. The parents of its children represent a wide range of occupations and incomes. Blue Rinse Primary is located on the periphery of a major city. Its catchment area consists almost entirely of large detached houses owned by a well-to-do professional and business community. Bleak Moor Primary is situated on the outskirts of a seaside resort. Most of its children come from a large council estate with a high unemployment rate. Almost all of the children at Taj Mahal Primary come from families with strong Indian or Pakistani connections. Many of these children have visited the Indian subcontinent, usually staying with relatives for perhaps six or eight weeks. The travel experiences of children at each school are summarized in table 5.3. It is not claimed that these figures are representative of any school population other than the schools from which they are taken but they do serve to illustrate the variety of travel experiences shared by children in contrasting schools. The figures may be compared with those of Esarte-Sarries (1989) who reported that 45 per cent of a sample of 200 primary school children had been abroad.

Mill Town children have travel experiences broadly comparable with the national pattern described earlier. Blue Rinse children have widespread and

Table 5.1: Numbers of holiday visits abroad by UK residents — 1975–1984

	000s
1975	7743
1976	7024
1977	6834
1978	8439
1979	9827
1980	11,666
1981	13,131
1982	14,224
1983 (provisional)	14,605
1984 (estimate)	15,200

(*Source*: Market Intelligence, December 1984, Mintel Publications)

Table 5.2: Destination of package holidays, 1977–1987

	1977 %	1987 %
Spain	47	37
Italy	10	5
France	9	12
Greece	6	13
Gibraltar/Malta/Cyprus	5	5
Yugoslavia	3	5
Portugal	3	5
North Africa	2	3
Belgium/Luxembourg	2	1
Austria	4	4
Eastern Europe	1	1
USA/Canada	*	2
West Germany	1	2
Netherlands	2	2
Switzerland	1	1
Scandinavia	1	*
Caribbean (Commonwealth islands)	*	*
Middle East	*	*
Other Africa	*	*
Other European	*	*
Elsewhere	*	*

(* = less than 1 per cent)

Source: Market Intelligence, Dec 1984, Mintel Publications; *Business Monitor: Overseas
         Travel and Tourism (MA6)*, 1987, Business Statistics Office of the Government
         Statistical Service, HMSO.

exotic holiday experiences including packages to Kenya where some had
visited the Tsavo East and Amboseli nature reserves. The percentage of
children from Bleak Moor who had been abroad surprised those teachers
who knew the catchment area but, of course, out-of-season packages to
Spain are probably the cheapest form of inclusive holidays available. In
1990, child prices for some Spanish holidays for those booking early were as
low as £25. The increasing popularity of travel to America became apparent

Table 5.3: *Travel experiences of Y5 and Y6 children from four schools*

	Mill Town %	Blue Rinse %	Bleak Moor %	Taj Mahal %
Spain	42	66	31	2
France	17	51	*	2
Greece	14	16	14	*
Italy	8	6	*	*
Germany	6	3	*	*
Malta	5	6	7	*
Belgium	2	6	*	*
Netherlands	2	*	3	*
Luxembourg	*	3	*	*
Bulgaria	*	*	3	*
America/Canada	6	13	7	*
North Africa	2	13	3	*
Sub Saharan Africa	*	*	*	5
Pakistan	*	*	*	33
India	*	*	*	22

(* = less than 1 per cent)

after discussions with children at all the schools. It was clearly the ambition of many to visit the United States and this seems to be seen increasingly as the achievable dream. Children from Taj Mahal Primary had the most exotic travel experiences but it is interesting to note that they had very little experience of Europe. Presumably, most of the resources allocated by their families to holidays was used in making visits to relatives.

No data was collected on the particular destination within each of these countries, but most children travelling to Spain would have visited the Mediterranean coast or the Balearic Islands, and in so doing experienced one of the world's most popular tourist locations (receiving in the mid-1980s something in the order of 30–35 million visitors per year). Resorts such as Benidorm, Lloret de Mar and Torremolinos form the 'tourist environment' *par excellence*. 'Such settings will create the transitory, insulated from danger, voyeuristic, occasionally exploitative, souvenir mentality ... characterizing the tourist experience' (Pearce, 1982). The most typical direct experience of distant people and places, therefore, that children receive is likely to be the Spanish Mediterranean resort, with its accompanying inauthentic attributes of placelessness (Relph, 1976). The destination of children travelling to the United States was, in every case, Orlando, Florida.

The quality and quantity of Orlando's tourist attractions have earned it the well-deserved title of 'Entertainments Capital of the World'. Walt Disney World is probably its biggest attraction — it takes at least three days to see it properly, so plan ahead! Then there's the EPCOT Centre, the natural beauty of the Cypress Gardens with nearly 10,000 rare flowers and plants, Circus World, Sea

World and of course the Kennedy Space Centre. (Travel Company Brochure)

The nature of the tourist industry, the way its clients are managed and the ways in which the 'tone' of resorts is developed and maintained is relevant to children's experience of distant places. There is the contention, for example, that tourists are controlled and managed to a high degree by the tourist industry (Pearce, 1980). If this is so, then *children* have even less power to control their own experiences as they are highly dependent on their parents. As consumers, families are probably faced with more constraints of cost than most other tourists and are therefore subject to marketing strategies with certain clearly defined features. Special reductions for children at certain hotels and resorts for example, as well as the extension of these reductions (at some hotels only) to single parents, the provision in hotels of 'family floors' and the availability (again, at certain resorts only) of the tour companies' 'children's clubs' are factors which tend to concentrate families in particular locations and therefore operate to promote a uniformity of experience for children as a subset of the standard Mediterranean package tour. These recognized features of the travel industry serve to isolate children still further from participation in what Relph (1976, see chapter 1) would call 'authentic' aspects of the country they are visiting.

By contrast, the children in the above study who travelled to India and Pakistan experienced everyday life in small villages 'off the tourist track' for the most part of their stay. Indeed, for many, the longest part of the journey came *after* arriving at Bombay airport! However, whilst there, they often travelled widely to other cities within the Indian subcontinent, such as Islamabad and Maipur, as well as to major tourist locations such as the Taj Mahal.

Nevertheless, it is intended to show below that whether children experience 'authentic' or 'inauthentic' places, travel provides them with a richness of experience which for them is memorable and enriching and which can be exploited in school to further help them understand the world.

Children's Travel Experiences

We do not believe that parents should actively keep their children away from school. But on the other hand, we believe the value and benefits to children of travelling abroad and experiencing a foreign holiday must be balanced against the loss of education when they are not in school for a week. (Mr. D. Goodman, spokesman for Thomson Holidays, quoted in *Times Educational Supplement*, 2 September 1988)

Record numbers of families booked foreign holidays in the summer of 1988, encouraged by cut price offers from the large holiday tour operators.

Children accompanying those parents who booked an early holiday to Europe for example were charged only £1, or £29 for a trip to Disneyworld, Florida. But what *is* the value and benefit to children of foreign travel?

Children in Yorkshire (aged 9–11) with travel experience of either India or Spain were given a word-association test and their written responses were compared with those of children who had not travelled to either country. For both countries, the children who *had* travelled were able to provide a richness of response (both quantitative and qualitative) that indicated the extent to which all their senses had been stimulated by the experience (see table 5.4). Of course, for these young travellers to India, their responses are influenced by more than just their direct experience of the visit itself. They also have a family experience that will have reinforced for them the positive and varied aspects of this faraway place that has for them special significance. Comparison of these responses reveals a complex reflection of the issues of bias and stereotypes discussed in chapter 3. For those children who had *not* travelled there, India was a place that was hot and dry, where people ate rice and curry and lived in 'huts' amongst herds of elephants. Many children confused Indian people with North American Indians, referring to face paints, totem poles, feathers and war dances (see figure 5.1). Those who *had* travelled to India mentioned bazaars, beggars, motorcycles, thieves, dogs, bare feet, jewellery, taxis, crowds, decorated trucks, mosques, wells and sleeping under the stars. For them, insects and snakes were far more typical of India's animals than tigers and elephants were. All the children who *had* been gave positive evaluative responses (such as 'nice', 'exciting', 'good', etc.).

For those who hadn't been to Spain, the country was a beach, with sun, flamenco dancers and bull fighting. But those young travellers who had spent a week or two there were able to add far more perceptive details of beach life: the brightness of the light, the 'skyscraper' hotels and the variety of icecreams. These impressions, however, were somewhat tempered with the realism of 'hooligans' and (sic) 'larger louts'.

As part of the same study, children with direct experiences of travel were interviewed in an attempt to assess further what they had learned and to begin to identify starting points for the study of distant places in the school curriculum. An interview schedule was used which tried to encourage children to reflect on what they saw as the principal differences and similarities between the country they had visited and their own, and to try to explore the nature of the stereotypes that were held about the country they had visited (see Esarte-Sarries, 1989 for a discussion of children's experiences of France).

Most children were able to develop and expand upon the impressions they had recorded in their word association responses.

(France) 'They have bread buns in the shape of a crab'.

(India) 'There was this man and on his hand there was no skin there.

Table 5.4:   *Word association responses to the word: INDIA from twenty-five NON-TRAVELLERS (aged 10–11) from Mill Town Primary. (Numbers indicate total number of responses received)*

sun/hot	25	Bombay	2
dry/drought	15	Delhi	2
curry/spicy food	15	lions	2
black/brown/'coloured' people	13	'awful'	2
elephants	8	Sikhs	2
rice	7	markets	2
poor people	6	dancing	2
(straw) huts	5	kebabs	1
totem poles/tents/face paints/feathers	5	buffaloes	1
jungle/trees	5	restaurants	1
Pakistan	5	rich people	1
camels	4	big families	1
crops	4	'cannibals'	1
sand	4	mountains	1
turbans	3	'funny' music	1
tigers	3	Sri Lanka	1
farms	3	Cape Town	1
different/'funny' language	3	big	1
crowded	3	swamp	1
temples	3	monkeys	1
'red spot on forehead'	3	bamboo	1
cricket	3	decorated cars	1
'tribes'	2	Salman Rushdie	1
Taj Mahal	2		

Word association responses to the word: INDIA from twenty-five TRAVELLERS (aged 10–11) from Taj Mahal Primary. Numbers indicate total number of responses received. (Note, ten of these children had travelled to Pakistan rather than India)

beggars/poor	25	far away	3
hot/sun	25	big	3
Bombay/Delhi/Calcutta	11	sleep outside	3
nice/beautiful/good	10	commonwealth	3
Taj Mahal	9	fighting	3
nice food	9	buses	3
crowded	7	taxis	3
relatives	7	rice	2
snakes	7	exciting	2
mud/wood/straw houses	6	rickshaws	2
mosques	6	thieves	2
rich people	6	dogs	2
bare feet	6	monkeys	2
jewellery	6	servants	2
muslims	5	weddings	2
wells	5	bicycles	1
shops	5	parks	1
elephants	4	tigers	1
hindus	4	farms	1
insects	4	drought	1
bazaars	4	untidy	1
camels	4	cheap	1
mountains	4	rain	1
Pakistan	4	cows	1
bungalows	3	prime minister	1
mangos	3	cinemas	1
no gas/electricity	3	fairs	1

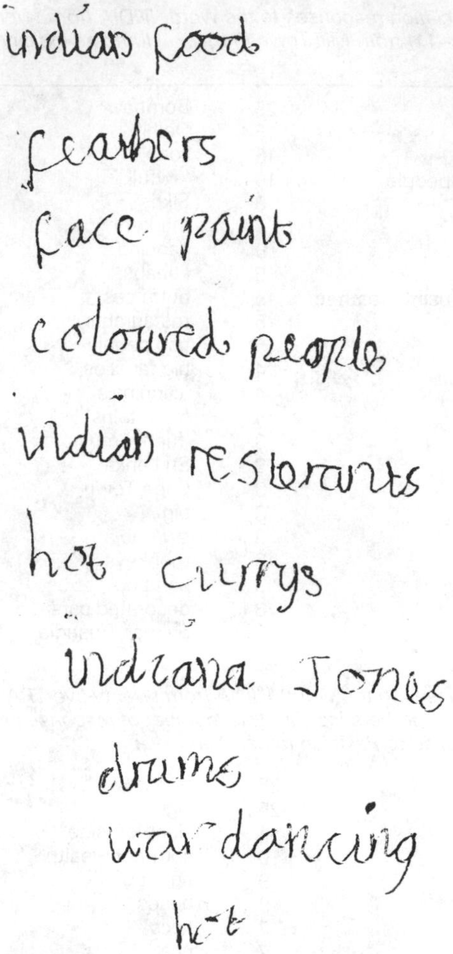

indian food

feathers

face paint

coloured people

indian resterants

hot currys

indiana Jones

drums

war dancing

hot

Figure 5.1: A 10-year-old's word association response to 'India'

He was near my Dad's brother's shop. There were about five poor people there. And there were these two ladies. They were really poor and we gave them some money. Not everyone is poor but most of the people are poor.'

At the most basic level, children who had travelled were able to accurately name the countries and resorts they had visited. These were proudly listed, for travel was universally seen as not only 'good for you' but something that counted for status. Many children could provide detailed information about the routes they had taken, including ferry crossings and airports and relate these journeys to an atlas map. The experience of travel had also given many children an indication of scale and distance.

'Could you go there for the weekend?'

'No way. It took nearly a whole day to get to Bordeaux in a car, never mind across the sea and the hovercraft.'

Many children had also learned a few words in the relevant foreign language and had had practice in converting currencies. Indeed, most still remembered the exchange rate after several years, and could comment on the relative prices of goods in the shops.

Because the context of most children's travel was the annual family holiday and because the most significant factor in choosing a holiday location is the weather (Market Intelligence, 1984; Business Monitor: Overseas Travel and Tourism, 1987), it is not surprising that this is the strongest remaining impression in children's minds. Almost all children when talking about travel, no matter where, recalled the heat.

'It was dead hot. It was like frying an egg.'

By no means all the children liked it and there were a few grisly descriptions of acute sunburn.

Most children had made some form of contact with foreign children or adults, either 'the locals' or other holidaymakers. These meetings, however brief, almost universally left positive impressions.

'Tell me more about the people.'

'Well, some of them were really nice. At one campsite a man helped us with our awning. He said, "Oh, you are English. Let me help you"'.

Gorman (1979) has illustrated the sense of cameraderie and shared purpose which can result from the shared experiences of adults travelling together in groups and for most of the children interviewed, the experience of being in an unfamiliar setting had served to unite their family. Children's interview responses often referred to family confrontations with local people and customs which clearly had served to draw the *family* together even if there had been fewer benefits in terms of *international* understanding! Many children had also obviously enjoyed comparing the responses of their parents to say, octopus salad or snails. The significance of travel as a family event cannot be overemphasized. Some of the strongest memories recounted by the children were family members' responses to particular situations encountered.

However, the fortunes of the family on holiday often seemed to influence strongly the children's responses to questions about the country concerned. Young children seem to find it difficult to separate their personal experiences from their attitudes towards the place as a whole:

'I don't like France at all.'

'Why not?'

'My Mum got poorly. She had to go to hospital. She got food poisoning.'

For the children who had travelled to India or Pakistan the visit had had special family significance and they talked with confidence about 'their' house and village. These children's experiences were especially vivid and they returned to the UK with a direct experience of homes, schools and daily life that had placed them in situations contrasting sharply with home.

'I didn't like the water. In some villages the water isn't very good. It isn't purified that much. Some villages, a very poor village we went to, some of my Mum's friends live there, they asked us to visit, so we went there, and the water is so dark, we took some purifying tablets with us and we gave them to them. The water tastes awful. But in our village, it's so big, we have really nice water in our village.'

———

'Did you go to school there?'

'I went for one day only. I didn't go back because it was too strict.'
'Tell me about it.'

'If you did anything wrong they hit you with a stick. I'm quite big so they put me in a higher form and I got it wrong. They hit me on the hand. There are no chairs to sit on. You just sit down on the ground. And there is all water coming through the roof. You write on a small blackboard with chalk. Or you can use ink pens. You get a break of one hour. You have to get up very early, at six o'clock. School is from seven until two o'clock. Sometimes I got scared about snakes.'

The most impressive feature of the conversations with children who had travelled was the revelation of a mature sense of balance in the way they described places. If there was one thing they had learned above any other it was that places are not what they might seem, that there is variety and that prior impressions can be wrong.

'What do you think the people who haven't been to Pakistan think it is like?'

'They think it is just kind of like one place but when they go there they would find that it is lots of different places.'

———

'What impressions do people who haven't been to Spain have of it?'

'Well, they might think that all the people are brown. But they're not. Some are, but not all.'

———

'What do you think that people who haven't been to France think about it?'

'They probably think that it's very hot. But in fact, sometimes the weather turns quite cold. You can get storms.'

––––––––

'What do you think people who haven't been there think about Pakistan?'

'They would think there are a lot of poor people.'

'Is that true?'

'Yes, but there are also rich people.'

It is this ability to be able to counteract previously held impressions, or the impressions held by those who haven't travelled that seems to be one of the most important benefits of travel for children. This also applies to the question of stereotypes. 'Travelled' children seemed more ready to view stereotypes more cautiously, matching them against their own observations. Some were also able to make the transfer to viewing critically the stereotypes of countries to which they had not been.

'What about the berets, the stripy tee shirts and the strings of onions?'

'Well, I'm not so sure about the strings of onions. I didn't see any of those. I think that's more of an olden day thing. The Second World War. You see it in "*Allo, Allo*". I think the berets are still in. You don't see as much of them as you would have done but they are still there.'

'What about the same sorts of pictures of other countries? What about Holland? What about clogs and windmills?'

'I think it's like the French berets. They're not quite out but not many people wear them.'

As well as their own direct experience, many children also pick up rich impressions of other countries from the stories told by friends and relatives who have been there. These can be vivid, even eccentric. Naturally, there is often much fascination with presents:

'My grandma and my uncle's been to Russia.'

'Have they?'

'Yes, and they brought, they had this wooden horse ands it had flowers all over it, you know, little flowers for the eyes and everything, and there was a doll ...'

––––––––

'My dad goes to lots of countries. He's been to Germany and he's been to Holland, and to Nigeria. He brings me foreign dolls and they've got the clothes they wear.'

'What does your Dutch doll have on her feet?'

'Clogs!'

'Can you describe what clogs are for the others?'

They're little wooden things and they're pointed at the toes. And one of my dolls, I think its from Portugal, and it's got a basket and she's got a kind of basket on her head, and I've got a Spanish doll and she's got castanets. But it's lost an arm ...'

'My dad works in Angola, they're having a war there. They speak Portuguese some of them.'

'Do you know why they speak Portuguese there?'

'It was captured by the Portuguese a long time ago.'

The notion that travel can change attitudes is implicit in much tourist literature. There is some evidence, for example, that travel can reduce ethnocentric and authoritarian attitudes among adults (Smith, 1955 and 1957) but where attitudes are deeply rooted they appear to be resistant to change and the methodological problems in separating any effect of travel from larger scale social and cultural influences are in any case, considerable. Virtually nothing is known about the effect of travel on children's attitudes to other peoples but it now seems clear that children *do* have considerable experience of foreign travel. The widely-held assumption that many children 'never go off the estate where they live' can be challenged. Many children do have experiences that can be built upon in the classroom, and their capacity to remember them is often powerful. 'Children enact their memories through description, conversation and play, sometimes outlining places and events with remarkable clarity and accuracy, at other times amalgamating a variety of memories into a kaleidoscope place' (Catling, 1988). At the very least they have powerful impressions that can be shared with other children. At best, some children begin to see the world from the point of view of other people — the essence of international understanding. One of the goals of geographical education is the development of a 'sense of place'. Some of the children interviewed above clearly demonstrate they have acquired that by the end of the primary phase. We could exploit this private geography of their 'known worlds' in the construction of learning experiences in the classroom.

School Journeys

The Central Bureau for Educational Visits and Exchanges is the national organization responsible for providing information and advice on all forms of educational visits and exchanges, and for developing and administering a range of programmes designed to promote better international understanding through mutual awareness. The Bureau is funded by a UK Government grant and has offices in London, Belfast and Edinburgh. The Bureau supports teacher exchanges, not only in languages, but also in other subjects; international study visits for educational specialists; a scheme for modern language students to spend a year working in school or college where their target language is spoken; overseas industrial placements; school exchanges; and an information service. Although progress towards the single market was focusing the Bureau's attention on contacts with Western Europe by the late 1980s, there were also at this time pioneering approaches to work in Eastern Europe and the Soviet Union.

No information is available about the extent of school journeys abroad but it is clear that in recent years the volume of primary school business has declined, not least because of DES guidelines on charging for optional out-of-school activities. Nevertheless, a substantial number of school journeys still continue to take place and the most popular destinations for primary schools appear to be North-west France, Belgium and Holland.

Companies specializing in primary school travel confirm that the visits are generally of five days (four nights) duration and involve parties of approximately forty children. There is generally a programme of historical and cultural sightseeing visits. Some indication of activities undertaken on such journeys may be obtained from a selection of pupil materials produced by the tour companies. These usually take the form of worksheets, inviting the pupil to keep a diary of the visit, record details such as the address of the hotel, the daily menu, distinctive features of the local buildings and so on. In places where English is widely spoken, such as the Netherlands, some schools undertake shopping surveys. Car park surveys also seem to be popular as is observational work based on shop displays or foreign language signs. There has also been work which has investigated the possibilities of linking environmental education and language learning (Mares, 1988).

Little is known about the role of teachers, tour guides and couriers in interpreting the host culture during foreign travel. There is some evidence from the literature of mainstream tourism that such people may provide a distorted view of the culture because of their own 'socially marginal' position within it (Smith, 1978). This analysis is however too far from *children's* experiences of other countries to offer helpful insights to teachers accompanying such parties but the experience children will have of a foreign environment as part of a school group is likely to be more restricted than a comparable environment in their own country. Because they are in a higher risk environment (they can't speak the language with ease, they are therefore less able to read the signs and danger signals, the traffic is on the other side of the road, etc.) they probably tend to be supervised more closely than usual and have the landscape and social situations interpreted for them rather than investigating more freely for themselves. This may make them more subject to the impressions of others. There is scope here for ethnographic research (Byram, 1989). Ethnographers attempt to understand other cultures by participating in them as insiders, whilst at the same time observing them as outsiders. Byram suggests that modern language student teachers would benefit from some ethnographic training. They would consequently be better placed to understand the target culture and thereby be able to interpret it for their pupils. Furthermore, it is quite possible that the approach of 'language for touring' and transactional language adopted by many GCSE courses is likely to foster ethnocentric attitudes as the culture is viewed solely from the outside. A balanced, structured and selective course is required which will enable pupils to learn how they can view other cultures as insiders.

International Villages

An interesting example of the travel experience of children (and of action research into international understanding) may be seen in the Children's International Summer Villages organization (CISV). CISV was founded by Doris T. Allen, a psychologist at the University of Cincinnati. The Village programme typically consists of a four-week international summer camp of forty-eight children aged 11, from twelve nations. Each participating nation sends a delegation of two boys and two girls together with an adult delegate. The multi-language camps feature a range of activities emphasizing international friendship, cross-cultural communication and cooperative living. The age of 11 was chosen by Allen because it was seen to represent some optimum point in receptiveness to the experiences the children would undergo. This includes being able to communicate unselfconsciously, being relatively stable emotionally (as opposed for example to later in adolescence) and not being inhibited about accepting new experiences. The programme goals are ambitious:

* to appreciate the likenesses and interdependence of all people while respecting and finding interest in their differences;
* to develop respect and appreciation for the way of life in other cultures;
* to provide the participants with experiences requiring cross-cultural cooperation in a national setting;
* to provide the participants with knowledge and experience about everyday life in another culture;

* to develop the ability to behave constructively and flexibly when interacting with persons of another culture;
* to provide all participants with better cross-cultural understanding by having interesting and stimulating experiences as 'family members' in another culture or as members of a 'global society' within a multinational camp;
* to develop effective communication skills even where there is no common language or cultural perspective;
* to develop skills in resolving conflicts without violence and stimulate a desire to work actively for peace;
* to promote international friendships and a sense of personal responsibility for family, community and national behaviour; and
* to provide a source of leadership for creating national and global communities respectful of cultural diversity, human rights and our physical environment. (CISV International Fact Sheet, 1987)

The villages themselves have stimulated research into changes in children's social attitudes as a result of such camps and the nature of communication between participating children. Doris Allen herself (1963) reports a number of studies demonstrating the characteristics of friendship formation across national boundaries. Sharing a common language was found to be *a* factor in determining friendships, but it was by no means the principal one. Gender is a much stronger determinant; 11-year-olds expressed a strong preference for friends of the same gender. There have in addition been some longitudinal studies of the long term 'sleeper' effects of such camps (Bjerstedt, 1960), indicating that children who have participated in the camps are often characterized by 'non-barrier thinking' and greater flexibility of thought in later life. Isolation of the camp as the significant factor is clearly problematic in such studies however. Other studies include analyses of the results of activities undertaken by the children whilst at the villages. An example of these is the 'Draw the World' activity (Allen and Anglin, 1988). Children in the first few days of attending a CISV village in Maine, USA, were given large sheets of paper and coloured crayons and told: 'We have come from different parts of the world. Today you have an opportunity to draw the world as you wish to draw it.' The exercise was repeated at the end of their stay in the village. Each child's two drawings were then compared. Allen quotes some (selected) examples of this comparison:

1st drawing: It shows a round world with continents of different sizes and water.
2nd drawing: The second drawing is also the round world but shows much more freedom of expression. It introduces a hope. The atmosphere is buoyant with trees and flowers, white clouds and rainbows. A large rainbow joins the world with clasped hands.

It has to be said that the methodology in accounts such as these is generally described uncritically and the children participating undergo a rigorous selection process which some might feel limits the general applicability of research findings. Nevertheless, such studies continue to support the belief of CISV that summer villages can promote the growth of attitudes favourable to world peace. In 1987 over 7000 participants from fifty-five countries took part in 225 international activities. In total, 40,000 children have participated in CISV villages between 1951 and 1987.

School and Class-to-class Links

The most comprehensive account of the principles and practice underlying school linking is to be found in Beddis and Mares (1988). This valuable book describes the experiences of primary school in Avon in making class links with schools overseas. The aims of class-to-class linking are:

* to encourage and help pupils develop a knowledge and understanding of themselves, their families and friends, their local neighbourhood and environment and their country using a wide range of study methods;
* to encourage and help pupils communicate to others this understanding of themselves, their community, environment and country, and their feelings and attitudes towards them. This may be done in a variety of ways — through writing, speech, images, sounds, models, music and artifacts. It may involve the use of electronic mailing and new information technologies, and offer support for the learning of a foreign language;
* to enable pupils to learn something of people, neighbourhoods, environments and ways of life in other parts of the world through the receipt and active study of similar communications from pupils of their own age;
* through this deeper understanding to counteract prejudice, develop sympathetic and caring attitudes to other peoples and ways of life, and a sense of responsibility for the environment, both globally and locally. (Beddis and Mares, 1988, p. 3)

Typically what happens in class-to-class linking is that pupils correspond with their peers in another classroom in another school in another country. One of the most significant benefits is that the communication is authentic, i.e. that the 'letters' that are written are real in the sense that they have a real recipient rather than (as was often the case in the past) being written for the teacher's eyes only. The task therefore has real purpose for the children involved. The whole class involvement enriches the traditional, individual 'pen-friend' exchange by acting as a forum for discussion and interpretation

Table 5.5: Primary school links in academic year 1987/88

Total number of schools with active links:	492
Number of schools with electronic mail:	49
Number of schools linked with: —	

France	159
Germany	44
Italy	11
USSR	6
Spain	4

and provides more liklihood of continuity. Pupils often start by sending a personal statement about themselves, which is followed by subsequent communications about their school life and neighbourhood. Communication is usually, but not always, in the mother tongue. Pupils in other countries frequently learn English earlier than is usual for foreign language learning in the UK. This, of course, works to the general advantage of British children. There have, however, been many successful links in second languages. Niemann (1987) has described a school link from the German perspective where the language of communication was in English. The German children had little difficulty with much of the correspondence as it tended to follow formulae with which they were well familiar. Typical letters began: 'My name is Claire. I am 9 years old. I live in Morecambe.' Niemann suggests that the personal name in the first sentence, the number in the second sentence and the place name in the third give the readers sufficient clues for them to decode the letter. Later, when interests are described, so many words are similar in German and English (for example, tennis, football, swimming, class, school) that the first, introductory letters are relatively easily read and the children are thus motivated to carry the link further. Where there is a language barrier, local secondary pupils have sometimes been able to provide translation (thus in turn giving *them* an authentic task) or the primary pupils themselves have devised ingenious ways of communicating, by, for example, the use of strip cartoons. Pictures, maps and models add to the variety of materials which can be exchanged.

Some indication of the extent of school linking may be obtained from table 5.5. This indicates the number of primary school participating in international links based on a questionnaire issued by the Central Bureau with a 70 per cent response.

E-Mail

A principal resolution of the European Ministers of Education standing conference in Istanbul (1989) was that education systems within the European Community should be encouraged to exploit to the full the educational potential of the new technologies and the media, particularly insofar as they can 'bring schools together in Europe and across the world' (Council of Europe document M ED-16–11).

In the school year 1987/88 there were forty-nine primary schools known to the Central Bureau to be communicating via E-mail with similar schools in other countries. Electronic mail is very similar to conventional mail in many respects. Basically, you need a microcomputer and a telephone. A modem connects the computer to the telephone line. You prepare as much text as you like in standard A4 format on a word processor. You then send that text instantly to the recipient. There can be one recipient or 100.

The benefit of E-mail as a vehicle for school to school linking is that it offers fast, written communication that is easy to edit. From the point of view of primary school children the immediacy of the communication avoids loss of interest during the inevitable time lag involved in conventional international post. Although there is some loss of the 'personality' of the communication in that it is in the form of print-out rather than handwriting, there is at least the considerable merit that the communication is legible! This is especially important if the letter is not in the mother tongue of the recipient.

How does E-mail work? The most common system in use in the UK is *Campus 2000*. This is a network which was established by The Times Network Systems Ltd and Prestel Education. There are two main elements of the network: databases of information and the electronic mail system itself which provides contact with the central resources and between users. The parent company, Dialcom, extends the network to the following countries: Australia, Canada, Denmark, Finland, Germany, Hong Kong, Republic of Ireland, Israel, Italy, Japan, Korea, Malta, Netherlands, New Zealand, Puerto Rico, Singapore and the USA.

A number of 'distant place-related' projects using E-mail formed part of the National Council for Educational Technology's Communications Project. Some of these are described in a special edition of the project newsletter (NCET, 1989). For example one project involving six schools was to write an 'epistolary novel' of the style of *Humphrey Clinker* by Tobias Smollett. In this novel the characters interact with each other while sending off correspondence to imaginary characters elsewhere. The primary school children worked with a writer in residence to start and then feed a fantasy based in the real world. The structure of the work is that an Old Man, once a courageous traveller but now old and infirm has recruited teams of explorers to continue his life's work. These are sent to exotic destinations and, once there, are given tasks to perform such as collecting artefacts. Regular reports are required to be sent to the Old Man. Here is a sample, which illustrates the possibilities for children's involvement in travel writing:

> I thought that the journey from Rome to L'Aquila was rather bumpy as the Renault did not have a very good suspension. But the views were beautiful, coming down the hills with the olive groves

Figure 5.2: Jane's letter to Arjun

Dear Arjun

Hello! How are you? I hope you're OK. I'm getting really excited about coming to visit you. I'm also a bit worried because I don't know much about India.

I hope you don't mind me asking lots of questions!

First, are there any diseases I should be vaccinated against? I hope there aren't too many, because I don't like injections. I've just had my BCG at school.

I don't like to look on the bleak side but if I'm ill, will I have to pay? I haven't got much money, so I hope not.

Talking of money, I was thinking of getting some Indian rupees before I set off. Will I be able to bring them with me into India?

If I can't, can you let me know when the banks are open in India, so that I can change my money when I get there? Oh yes, by the way, how many rupees do I get for £1?

Although it's lovely and warm here now, we had an awful winter. Lots of snow and very cold. What will the weather be like in India when I get there? What kind of clothes do you think I should wear?

A friend at school said I would need something called a visa before I can visit you.

Do you know where I can get a visa in England? Also, what will I need to get one?

When I get to Bombay, I shall get on a train to Jaipur. That's one of the things I'm looking forward to most — travelling on a real Indian train.

My friend Gemma has already been to India. She says I should buy a 7-day Indrail pass. How much are they?

She also said I should go to the Palace on Wheels — if I can afford it! Could you tell me about it?

Finally, I've heard that there are some very beautiful temples in India. I'd love to visit some of them. Can you tell me where some of them are?

My teacher said they don't have lions in the wild in India. I'd like to see some if I can, though. Are there any special places where I could see lions?

One last question, are there any parts of India I can't go unless I have a special pass? I don't want to get into trouble!

Well, Arjun, that's it. I do look forward to hearing from you.

Bye for now,

Jane.

(Reproduced, with permission, from Marshall, 1989)

---

and lemon and lime groves. It doesn't seem fair though, all the women seem to work in the fields in the hot midday sun. Whilst the men just drive tractors shielded by a canopy. In fact the women hold the place together. (*ibid*, p. 4)

E-mail links are still in their infancy but the potential is considerable. The direct link with other people provides an immediacy which reinforces understanding of real world problems and promotes collaborative learning. Children could find out about real issues in other parts of the world by supplying and collecting their own evidence. In so doing they would become involved in the processes of considering bias in the materials they received as well as the representation of their own locality. There are a number of examples of school links using email in the Campus 2000 handbook for 1989/90 (Marshall, 1989). One topic, for example, focuses on Jane, a fictitious character with penfriends all over the world. Jane has written to Arjun, her Indian friend and asks a number of questions about a forthcoming visit (figure 5.2).

A group of 10-year-olds were given a copy of Jane's letter and used the PRESTEL database on India to find out the answers to some of Jane's questions. This investigative activity simulates the way real travellers might use a travel agent. Of course, the same activity could be undertaken using reference books, the telephone and conventional mail and some colleagues may wish to provide practice in some of those skills in addition to using PRESTEL. This type of exercise is easily constructed for any country the class might be studying.

It is worth summarizing the experiences of those teachers who have undertaken international E-mail projects: It seems to be agreed that it is probably better to focus on the subject matter of a particular project rather than trying to establish pupil 'pen pal' type relationships at the outset. Teacher *rapport* however is essential from the beginning to maintain the impetus. The initial link seems to have been mainly stimulated through personal friendships, although some teachers have been put in touch with each other through organizations such as the Central Bureau. From the British perspective, almost all reported contacts appear to have been in English. Compatibility of age of the pupils participating and some commonality of curriculum are important issues. There has to be 'something in it' for both sides of the link. There are also some technical matters that govern links with Europe. France for example uses a completely different system from that available in the UK. The French use 'Minitel', a Viewdata type of service which is not compatible with either PRESTEL or Campus 2000. For contacts with French schools to take place therefore, either they have to subscribe to the UK system or UK schools have to subscribe to theirs! Germany is easier to contact as the 'Telebox' system is compatible.

Chapter 6

Teaching About Places

By means of description, comparison and handwork, you wish to teach children of six, in two lessons, about the characteristic mode of life of some of the inhabitants of *either* the Sahara *or* the Melanesian Islands. Indicate your method, and outline the matter of your lessons.

You wish to teach the geography of *either* Holland *or* Switzerland to children of ten years. Show what preliminary work you could do in your home area, in connection with the physical conditions and human activities, in order to help the children to a fuller understanding of the relative conditions in the other country.

(Teacher's Certificate specimen examination questions, National Froebel Union, St. Mary's College, quoted in Bown, c. 1920)

This final chapter builds on the evidence presented in previous chapters about children's understanding and experience of places and makes some suggestions for classroom practice. These suggestions are grouped for convenience under the headings *knowledge*, cross-curricular *skills* and the formation of *attitudes and values* in relation to people and places.

There are a number of key books which I can recommend as sources of teaching ideas (figure 6.1). Some of the suggested activities in this chapter are derived in part from some of these books but it has to be said that the true origin of many of these ideas is now obscure.

The purpose of this chapter is not to repeat the suggestions made in these books. They can do that better, especially as they are mostly highly illustrated and in large format. What I shall try to do, however, is to make some connections between appropriate activities and the National Curriculum and raise some issues about those activities.

Button, J. (Ed.) (1989) *The Primary School in a Changing World*, London, Centre for World Development Education.
Starting Together: Development education and young children
Clark, B. (1979) *The Changing World and the Primary School*, London, Council for World Development Education.
Fisher, S. and Hicks, D. (1985) *World Studies 8–13: A Teacher's Handbook*, Edinburgh, Oliver and Boyd.
Fountain, S. (1990) *Learning Together: Global Education 4–7*, Cheltenham, Stanley Thornes.
Fyson, N.L. (1984) *The Development Puzzle*, 7th edn, London, CWDE and Hodder and Stoughton.
McFarlane, C. (1986) *Development Education in the Primary School, Books 1–3*, Birmingham, Development Education Centre.
World Studies Project (1976) *Learning for Change in World Society*, London, One World Trust.
Nicholas, F.M. (1987) *Coping with Conflict*, Wisbech, Learning Development Aids.
Pike, G. and Selby, D. (1988) *Global Teacher, Global Learner*, London, Hodder and Stoughton.

Figure 6.1: A short list of staffroom reference books on teaching about places

Activities to Develop Locational Knowledge

The National Curriculum requires that children should have a framework of locational knowledge. I do not disagree with this. Place knowledge is important. In fact, place name *ignorance* is national news. Helgren (1983) describes how a first day of term quiz on place knowledge amongst students at an American university, the (admittedly fairly shocking) results of which were reported in the campus newspaper, provoked a national outcry. Neither are scare stories of lack of locational knowledge unknown in the United Kingdom. An international Gallup survey on geographical knowledge (1988) revealed British adults as coming near the bottom of the league of the nine countries involved in the study. Most Britons, given a map of the world, were unable to correctly identify central America, Japan, the Persian Gulf, Mexico, Sweden, Egypt or Vietnam. Thirteen were also unable to locate the British Isles and more than half could not locate Germany. In an Observer/Harris poll in 1990, British interviewees were given a map of Europe and asked to match the names of eight capital cities with eleven dots on the map (three of the dots were put in as dummies). Only about half of the respondents were able to correctly locate Brussels, Copenhagen and Paris. At times when hard news is in short supply, surveys such as this fuel the readily-combustible debate about standards in education. It's easy to see why. The potential content to be tested is immense. Many place names are in daily use and the news provides a constant supply of unfamiliar places to be known. Besides which, testing to reveal ignorance is a relatively straightforward matter.

There is broad agreement that children need some place knowledge to provide them with points of reference that enable them more easily to locate other places and appreciate broad spatial relationships. 'The names of places are embedded in everyday conversation and discourse, in newspaper, radio and TV items, and are part of the general culture which people need immediately to hand if they are to make sense of the world around them.' (DES, 1990d). Of course, it is to be hoped that they will accumulate this in the context of a variety of classroom activities and frequent incidental reference to atlases and globes. But that's not guaranteed and a 'realistic minimum' of particular places to be known is identified by the National Curriculum. Place knowledge includes having the skills to find *absolute* locations (for example, on simple letter and number map grids or by using more complex systems such as latitude and longitude) as well as being able to identify *relative* location (expressed by terms such as 'north of . . .', 'towards the coast', etc. as well as understanding the 'nesting' arrangements of places described in chapter 2). Children also need to learn some *facts* about places. This includes facts related to magnitude — such as area, population size, the height of mountains, etc. and these need to be compared with what is already known of the home region and country. Facts relating to the physical, economic and cultural characteristics of places will increasingly be seen as patterns, for example, patterns of temperatures around the world.

However, it was never intended that the locational requirements of the National Curriculum should be time consuming or irksome or learnt by rote. So how might children's general place knowledge be developed? What follows is a list of suggested activities for developing basic locational and factual knowledge which might be seen as short teaching units in their own right or as starters to project work on places.

We have, of course, used large classroom-wall news maps and maps to show food labels, sporting events, royal and head-of-state world tours for years. But these are still effective devices for children to store information and plot events. I think it's best to have two or three (The British Isles, Europe and the World) at different scales, and displayed at child height in the classroom. A *blank* wall map is extremely flexible to use. The locations of places in the news, football teams and so on can be easily marked on it by children or their teacher. A 'country of the week' can provide the focus of research and library skills for an end-of-week round-up to see how much has been discovered about it. The basic blank map can be elaborated to include 'advent calendar' type windows. Collage maps of particular countries also serve a useful purpose. A Commonwealth Institute activity booklet for example suggests making a collage map of Canada: 'Use green materials for the forests, brown for the mountains with white felt triangles for the snowy peaks. Yellow for where cereals are grown and blue for the lakes'. I also like the idea of each child having a 'personal organizer' which includes some blank maps (at different scales, i.e. perhaps the UK, Europe and the world). Children readily find uses for these, colouring in towns, rivers, countries etc. as they 'know' them, those they've been to, those they want to visit, in order of preference, those they have stamps from and so on. Blank maps can also store information collected about countries from class questionnaires. Which places have been visited, where do relatives live, where do letters come from?

Wall maps also form the backdrop to exhibitions and collections. At the very least these can be of souvenirs, dolls, flags, currency, postcards, stamps and symbols. It's worth pursuing some of these items further. What, for example, is the purpose of souvenirs? What sorts of things make good ones? What do they tell us about the places they come from? There are possibilities here for project work in design and technology (Attainment Target 2) — design a souvenir! The design generation stage involves talking about the proposed souvenir, choosing memorable symbols to represent the location and working the idea up by drawings and models. Class collections of everyday objects from other countries stimulate discussion. What is it? What is it used for? Why do people need it? An activity table task which I have generally found to be successful is to display objects together with cards that give their names and describe their function. Children have to match the objects with the cards (figure 6.2). It's possible to build up collections of artifacts from around the world quite cheaply, but there are also museum loan collections available in some areas. Although they can't always be borrowed or handled, many museums in Britain have outstanding ethnographic collections. Some museums have specialist posts for ethnic arts or multicultural officers and the city museums in Bradford, Kirklees, Leicester, Ipswich and Manchester have been working hard at collecting contemporary everyday artifacts related to the history of immigrant groups.

Another idea for map plotting is to use twin towns. The town twinning movement is now very strong in Europe and almost all large towns and many small ones have a 'twin' in France or Germany at least. Free information about the twin is often readily available from civic centres and tourist offices. Towns are usually matched to some degree by size and function so the twin provides a good starting point for a study of another locality outside the UK.

Children seem perennially to be interested in extremes. Some of the world's 'record breakers' are listed below for plotting on class or personal blank maps (see also *Oxford Rainbow Atlas*, 1987, p. 45). Further extremes can of course be investigated with the *Guinness Book of Records*.

Wettest place in the world	Mount Waialeale, Hawaii
Driest place in the world	Atacama Desert, Chile
Hottest ever place	Al'Aziziyah, Libya
Coldest ever place	Vostock, Antarctica
Windiest ever place	Mount Washington, USA
Snowiest ever place	Mount Rainier, USA
Highest waterfall	Angel Falls, Venezuela
Longest river	River Nile

Figure 6.2: Matching objects from other countries with identifying labels

A further plotting idea is the supermarket map. Local supermarkets sell an increasing variety of exotic fruits and vegetables. A visit to my local supermarket in November produced the following list:

kiwi fruit	from:	France
avocados		Israel
guavas		Egypt
grenadillos		West Indies
lemons		Cyprus
mushrooms		Ireland
peppers		Netherlands
curly kale		Scotland
honeycomb		New Zealand
coconuts		Windward Islands
pineapples		Ivory Coast
mangoes and pawpaws		Brazil
pears		USA

In the supermarket example the map is the *starting point* for a number of possible investigations, not an end in itself. Do these fruits and vegetables for example *always* come from those locations? Comparisons can be made with other supermarkets and other times of the year. Information like this can be stored on a simple database for later interrogation. Patterns should emerge if enough data is collected. For example, citrus fruits (such as oranges, lemons and grapefruit) and grapes (and therefore sultanas, raisins and wine) generally come from Mediterranean countries and other places with a Mediterranean type of climate — such as California, Chile, South Africa and Western Australia. Some produce is particularly good for seeing the effect of climate and technology on the area and time of production as the growing season progresses. There is a lot of economic understanding in the tomato! Early in the season tomatoes come from further afield and are expensive. Later, as the temperature increases nearer home they are grown under glass and finally become cheapest of all when most people in Southern England at least can pick their own home-grown outdoor crop.

There are all sorts of variants of the *matching* game for introducing locational knowledge and factual information. Try making playing cards showing the following information so that they can be used as matched pairs in games:

> country shape outlines or cut-outs
> country names
> capital city names
> pictures (start with well known symbols, go on to more subtle pictures of scenery)
> continent shape outlines or cut-outs

name of highest mountain
name of longest river
name of currency
picture of flag

The matching tasks can become progressively more demanding. Matching the highest mountain in a country and the longest river of the same country for example is more testing than matching the country name with its capital. Once you have a basic set of information, you can use it in various ways. The facts can be presented in 'playing card' format or on 'dominoes'. Children will readily invent their own games such as versions of Happy Families, picture dominoes or the Memory Game (pelmanism). Best of all of course is where children manufacture their own games, researching the information they need. Children can also produce travel board games, where counters are moved around a map 'board' and progress is determined on the throw of a dice by geographical fortune and misfortune ('Sandstorm!, miss one turn', etc.). Postcards also offer opportunities for matching games. They can be matched with placenames or cards marked with words that describe landscapes. These can be either topographic names such as hill, mountain, lake, river (see Geography Attainment Target 3) or evaluative names such as noisy, quiet, dull, interesting, beautiful (see Geography Attainment Target 5).

Jigsaw picture puzzles combine trivial pursuit questions with a picture of the country concerned. Children make these for each other. Start with a picture of a particular locality, region or country, from a colour supplement or travel brochure. Mount the picture on a piece of card. Next, make a card folder for the picture (see figure 6.3). Divide the inside face of the folder into four or six or eight sections, (depending on age or ability). Research and write a question about the country in each section. Cut the picture into pieces to fit on each section of the folder and write the answers to the questions on the back of each picture section. When the game is played, the player reads the questions and selects the appropriate answer card, putting it face up on the question section. When this is done, the folder is closed, turned over, and, if the questions have been correctly answered the player is rewarded with a picture of the place. There are a lot of design and technology skills in this activity. The planning stage includes choosing pictures for their interest and content and devising suitable questions. The making stage involves careful measuring and cutting. Information for making cards used in matching activities and games based on geographical knowledge (such as *Trivial Pursuit*) can be found in sources such as *Whitaker's Almanac*, *Pears Cyclopedia* and the *Everyman Factfinder*. Perhaps the best reference source for children to use is the *New Oxford Children's Encyclopedia* (OUP, 1991) which has an entry on every country with an accompanying marginal 'fact-file' section giving basic information.

You can also play guessing games with the help of atlases. Children

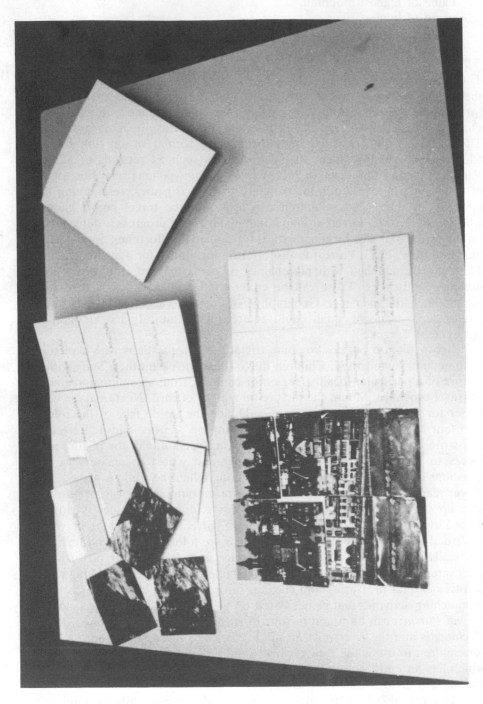

Figure 6.3: Jigsaw picture puzzles
(I am indebted to Jorma Ojala of the Department of Teacher Training, Jyvaskyla University, Finland, for this idea.)

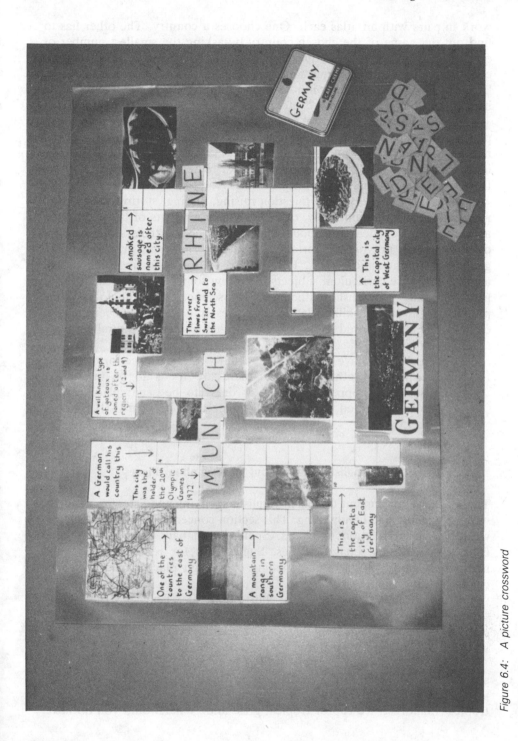

Figure 6.4: A picture crossword

work in pairs with an atlas each. One chooses a country. The other has to find out the name of the chosen country by asking the smallest number of questions. Answers to those questions can only be yes or no. The children come to realize that good questions to ask in order to narrow the field are: 'Is it on the equator?'; 'Does it have a coastline?'; 'Is it in continent X?', 'Is it in the northern hemisphere?' etc.

Another starting point for place knowledge is simply the name of a place. 'Write down ten things that come into your mind when you hear the name...'. Each idea could be written on a separate postcard so that the ideas can be sorted, grouped and classified. Where do these ideas come from? How can we find out if they are true?

The skills of observation, question raising, finding, storing, sorting and representing information apply, of course, to other parts of the curriculum as well as simply to learning about distant places. Nevertheless, the study of other countries provides important content for children's practice of language and mathematical skills. For this reason the following sections are arranged by core curriculum subjects to review some of the possibilities for practicing skills in English, mathematics and science and technology. In the practice of all these skills relating to places it is especially beneficial if children are already used to living and working in a multicultural context.

London children have a greater opportunity to experience for themselves aspects of other cultures. There are foods to be tasted, markets to be shopped in, styles of dress to be seen, places of worship to be visited, languages and dialects to be heard. (ILEA, 1984, p. 15)

Activities in English: Talking and Writing about Places

There are five attainment targets in English: speaking and listening, reading, writing, spelling and handwriting. This section concentrates on speaking and writing skills in relation to places. Spelling and handwriting will not be considered here as separate issues. Suggestions for reading (fiction and non-fiction) and aspects of the spelling of foreign place names were discussed in chapter 4.

Countries make good topics for short pupil talks (English AT 1, level 4) or pieces of non-chronological writing (English AT 3, levels 3 and 4). Two starting points are suggested here for activities in English: starting with stories and starting with pictures.

Topic work on places offers numerous opportunities for starting with stories. One possibility is to continue after the cliffhanger. Read (or make up) a survival story. End with a shipwreck or plane crash in the desert, tropical rainforest, ice cap or tropical grassland. What would you do next?

What are the priorities for food and shelter? What resources are likely to exist for these? In order to continue the story, children need information. This can be organized under headings such as plant and animal life, weather and climate, likely building materials, landscape, etc. This sort of activity can also be supported with computer software. *The Inhabitant* (Longman, 1984) allows children to explore the language of environments and basic needs and *River* (BBC, 1984) is a simulation of a plane crash which offers scope for learning about topography, drainage basins and mapreading.

Places have always had strong associations with the imagination of childhood. After Branwell Brontë was given a set of wooden toy soldiers by his father in 1826 the Brontë children began writing miniature books for them. These books chronicled imaginary worlds. Emily and Anne invented the land of Gondal, Branwell and Charlotte the kingdom of Angria. These worlds had landscapes, societies and courts (Alexander, 1983). A way of developing this theme in the primary school is to consider whether the place where a story is set is *real*. The environment of *Treasure Island*, for example, is described clearly enough by Robert Louis Stevenson but did the island actually exist? If it did where in the world is it likely to have been? What is the topography like of fictional places such as C.S. Lewis' *Narnia*, Ursula le Guin's *Earthsea* and Tolkein's *Middle Earth*? What are the clues in the text and can children fill in and compare the gaps using their imagination? Perhaps too subtle for primary children is the recognition of the American-ness of the land of *Oz*, created by L. Frank Baum and described as 'the first distinctive attempt to create a fairyland out of American materials' (Wagenknecht, 1929, p. 17). And yet Oz *does* have a distinctively American provenance and perhaps the story is enhanced if children are aware that, whilst Oz is a fairyland, Kansas (Dorothy's home) most certainly is not.

English Attainment Target 2 (reading) requires that children broaden their experience of a variety of forms of non-fiction and develop their abilities to use inference and deduction. Travel writing offers good opportunities for this, although it has been little used in primary classrooms to date. Eric Newby's marvellous collection of *Travellers' Tales* (Picador, 1985) and the superb anthology of travel writing from *The Spectator*, *Views From Abroad* (edited by Philip Marsden-Smedley and Jeffrey Klinke, Paladin Grafton Books, 1989) are really for adults but they do contain gems that with some adaptation by teachers could be used very well in the context of, say, the history study unit on exploration and encounters. If I had to choose just one travel writer to introduce to children, however, it would be Dervla Murphy. *Eight Feet in the Andes* is the amazing story of the author's walk with her 8-year-old daughter and a mule along the length of South America. *Full Tilt* (Murray, 1965; Century Publishing, 1983) is an account of an extraordinary cycle journey to India. In the following extract, her cycle has had a puncture and so she completes the day's journey by bus:

About 2 miles beyond Bulola the engine broke down; it was now dark and raining, and the repairs, during which the headlights were put out of order, took very nearly an hour. At 7.30 p.m. we resumed the journey up and over a 10,000 foot pass on a corkscrew 'road', barely wide enough for one vehicle, with sheer drops which I could imagine but happily not see, as there was no light. Then quite soon there *was* light — lots of it — when the daily spring thunderstorm began. For several minutes lightning was continuous — not flashes as we know them, but glaring sheets of blue illumination, revealing gaunt peaks on one side and sickening ravines on the other; yet it was all so beautiful and awe-inspiring that one simply forgot to be afraid. The thunder reverberating in the mountains was deafening — peal after peal, the echoes of each being drowned in the crash of the next. With all this came gusts of gale-force wind carrying enormous hailstones which took the skin off my nose where they struck it as I sat next to the window-that-wasn't. There are limits even to Afghan toughness and when this demonstration started the bus stopped for the nine men on the roof to come below. As the 'inside' was already overcrowded beyond belief this meant that I had three children on my lap for the rest of the journey; I had only one 2-year-old at the beginning. We waited for about fifteen minutes until the worst was over because to attempt to negotiate that winding track with the driver intermittently dazzled by lightning would have been suicidal. (To my mind the whole trip wasn't far short of suicidal anyway.) Yet what an experience to see a landscape, dramatic in itself, under such melodramatic conditions — like some inspired choreographer's setting for Faust.

Soon after we had restarted a melodrama of a different kind began. The system on these privately owned buses is that the driver's assistant, usually an adolescent known as a *bacha*, collects the fares during the journey. The *bacha* now asked twelve *afghanis* from everyone and a number of passengers protested that ten had been agreed at the start. Hell then broke loose and while I was bundling the children under the seat an infuriated tribesman, brandishing his rifle, climbed over me, trying to get at the driver; the *bacha* pushed him, and he fell backwards, striking me a frightful blow on the ribs with the rifle butt. I looked round to see a terrifying forest of rifle barrels behind me — terrifying because in a jolting bus I imagined them going off accidentally; but of course these men know exactly what they are doing with their triggers, if not with their butts, and nothing of the sort happened. The unarmed *bacha* continued his heroic defence of the driver, the bus stopped yet again, and the driver got out and stood grasping *his* gun and refusing to go another yard until everyone had paid their twelve *afghanis* and I hastily produced mine, hoping to set a good example. But I was completely ignored while the verbal battle raged and everyone fingered his trigger menacingly as though it wouldn't be verbal much longer; the angry shouts of all concerned almost drowned both the thunder and the hiss of the hail slashing down. Finally one of the passengers threatened to smash the inside light with his rifle butt. Then a compromise of eleven *afghanis* was accepted, whereupon the driver resumed his seat and off we went again. (Murphy, 1965, pp. 72–3)

The BBC television documentary series and accompanying book *All Our Children* (Judith and Martin Woodhead, Ringpress, 1990) offers good non-fiction material for discussing other children's lives. The book is arranged in sections (babies, health, homes, work, schools, talents, music, beliefs and the passage from childhood), each with half a dozen biographical pieces of writing that need in some cases, a little editing by the teacher. Eliza is a refugee from Mozambique living in the Ukwimi refugee settlement in South-eastern Zambia. Kavita lives in Delhi. She has polio and will spend the rest of her life with her legs in heavy iron calipers. Belinda lives on the Mount Elm sheep station in Southern Australia. Together with other isolated children living in the Bush, she receives her education through the School of the Air. Edison is a shoe shine boy in Quito, Ecuador, whilst Melinda scavenges for scrap on the rubbish tips of Manila in the Philippines. Some of these mini biographies are immensely moving and there is much material here for discussion with children in small groups. Far less vivid, but equally authentic is a little collection of children's own accounts of their lives in *Where and How I Live* (Haubrich, 1987).

I think perhaps that the best use of these materials would be after the children's own autobiographical writing so that the teaching sequence is something like: myself (my home, family, school, interests), followed by reading with the teacher about the life of another child in a distant place, followed in turn by a clarification of similarities and differences in way of life. Attention then turns to the locality itself and use of information skills to find out more about the place where x lives.

There are over 4,000,000,000 people on Earth and Peter Spier's book, *People* (World's Work, 1980) introduces their variety. Excellent for browsing or for observational work in art, the book covers how we all differ — eyes and noses, clothes, homes, preferences for food and pets, worship and language.

Pictures of places, especially photographs, offer opportunities for stimulating pupil talk (English Attainment Target 1). All children have experience of media such as photographs when they first come to school but they may need help in making sense of the images they see (Davies, 1989). But what images *do* children 'see'? An important starting point is to establish the basic content of the picture. How many people are there? What are they doing? Where are they going? Then lead on to questions that push the children further. What are they going to do next? Would you like to do that? What would you like to know about these people? Another starting activity is to play 'Kim's Game' with pictures. Look at the picture for a minute. Cover it and try to remember everything the picture showed. Check to see if you were right. Pictures can also be used for sorting activities. Sort the photographs into those showing people and those with no people. Or sort into places that you think are hotter than where we live and places that are colder. Or places that are like where we live and places that are unlike where we live. The valuable part of the sorting is the identification and discussion of the criteria used. A good question to pose is: 'Do you think the photo could have been taken in ... (name of town where the children live)?'

'Photos tell fibs'. Or at least they can do. It often depends on how much of the photograph you can see. You can test this by collecting a number of photographs of places and investigating the effect of looking at only part of the picture by using a cut out 'window' smaller than the original picture. Do you get a different impression of the place if you put your window *here* compared with *there*? A development of this activity is to cut out a picture, mount it in the centre of a piece of drawing paper and then complete what you think might be the scene on either side of the original picture. A class of 9-year-olds had great fun in this way with travel brochure pictures — the original (highly attractive) illustration from the brochure was put in the middle of their paper and they drew around it what they imagined the camera had deliberately not shown — gasworks, smoking chimneys and sewage outlets — just outside the picture.

The *caption* to an illustration often influences the way we 'read' the picture. A travel brochure picture of a deserted beach for example could be described as 'perfect peace' or 'dead boring'. The same effect is achieved if you add speech or thought bubbles to the people in travel pictures. At its simplest level, children can thereby make people on the beach think about whether they like the heat, or what they are going to do next or even worry about whether they've left the gas on at home.

In addition to the obvious sources of pictures from travel brochures, colour supplements and magazines such as the *Geographical Magazine* and *National Geographic*, there are a number of excellent published photo packs dealing with places to be found in the catalogues of the major educational suppliers. The ILEA Learning Materials service has a number of good packs as well as the Centre for World Development Education and many of the Development Education Centres. The latter are an especially useful source of images that counter the usual stereotypes held about places.

A further way of stimulating talk and 'looking' at places is to compare photographs with artwork of different types — linework for example, as well as paintings. Many children enjoy the Van Gogh landscapes of swirling wheatfields and cypress trees as well as the subtle landscapes of Constable. But how do these compare with the background landscapes of the Italian Renaissance or the strange landscapes painted by Salvador Dali? Which is more 'real'? That brings us back to whether or not places in literature are real. Of course, this is very demanding stuff. I'm trying to argue for the use of places as a stimulus for thinking about experience and suggesting directions to move towards rather than finite goals.

Activities in Mathematics: Shape, Space and Data Handling

There are a number of ways of promoting shape awareness in relation to place. Flash cards of country shapes are, of course, easily made, either for playing recognition games or forming a small pile of countries that are to be researched with the aid of an atlas. Card outlines can be provided with instructions to (for example) use the card as a template to cut out the country shape on paper, use the atlas to find which country it is, add its capital city, the main rivers, etc. and make a label before adding to a display. (It's essential to indicate which side of the card is the 'right way up' so that children don't search for the mirror image in error!)

The same cards can be used to investigate relative country area. Start with considering '*How big* is Britain?' It's helpful to remember that it's about 1000 km from Land's End to John O'Groats, as the crow flies, but distances expressed in linear units do not mean a great deal to young children. It's better to consider journey time. How long would it take to fly this distance? About two hours? (Compare the distance with a London to Spain holiday flight) How long would it take to go by car? About two days? (Remember that only part of the journey could be done by motorway.) And how long might it take to *walk*? (Remember that the journey by road is longer than the straight line distance — about 1400 km.) Ian Botham's 1985 charity walk took him thirty-six days. But how does the size of Britain compare with the size of other countries? Compare cut out shapes of countries that children know with a cut out of Great Britain. Which is bigger? (Make sure that the cut outs are at the same scale!) List countries that are bigger than/smaller than/about the same size as Britain. Many of the places that children seem to know about early on in childhood (see chapter 3) are much bigger than Britain. Use an outline map of Australia, or the United States or China and a template of Great Britain. Draw around the template as many times as possible in the outline map. How many times does it 'fit into' the other country? But Great Britain is a very irregular shape. What about the gaps between the drawn outlines? Is there a better way of comparing country areas using statistics and your calculator? Is there a relationship between the area of a country and its population? Can what you have found out be shown on a graph? Can countries be grouped into 'crowded' and 'empty' countries?

For the National Curriculum in geography children are expected to be aware that the globe can be represented as a flat surface (Gg/1/5e). The nearest statement to this in the mathematics National Curriculum documentation seems to be later, at level 6: 'recognize and use common 2D representation of 3D objects' (AT10). Nevertheless, recognition of the problems of representing the globe on a flat surface may be demonstrated quite easily. First, forget the orange! Almost all books ever published on primary geography have recommended trying to peel an orange to show that the skin won't lie flat afterwards. It won't, but the method is extremely messy (especially if the children attempt it themselves) and drawing outlines of the continents on the outside of the orange first is much harder than it looks. And even the waterproof marker pens don't seem to be orange juice proof. Instead, buy two inflatable globes. These are like beach balls and come in a variety of sizes. Some High Street shops sell them but they are also available quite cheaply from the major school equipment suppliers. Hang one up on permanent display where it can be easily seen. These globes are not as accurate as the more expensive sort but they are appealing to children. When the time comes to explain about the round globe/flat map issue, show the children the inflated globe and the deflated one. The deflated one is not 'flat' of course, but bunched up. Now use your strong scissors and cut it (yes!) along the 0° and 180° lines of longitude, so that it is divided into two hemispheres (East and West). Neither lies flat. Cut each hemisphere again along (say) the 90° East and West lines of longitude. These lie flatter. Repeat until you have a number of strips or 'gores' that will lie flat. The globe can then be laid out in this dissected form so that all the gores are touching at the equator. This is an accurate map of the world but it's difficult to use because there are gaps in the land and sea. So, map makers have to find ways of stretching the meridians and parallels to close the gaps. I know it destroys inflatable globes, but they are not that expensive and the cut up pieces can be used again another year, albeit with some loss of impact, (here is one I prepared earlier ...).

Jahoda's (1963) work on children's understanding of the 'nesting' spatial relationships of many geographical units — for example, the locality — region — country — continent relationship was described in chapter 2. Jigsaws are really useful for establishing this principle. It's fairly easy to make cut outs of say, Roundhay, Leeds, West Yorkshire, England, etc. so that they can be superimposed to illustrate that you *can* live in each at the same time. As for understanding how parts of the British Isles and other countries fit together, there are some good jigsaws on the market but also some terrible ones. If countries or continents are to be named they have to be named on each cut out piece, because it's the picking up and looking at each piece in its own right that helps establish the shape and relative size in children's minds. This means that the pieces must not be too small. What is really needed here is the formula: parent (or grandparent) + fretsaw + free time. A tall order but jigsaws really are valuable in developing place concepts.

Places lend themselves especially well to data collection and handling (mathematics attainment targets 12 and 13). Computer databases can be used to collect and access information such as climatic statistics, population figures and data about the quality of life, for example infant mortality, life expectancy, literacy and levels of energy consumption. All this sort of information is available in regularly published sources such as *Whitaker's Almanac, Social Trends,* the *Census of Population, Philips' Geographical Digest* etc. Simple statistical processing such as finding arithmetic averages can be carried out on this type of data and patterns on the map can be investigated. The data can be represented in the form of block graphs, bar charts, pictograms and tree diagrams.

Activities in Science and Technology

Science attainment target 16 (The Earth in Space) is inseparable from the study of places. The explanation of why night occurs, the changes in the length of daytime and the differences in time at different points on the Earth's surface are essential aspects of the study of places. If children are studying a distant place it's helpful to have a clock set to the appropriate time difference in the classroom. What are *they* doing while *we* are getting up, or having lunch, or going home from school...? By extension, a check can be kept on the seasons and harvest. Similarly, comparisons need to be made with the weather. The weather has a powerful effect on people's lives but beware the use of climatic statistics without making reference to comparable figures for the local area. These are usually easily obtained from a good atlas, but as a general guide the winter average temperature for much of Britain would be, say, 2°C, and the average temperature in July would be about 15°C. As for rainfall, it's rather variable across Britain, but 600–800 mm per year would be right for most areas.

We are, of course, familiar with those fairly well-worn primary topics such as clothes and homes around the world, but with the advent of technology in the National Curriculum, these topics take on a rather different emphasis. The use of fabrics in clothing is related to location. White fabrics, for example, reflect heat and loose clothes trap air. Similarly, the design of houses is usually matched to environmental conditions. In areas of high, dry snowfall, shallow pitched roofs are designed to keep an insulating layer of snow on top of the house. Steep pitched roofs in wet areas are designed to remove the rain and snow rapidly. Double (or triple) glazing in Finnish homes keeps the residents warm but there are other features of homes in cold climates that are worth attention. Porches, for example, tend to be large (to accommodate all those bulky outdoor clothes and snow boots) and the homes probably have saunas. Further north still, homes may be built on areas of permanently frozen ground. The heat from conventionally constructed buildings in these areas would melt the ice and the house would disappear into a sludge of mud. Houses are therefore built on stilts so that cold air can circulate underneath or on gravel pads so that if there is any settlement of the structure during the summer months it is absorbed by the flexible base material. Services such as gas and electricity and water supply are delivered in Northern regions, not by underground pipes but in *utilidors*, above-ground conduits. Vehicle design too is also affected by climate. Studded tyres for winter, car parking spaces that have a 'plug in' facility to keep the engine warm overnight, heated seats in cars and lights that come on whenever the engine is running are all responses to cold, dark, Northern climates. It isn't necessary to have a great deal of specialist knowledge to extract principles such as these. A good start can be made with advertisements in Britain — for anti-rust paint for cars, house paint, double glazing, cavity wall insulation, replacement door and window frames, wood preservatives, fungicides, etc. What do all these have to say about our weather conditions and how we can protect against them?

Environmental characteristics such as climatic conditions can be especially well investigated through animals and plants. At a very simple level, children can match pictures of environments with animal cut outs (the polar bear cut out goes on the ice picture etc.). But these tasks can become progressively more complex and the task of placing a set of animal cut outs on a world map is quite a demanding one that would involve quite a lot of reference work and a fairly high level of information skills from pupils. Try the following set of animals: penguin (only in the Antarctic and surrounding areas), polar bear (only in the Arctic and surrounding areas), kangaroo, African elephant, tiger, panda, llama, armadillo, camel and caribou.

Promoting International Understanding
— A Cross-curricular Dimension

Just teaching *about* other people and places isn't enough. We have to extend children's understanding beyond stereotypes and biased views. But how are we to promote empathy and develop that 'reciprocity in thought and action which is vital to the attainment of impartiality and affective understanding'? (Piaget with Weil, 1951, p. 578) One of the first requisites is a strong knowledge base. You really have to have found out a good deal before you can tackle an activity such as 'pretend you are an Inuit boy or girl' ... (Note, incidentally, the powerful examples of this sort of imaginative writing in the anthology of pupils' work compiled by Chris Searle in *The World in a Classroom*, (1977, London, Writers and Readers.) Children need pictures to help them think themselves into the scene, to have detailed and structured information about food, clothing, temperatures, landscape, etc. before they attempt such a task. However, the mere provision of information about distant peoples isn't enough either. International understanding starts in the classroom by using teaching and learning styles that reflect mutual respect and tolerance. It goes without saying that all pupils should be accepted equally, that learning should be 'active' and that the children should be 'involved' and that they should spend much of their time 'on task'. All these are features of good teaching and effective group work is an important prerequisite. Children enjoy participating and small groups help children to think through their ideas in a less threatening way than in front of the whole class. This builds confidence. But, such group work needs to be very carefully structured if these goals are to be met. Richardson (1982) offers some suggestions for ways in which group work can be used:

* Have tangible things for children to pass around to focus the discussion. Use pictures, lists, artifacts. These can be sorted and arranged physically. It may help to have a microphone or other object to pass around to establish the rules for listening and speaking. Only the person holding the microphone can talk. This principle will be known to many readers as that used by the castaway children in William Golding's novel, *The Lord of the Flies*, where a conch shell was passed around the group.
* Give each group a *precise task*, and perhaps each member of the group a precise task also. For example: 'Here are pictures of six homes in other lands. Sort them into whether you think the climate in each place is hotter or cooler than our own'.
* Choose cooperative tasks where all the children must take part. Cooperative learning strategies allow children to experience their own peers not as a collection of individuals but as members of an interrelated system in which everyone's actions affect everyone else. This provides early experience of the complex concept of interdependence.
* Choose a controversial topic so that the group members have plenty to contribute.
* Get the match of task and ability right.
* Get the children to reflect afterwards on the success of the group activity — what parts of the discussion went well?

Many advocates of global education or world studies favour cooperative games as a way of promoting a sense of interdependence in children. The assumption is that by participating in such activities they can, at a very early age, gain personal experience of the notion of interdependence. Resolving conflicts requires cooperation. But many personal and social (as well as national) relationships are characterized instead by competition.

Research evidence supporting activities designed to promote empathy is, sadly, in short supply. On the other hand, this may be one of those aspects of education that we simply have to take on trust. There is no doubt that learning to cooperate is a highly desirable aim in education. Children need to build respect for themselves and others, value diversity, identify and feel comfortable with their own feelings and have respect for the feelings of others. Other points of view have to be considered and conflicts resolved peacefully. But exactly how cooperation in the classroom extends to an understanding of interrelationships at a global scale is less clear. Understanding of people who live in different places is a cross-curricular approach, and cooperative learning needs to be established over a long time period. This has something to do with the individual teacher's outlook — that's one of its weaknesses and it calls for a whole school and staff policy rather than a set of specimen 'lessons'.

What are the first steps in teaching for international understanding? For very young children it is necessary to start with themselves (see a number of activities described in Fountain, 1990). All children bring their own experiences to school with them and they need to be helped to value this experience. There are many activities which are often recommended to promote self-esteem in very young children and to help them make statements about others. It's good, for example, for children to learn to introduce themselves as well as other children ('I'm Katy and this is my brother Christopher'). This can be developed into making statements about (for example) favourite foods ('I'm Christopher and I like chips'). The personal statements can be extended to TV programmes, pets, favourite colours and so on. Teachers often do this with the children sitting round in a circle so that they can then try to remember who likes what. Older children can attempt to devise an interview schedule based on questions such as these, carry out the survey and report on the results of their investigation. Further developments on this theme include making badges that describe some outstanding characteristic that each child feels reflects his or her own identity or participating in drama sessions where children take part in a 'lost child' adventure in which a description of the lost child must be given to a police officer. Observation of others is encouraged in art by drawing and painting from life. Making a 'rogues' gallery' of the whole class is a widely undertaken activity, and sensitive handling of individual differences and similarities in skin colour and facial features amongst the children in the class is an important step on the way to understanding people far away. Useful resources to extend this sort of work include the 'Talk about' materials such as *I'm Special: Myself* (from the ILEA Learning Resources Centre).

Activities such as those above are appropriate for children at key stage 1. But how can these be developed for older children in the primary phase? The interview technique is worth exploring. The first step is the simple interview, based on factual questions and preferences. Children then change roles and each has to answer the questions as they think the other would answer. This forces them to think themselves into what it would be like to be someone else. The next step is to investigate the way of life of someone in a different locality — perhaps in the economically developing world. The interview is repeated with children replying as if they were a person from the place they have researched. The whole exercise is valuable but needs careful handling as children switch in and out of role. Discussion after the activity identifies those answers the children weren't sure about, which in turn gives further scope for information finding.

I would support all these activities on the grounds that they should be part of any good primary teacher's collection of teaching strategies, but except insofar as they may develop self-esteem and promote cooperative learning (which are essential foundations for learning about others), very few of such activities actually focus on place. Yet it's important for children to be aware of the links they already have with the wider world. Those links can be easily demonstrated. For example, I'm typing the manuscript for this book using a keyboard made in Korea and a printer made in Japan. My desk is made of chipboard (probably from Scandinavian trees) and covered with mahogany veneer, probably from West Africa, whilst my mug with its *Peanuts* cartoon (drawn in the USA) contains the remains of coffee from beans grown in Colombia and Brazil. But when I looked at the packet to check that I noticed that it had been packed in Germany. 'Global connections' such as these are easily extended to the immediate locality of the school. Leeds, for example, has what appears to be a Florentine campanile which is nothing more than a mill chimney in disguise, as well as Marshall's Flax Mill built in the style of an Egyptian temple with massive palm columns copied from buildings at Tanis. And in Park Square there is a wool warehouse that imitates a Moorish palace, complete with minarets; while the Town Hall, (perhaps the finest Victorian architectural set piece in Britain) is decorated with massive Corinthian pillars. There is also a tropical house with exotic plants and a Japanese garden. Global connections are also readily seen in the names of restaurants, such as these from the Leeds telephone directory:

Bella Napoli
Bella Roma
Dynasty Cantonese
Hong Kong
Indus Valley
Java
Kashmir
Khyber
Marrakesh
New Shalamar
Old Delhi
Sorrento
Star of Bengal

I'm suggesting here that study of the local area (such as an examination of the land use and buildings) goes hand in hand with a study of more distant places so that children come to see themselves from the outset as part of a much wider community.

Places Through Topics on Localities

The National Curriculum is set up to allow and encourage cross-curricular ways of working. This book deals principally with issues that many regard as geographical but there's no reason at all why places should be taught as a separate part of the curriculum. Good topics for dealing with places could be labelled: celebrations, communications, journeys, shelter, homes, food and hats. (These particular topics are suggested and developed by Ruth Hessari and Dave Hill in their book *Practical Ideas for Multicultural Learning and Teaching in the Primary Classroom*, Routledge, 1989.) It is likely, however, that teachers will want to include in their planning some topics that deal with a specific place. The greatest challenge posed by the National Curriculum in geography is that these places must be specific small-scale localities, comparable with (indeed, they *are* to be compared with) the immediate locality of the school. Two issues immediately emerge. Which places to choose and where to get the information? Just as some topics are better than others (because they encapsulate more learning potential or provide access to a broader range of human experience), so it is with places. Some localities will provide more opportunities for comparisons of landscape and ways of life than others. It is as well to be aware of some possible criteria for the selection of localities to study. The National Curriculum already provides for an 'economically developing' country, but there are other criteria that could be considered in addition to economic factors. Climate is worth considering for example (indeed, one of the earlier drafts of the National Curriculum in geography referred to tropical or subtropical localities). Another is the extent of the children's existing knowledge about the world and it is hoped that the 'known world' material in chapter 3 will provide some pointers in this direction. Places could be chosen for study on the basis of whether they are already partially known or whether they are as yet totally unknown. Teachers can easily establish the extent of their own class' knowledge by replicating the investigations described in chapter 3. A baseline of information about travel and other experiences is really an important starting point for selecting an appropriate locality for a project.

But these places must be 'specific localities'. This means that *detailed* case study material needs to be found. Suppose you want to help children compare their own surroundings with those of a French village. What are the minimum resource requirements? You'll need some photographs of the village, particularly of shops, houses and other significant buildings as well as pictures of 'people who help us'. Some of these might be slides for showing to large groups, some might be prints (probably laminated for passing around, sorting and classifying) for small group work, and some might be made into posters through the High Street photo shop. The local 'Ordnance Survey' equivalent map could be used as the base for a simplified poster-size wall map of the village. Postcards would help too, as well as any tourist material that is produced locally. Some 'real things' that are used or made there would also be good — perhaps comics or sweets or school books. There are books about other countries on the market (see chapter 4) — and many of them are very good. But in the number of pages they have available they can't create the atmosphere and level of detail that you really need for very young children to understand what 'being there' is like. This means that someone on the staff has to collect this stuff — well, *someone* must be going to Europe this summer! The highest priority are the pictures. Stories about the postwoman, the garage owner, the baker, the teacher and so on, can be developed later. In fact a small amount of authentic material goes a long way and can be boosted by activities that are not too precisely place-specific. I was much impressed by one primary school's 'French breakfast' recently — hot chocolate and croissants! It is important though that the places chosen for study are not always those that are popular for holidays. Children will, in any case have their own holiday experiences to relate to and there is a danger that far places come to be seen only as resorts — places where 'they' provide holidays for 'us'.

However, you also need material like this for *beyond* Europe — specifically for a locality in an economically developing country. If your school (or one nearby) has families with strong South Asian or Caribbean connections you're halfway there. Some schools involve community experiences of other parts of the world very successfully. Visitors to the class are a valuable resource for providing detailed 'on the ground' information. Many schools are fortunate enough to be located near to a college or university with large numbers of overseas students — a rich source of first hand information. But the class need to decide in advance what information they require from their visitor. And the visitor him or herself needs to be well briefed. It's often useful if personal belongings can be brought and discussed. Pictures of home and family are 'real' and in many teachers' experience stimulate genuine interest from the children.

In the absence of first hand information sources, there is some good case study material available in book form. At the time of writing, there is good material relating to a family in the Gambia in Bruton, J. *et al* (1987) *Whose Development?* published by the Development Education Centre, Birmingham (see address section). The book is primarily intended for secondary pupils but it contains much detail that could be exploited by teachers for primary school use. For example, there is a sketch of one family's compound, a street map and several photographs of Banjul. The Centre for World Development Education (see addresses) has much source material on economically developing countries. For example there are a number of six-sided A4 fold-out photo/information sheets about a range of commodities and countries. A teaching pack on *A Rain Forest Child* (Greenlight Publications, 1989 and available through CWDE) is useful. There are also slide sets on changes in Nigeria and the Caribbean. From commercial publishers there are a number of possibilities and these will grow as the National Curriculum takes shape in our schools. A. and C. Black produce several series such as *Beans* and *Wide World* which look at the experiences of particular children and the ways of life in other countries. Hamish Hamilton's *Focus on* ... series has both informative text and good quality photographs. Macdonald's *My village in* ... series has good resources on particular communities, in for example, Morocco, India and the Sahara. Wayland have a series on food and drink (in Africa, the Caribbean and India). These books describe the food and drink of each area in relation to people, culture and geography and each includes simple recipes. Note also Wayland's *Families Around the World* and *My Country* series, the latter giving accounts of a selection of people and their occupations. Anandra in *Anandra in Sri Lanka* (by Carol Baker, Hamish Hamilton) describes his routine everyday life. Note too the resources published regularly in periodicals such as *Child Education* and *Junior Education*. See especially the *Junior Education* issue of November 1990 which features a topic pack on faraway lands and includes a colour poster on growing up in the Caribbean. Further case study visual material is available in the form of slide sets which illustrate the life of children in developing countries. *Kwadwo of Ghana*, *Sujan of Bangladesh*, *Fatimettou of Mauntama* and *Pauline of Malaysia* are available from UNICEF (see the appendix for address).

As regards the structure of the project, it is a good idea for children to start by reviewing all the ideas they already have about the place or the country that will be studied. These ideas can then be collected and grouped and some generalized images constructed. How can we find out whether these images are true or not? Where did the information come from? Particular lines of investigation can then be researched (such as what sorts of food are eaten there, what sorts of clothes people wear, what work do they do?).

What *activities* are appropriate for such a project on place? It may be helpful to consider at the beginning the focus or outcome of the project. I like the idea of children preparing their own book about the place they are studying. But if they are going to learn something about secondary representations of places (see chapter 4) they need to be faced with constraints. Suggest that the book must have only four pages, a finite number of pictures, that the language must be easy to understand for younger children. The project then becomes not just an exercise in collecting information, but, especially for older children, one of selecting information and making judgments about representativeness. It may be best to run through these stages first with the local area.

There are, of course, a number of possible foci for place projects. In addition to locating the place using a globe and atlas and finding out how far away it is (in time and cost as well as distance), is it possible for children to participate (albeit at second hand) in the way of life there? For example, a class studying Malaysia, might make up a play using Malaysian shadow puppets, do some batik work and make and fly kites. Can they also make and eat some regional recipe? Recipe books from other countries are plentiful in book shops and public libraries. Children are probably already familiar with Indian and Chinese food (at least in their takeaway manifestations). Of course ingredients can be expensive and cooking might be a problem. It's best to go for something simple therefore. Rosalind Kerven, in a resource book for Commonwealth Day, from the Commonwealth Institute, suggests a fresh fruit salad using (for example) oranges from Cyprus, apples from Australia, Canada or New Zealand, bananas from the Caribbean, pineapples from Kenya, mangoes from Africa or the Caribbean, grapes from Australia or Cyprus and desiccated coconut from Sri Lanka or Mauritius. What about possibilities for music? *Mango Spice* is a songbook containing words and music of forty-four Caribbean songs with piano accompaniment and guitar chords. Audiotapes of music from a number of countries are available from the ILEA Learning Resources Centre, from *One World* shops and public libraries. *Songs for a New Generation* by Evelyn Challis (Oak Music Sales Ltd, 78 Newman St., London W1) also has lots of songs from different countries.

Play a game! Good source books are: Millen, N. (1965) *Children's Games from Many Lands*, Friendship Press, New York; and Masheder, M. (1989) *Let's Play Together*, Green Print (available from CWDE). A good game to start with is *ayo*, perhaps the world's most widespread game. It's very popular in Africa where it goes under a number of local names. The game consists of a board into which two rows of six holes have been hollowed out. Seeds, pebbles or nuts are distributed in the hollows and the two players each try to gain possession of their opponent's counters. The game is often played simply by scooping hollows in the sand, but it can be recreated in the classroom by using egg boxes. You can often find inexpensive boards in 'One World' shops.

Any attempt to provide children with authentic experiences of places (even though they will be largely second hand experiences) has, at some stage to confront the issue of foreign language. In practice, there is little foreign language teaching in primary school — not because children of this age cannot successfully learn a foreign language but because there are too few teachers equipped to teach one. And yet distant places and foreign languages are inextricably linked. It is now recognized that it is desirable to identify the steps that need to be taken to make foreign language teaching more widespread in primary schools (DES, 1990c) and a House of Lords Select Committee has made recommendations to this effect (House of Lords, 1990). But in the meantime, not only should pupils be made aware of the great variety of world languages but also perhaps be introduced to the sounds and common expressions of some of them. Reference has already been made to identifying the characteristics of place names and their anglicised versions in atlases in chapter 4, but to what extent is it possible to give pupils a feel for language in the context of a topic on another country? Menus provide good starting points — collect these from the local Indian, Chinese, Italian or Greek restaurants and look for similarities and differences in dishes and ingredients. The children themselves may have information from home.

When learning about distant places children need authentic resources and to be able to relate what they learn to their own experience. In a topic on Germany (Wiegand, 1990) I decided to start by attempting to provide English children with a simulated experience of being at school in Germany for a day. It was decided to start the topic with school because that is part of the everyday experience of children themselves and offers potential for comparative material. The theme of using school as a basis for promoting empathy and geographical understanding has been more fully developed by Marsden (1988).

For this topic, the class had been told that they would have a German teacher as part of their term-long project on the European Community. Their class teacher had told them that, to start with at least, I would only speak German to them and they were well-rehearsed to reply 'Guten Morgen Herr Wiegand' when I greeted them. We started with some simple introductions in German ('My name is . . .', 'I am . . . years old'.) We did some simple counting with picture flash cards.

I then explained, in English, that I had visited a German primary school and a class exactly the same age as themselves. Would they like to see some pictures? They would. I showed about twelve slides of the class at work. I gave no commentary at all. The children were to ask questions if they wanted to. My intention was for the children to use the pictures as *evidence* for another part of the world. Most of the questions were personal at first (What are their names? How do they travel to school?). Later they began to ask questions about the school itself, and then about the curriculum.

In response to these questions I then produced copies of the class timetable. What questions would they like to ask about this?

Why do they start school so early?

Why don't they do English?

Where do they have dinner, and what do they have?

I then asked what the class would like to do with the information they had so far. One group decided to draw a picture of the class at work from one of the slides. Another group wanted to find where the school was on a map of Germany. Another group decided to find out which group of children worked harder (i.e. the longer number of hours) in a day, week, term . . . by comparing the German timetable with their own. Sizeable calculations ensued.

After playtime I wanted the children to experience some reading and writing in German. I used some materials adapted from a language scheme designed for the children of *Gastarbeiter* (guest workers), whose mother tongue is not German. The children were given a worksheet with spaces for pictures of members of their family. Under the spaces they were to copy one or more of:

Das ist meine Mutter
Das ist mein Vater
Das ist meine Schwester
Das ist mein Bruder

Colours were learned using a picture of a clown holding balloons which were to be coloured in, each balloon with a label (*blau*, *schwartz*, *rot*, *gelb*, *grün*, etc.) indicating what colour crayon to use. Most children guessed the colours ('*Blau* is just like "blue" isn't it sir?').

Later, I read some poetry to the class. *Struwwelpeter* by Heinrich Hoffman. (Hilaire Belloc based some of his *Cautionary Tales* on these poems. They are similar in style.) The children had copies of the poems and the pictures that illustrate them. I read the poems in German. The children had to tell me what was happening. In one poem, *Paulinchen* (the prototype of Belloc's *Matilda*), plays with matches despite the repeated warnings by the cats, Minz and Maunz, that her parents have told her not to. Needless to say, the story ends in tears. She is burned and all that is left of her, and the house, is a little heap of ash and two shoes. The class enjoyed hugely the sounds of the poem and looking for familiar sounds and shapes to words (*miaow*, *Katzen* = cats, *Haus* = house, *allein* = alone, etc.). *Paulinchen* was followed by the poem about *Konrad* — who sucks his thumb. Konrad's mother is going out. He is to stay put and *on no account* to suck his thumb. If he does the tailor will come and cut his thumbs off.

Fort geht die Mutter und
wupp! den Daumen in den Mund.

Out goes his mother and, wupp! Thumb in mouth! With breathtaking speed the door bursts open, the tailor rushes in and 'klipp, klapp'; both thumbs are cut off. The children were outraged. 'But sir, he didn't even get a second warning!' We discussed the events of both poems for ages. The nature and necessity of 'second warnings', how it feels to be left alone in the house, how it feels to do something you've been told not to do, as well as the dramatic effect of the two-line, scene setting introduction to both poems:

Paulinchen war allein zu Haus,
die Eltern waren beide aus.

Paulinchen was alone in the house; both parents were out. Straightaway you have a risky feeling!

We finished the day by examining a graph which had been produced by one of the German children about his favourite food. Preferences were compared — the translation being easy in most cases (Schokolade, kiwi, spaghetti, eis, etc.) The class made their own graphs. At the end of school the children left shouting *'Tschüs!'* ('Bye!') to each other and to me — in just the same way as German children do.

What I had tried to do during this day was reinforce some simple messages about people and places. German children go to school just like you. Much of what they do is the same. They like many of the same things. But there are some differences too. After this introduction the children became keen to learn more about the country itself — houses, transport, work, holidays, etc. The actual activities the children engaged in were fairly like those they might ordinarily have undertaken. What was, I suppose, different was that the stimulus to discussion and activity was in a different language. Source material for lessons like this could come from an overseas school link (see chapter 5) but there should be a high school nearby with specialist language teachers who may be able to provide authentic materials and may even welcome the chance to do an introductory lesson or two with the children they will receive the following year.

Some Final Thoughts

We don't really know very much yet about what children understand about place. This book has concentrated primarily on *distant* places because the existing literature is very thin on this aspect of the primary school curriculum. This is partly a result of a mistaken, but widespread, belief that children are only capable of understanding their local and immediate environment. And yet children do appear to have greater knowledge, experience and understanding of distant places than they have generally been given credit for. I have tried to illustrate this from the limited amount of evidence that is available. Many of the activities suggested, however, need to be taken on trust as this area of the curriculum has rarely received attention from research funding authorities. Nevertheless, place is an important concept and is one of the building blocks of international understanding. And at the time of writing in particular (the beginning of the Gulf War) we could do with more of that. Of all the words that have been used to help clarify the meaning of the curriculum in recent years the one that stands out for me is entitlement. Children are *entitled* to know more about the wider world and the National Curriculum for primary school children offers a good (though limited) deal in this respect. Although far from what the expert geography groups envisaged, it does at least attempt to ensure that children will learn something about other people and places, and will thereby discover something about alternatives to their own way of life. It literally extends their horizons.

Appendix:

Addresses of Organizations Referred to in the Text

Central Bureau for Educational Visits and Exchanges
Seymour Mews House, Seymour Mews, London, W1H 9PE.

Centre for Global Education
University of York, Heslington, York, YO1 5DD.

Centre for World Development Education
Regent's College, Inner Circle, Regent's Park, London, NW1 4NS.

Commission for Racial Equality
Elliott House, 10/12 Allington Street, London, SW1E 5EH.

Commonwealth Institute
Kensington High Street, London, W8 6NQ.

Council for Environmental Education
School of Education, University of Reading, London Road, Reading, RG1 5AQ.

Development Education Centre
Selly Oak Colleges, Bristol Road, Birmingham, B29 6LE.

Friends of the Earth
26–28 Underwood Street, London, N1 7JQ.

The Geographical Association
343 Fulwood Road, Sheffield, S10 3BP.

Horniman Museum
London Road, London, SE23.

ILEA Learning Materials Service
Highbury Station Road, London, N1 1SB.

Information and Documentation Centre for the Geography of The Nether-lands
Heidelberglaan 2, Postbus 80115, 3508 TC, Utrecht, The Netherlands.

Museum of Mankind
6 Burlington Gardens, London, W1X 2EX.

National Association of Development Education Centres
6 Endsleigh Street, London, WC1H 0DX.

One World (offices and warehouse)
Unit B305, Lawrence Street, York, YO1 3BN.

Pictorial Charts Educational Trust
27 Kirchen Road, London, W13 0UD.

Save the Children Fund
Mary Datchelor House, 17 Grove Lane, London, SE5 8RD.

Survival
310 Edgeware Road, London, W2 1DY.

United Kingdom Centre for European Education
Seymour Mews House, Seymour Mews, London, W1H 9PE.

UNICEF UK
55 Lincolns Inn Fields, London, WC2A 3NB.

World Wide Fund For Nature (WWF)
Panda House, Wayside Park, Godalming, Surrey, GU7 1XR.

Bibliography

ABOUD, F.E. (1988) *Children and Prejudice*, Oxford, Blackwell.

ABOUD, F.E. and MITCHELL, F.G. (1977) 'Ethnic role taking: The effects of preference and self-identification', *International Journal of Psychology*, **12**, pp. 1–17.

ADORNO, T.W., FRENKEL-BRUNSWIK, E., LEVINSON, D.J. and SANFORD, R.N. (1950) *The Authoritarian Personality*, New York, Harper and Row.

ALEXANDER, B. and C. (1988) 'Canada's U turn', *The Geographical Magazine*, November, pp. 10–15.

ALEXANDER, C. (1983) *The Early Writings of Charlotte Brontë*, Oxford, Basil Blackwell.

ALLEN, D. and ANGLIN, A.M. (1988) '"Draw the world" research in 1987 — A pilot study for CISV', *Interspectives*, **7**, pp. 38–41.

ALLEN, D.T. (1963) 'Growth in attitudes favourable to peace', *Merril-Palmer Quarterly of Behaviour and Development*, **9**, 4, pp. 27–38.

ALLISON, B., CONWAY, E. and DENSCOMBE, M. (1982) *Development Education in the Primary School Project: Final Report*, Leicester Polytechnic, Leicester.

ALLPORT, G. (1954) *The Nature of Prejudice*, Reading, MA, Addison-Wesley.

ALVIK, T. (1968) 'The development of views on conflict, war and peace among school children', *Journal of Peace Research*, **5**, pp. 171–95.

ASCH, S.E. (1946) 'Forming impressions of personality', *Journal of Abnormal and Social Psychology*, **41**, pp. 258–90.

ASHMORE, R.D. and DEL BOCA, F.K. (1981) 'Conceptual approaches to stereotypes and stereotyping' in HAMILTON, D.L. (Ed.) *Cognitive Processes in Stereotyping and Intergroup Behaviour*, Hillsdale, NJ, Erlbaum, pp. 123–78.

ATKINSON, D. (1989) *The Children's Bookroom: Reading and the Use of Books*, Stoke-on-Trent, Trentham Books.

BAILYN, L. (1959) 'Mass media and children: A study of experience habits and cognitive effects', *Psychology Monographs: General and Applied*, **471**, 73, 1, pp. 1–48.

BALE, J. (1987) *Geography in the Primary School*, London, Routledge & Kegan Paul.

BANFIELD, B. (1980) 'Racism in children's books: An Afro-American perspective' in PREISWERK, R. (Ed.) *The Slant of the Pen: Racism in Children's Books*, Geneva, World Council of Churches, pp. 13–26.

BAR-GAL, Y. (1984) 'There are no butterflies there: An intercultural experiment in landscape perception' in HAUBRICH, H. (Ed.) *Perception of People and Places Through Media*, Freiburg, Paedagogische Hochschule, pp. 134–54.

BARON, B. and BACHMAN, P. (1987) 'Study abroad in Western Europe: A bibliography', *European Journal of Education*, **22**, 1, pp. 101–13.

BARTZ, B. (1965) *Map Design for Children*, New York, Field Enterprises Education Corporation.

BAY, C. (1965) *The Structure of Freedom*, New York, Athenaeum.

BAYLISS, D.G. and RENWICK, T.M. (1966) 'Photograph study in a junior school', *Geography*, **51**, pp. 322–9.

BAZALGETTE, C. (1989) *Primary Media Education: A Curriculum Statement*, London, British Film Institute/DES Working Party for Primary Media Education.

BECKER, J. (1973) 'Racism in children's and young peoples' literature in the Western world', *Journal of Peace Research*, **10**, pp. 295–303.

BECKER, J. (1976) 'Es ging spazieren vor dem Tor ein kohlpechrabenschwartzer Mohr' in *Schuler und Dritte Welt Texte und Materialen für den Unterricht*, Federal Ministry for Economic Cooperation, **48**.

BECKER, J. (Ed.) (1979) *Schooling for a Global Age*, New York, McGraw-Hill.

BEDDIS, R. and MARES, C. (1988) *School Links International*, Brighton, Avon County Council/Tidy Britain Group Schools Research Project.

BEITTER, U.E. (1983) 'Twenty years of cliches: An investigation of the image of Germans and Germany in first year American college texts, 1950–1970', *Internationale Schulbuchforschung*, **2**, pp. 109–31.

BELL, G.H. (1979) 'Cooperation in teacher education in the European Community', *Revue ATEE Journal*, **2**, pp. 59–68.

BELL, G.H. (1987) 'Developing intercultural understanding: An action research approach', *School Organization*, **7**, 3, pp. 273–9.

BELL, G.H. (1989) 'Europe in the primary school: A collaborative venture between schools and teacher trainers', *British Journal of In-Service Education*, **15**, 2, pp. 86–92.

BELL, G.H. and LLOYD, J.T. (1989) *Europe in the Primary School: A Case Review Report*, Sheffield, PAVIC Publications.

BELL, G.H., MILES, A.G. and OVENS, P. (Eds) (1989) *Europe in the Primary School: In England, A Case Study*, Sheffield, PAVIC Publications.

BERRY, G.L. and MITCHELL-KERNAN, C. (1982) *Television and the Socialization of the Minority Child*, New York, Academic Press.

BETTELHEIM, B. (1977) *The Uses of Enchantment: The Meaning and Importance of Fairy Tales*, London, Thames & Hudson.

BIRKENHAUER, J. (1984) 'Perception of landscapes and landforms' in HAUBRICH, H. (Ed.) *Perception of People and Places Through Media*, Freiburg Paedagogische Hochschule, pp. 68–107.

BISHOP, J. and FOULSHAM, J. (1973) *Children's Images of Harwich*, Architectural Psychology Research Unit Working Paper No. 3, Kingston, Kingston Polytechnic.

BJERSTEDT, A. (1960) *Glimpses from the World of the School Child*, New York, Beacon House.

BLANK, M., ROSE, S.A. and BERLIN, L.J. (1978) *The Language of Learning: The Pre-school Years*, New York, Grune and Stratton.

BLYTH, J. (1984) *Place and Time with Children Five to Nine*, London, Croom Helm.

BLYTH, W.A.L. (1990) *Making the Grade for Primary Humanities*, Milton Keynes, Open University Press.

BODEN, P.K. (1977) *Promoting International Understanding Through School Textbooks*, Braunschweig, George Eckert Institute for International Textbook Research.

BOEHM, R.G. and PETERSEN, J.F. (1987) 'Teaching place names and locations in grades 4–8: Map of errors', *Journal of Geography*, July/August, pp. 167–70.

BOGATZ, G.A. and BALL, S.J. (1971) *The Second Year of Sesame Street: A Continuing Evaluation*, Princeton, NJ, Educational Testing Service.

BOOTH, A. (1970) 'The recall of news items', *Public Opinion Quarterly*, **34**, pp. 604–10.

BOWDEN, M.J. (1976) 'The great American desert in the American mind: The historiography of a geographical notion' in LOWENTHAL, D. and BOWDEN, M.J. (Eds) *Geographies of the Mind*, New York, Oxford University Press, pp. 119–48.

BOWN, E. (c. 1920) *The Approach to Geography: A Suggestive Course for Students and Teachers in Kindergartens and Preparatory Schools*, London, Christophers.

BRODERICK, D.M. (1973) *Image of the Black in Children's Fiction*, New York, Bowker.

BRUNER, J.S. and GOODMAN, C.D. (1947) 'Value and needs as ongoing factors in perception', *Journal of Abnormal and Social Psychology*, **42**, pp. 33–44.

BUNGE, W. (1965) 'Racism in geography', *Crisis*, **2**, 8.

BURGESS, J. and GOLD, J. (1985) *Geography, the Media and Popular Culture*, London, Croom Helm.

BURRISS, G. (1983) 'Stages in the development of economic concepts', *Human Relations*, **36**, 9, pp. 791–812.

BURPEE, P. (1981) 'Teaching about the Inuit', *Teaching Geography*, **6**, 3, pp. 113–5.

Business Monitor: Overseas Travel and Tourism (MA6) (1987) Business Statistics Office of the Government Statistical Service, London, HMSO.

BYRAM, M. (1989) 'A school visit to France: Ethnographic explorations', *British Journal of Language Teaching*, **27**, 2.

CAPPS, F.K. (1986) 'The search for global perspectives in Social Education's history articles: 1937–1982', *International Journal of Social Sciences*, **1**, 2, pp. 90–8.

CARNIE, J. (1971) 'The development of junior children's ideas of people of different race and nation', unpublished PhD thesis, London, University of London.

CARNIE, J. (1972) 'Children's attitudes to other nationalities' in GRAVES, N.J. (Ed.) *New Movements in the Study and Teaching of Geography*, London, Temple Smith, pp. 121–35.

CATLING, S. (1979) 'Maps and cognitive maps: The young child's perception', *Geography*, **64**, pp. 288–96.

CATLING, S. (1988) 'Children and geography' in MILLS, D. (Ed.) *Geographical Work in Primary and Middle Schools*, Sheffield, The Geographical Association, pp. 9–19.

Children's International Summer Villages (CISV) Fact Sheet/Village Guide, Newcastle, CISV.

CHRISTENSON, P.G. and ROBERTS, D.F. (1983) 'The role of television in the formation of children's social attitudes' in HOWE, M.J.A. (Ed.) *Learning from Television: Psychological and Educational Research*, London, Academic Press, pp. 79–100.

CLARK, B. (1979) *The Changing World and the Primary School*, London, Council for World Development Education.

CODOL, J-P. (1986) 'Estimation et expression de la réssemblance et de la différence entre pairs', *L' Année Psychologique*, **86**, pp. 527–50.

COHEN, R. (Ed.) (1985) *The Development of Spatial Cognition*, Hillsdale, NJ, Erlbaum.

COLE, J.P. and WHYSALL, P. (1968) 'Places in the news: A study of geographical information', *Bulletin of Quantitative Data for Geographers*, **17**, pp. 67–72.

COMBES, G. (1990) *Where to Next? An Evaluation and Review of the Work and Achievements of the Development Education Centre Primary Project*, Birmingham, Development Education Centre.

CONNELL, S. and DRISCOLL, V. (1977) *Lands of Ice and Snow*, London, Macdonald Educational.

COOPER, P. (1965) 'The development of the concept of war', *Journal of Peace Research*, **2**, pp. 1–17.

COUNCIL FOR EDUCATION IN WORLD CITIZENSHIP (1987) *Citizens of the World*, London, CEWC.

Cox, C. and Scruton, R. (1984) *Peace Studies: A Critical Survey*, London, Institute for European Defence and Strategic Studies.

Creery, I. (1982) *The Inuit (Eskimo) of Canada*, London, Minority Rights Group, Report No. 60.

Cullingford, C. (1984) *Children and Television*, Aldershot, Gower.

Cunliffe, L. and Usborne, K. (1985) *My Passport to France*, London, Fontana Lions.

D'Amore, L. (1988) 'Tourism — The world's peace industry', *Journal of Travel Research*, **27**, 1, pp. 35–40.

Darvizeh, Z. and Spencer, C.P. (1984) 'How do young children learn novel routes? The importance of landmarks in the child's retracing of routes through the large scale environment', *Environmental Education and Information*, **3**, pp. 97–105.

Davies, A.F. (1968) 'The child's discovery of nationality', *The Australian and New Zealand Journal of Sociology*, iv, pp. 107–25.

Davies, M. (1989) *Get the Picture! Developing Visual Literacy in the Infant Classroom*, Birmingham, Development Education Centre.

Davies, R. (1987) *Hopes and Fears: Children's Attitudes to Nuclear War*, Occasional Paper No. 11, Lancaster, The Richardson Institute for Peace Studies.

Davis, V. (1985) 'Ethiopia: That's the name of a pop record innit miss? Ethiopia — What does it mean to you?', *Multi-ethnic Education Review*, summer/autumn, pp. 25–29.

Dennis, J., Lindberg, L. and McCrane, D. (1972) 'Support for nation and government among English children', *British Journal of Political Science*, **1**, pp. 25–48.

Department of Education and Science (1986) *Geography from 5 to 16; Curriculum Matters 7, an HMI Series*, London, HMSO.

Department of Education and Science (1989a) *English in the National Curriculum*, London, HMSO.

Department of Education and Science (1989b) *Mathematics in the National Curriculum*, London, HMSO.

Department of Education and Science (1989c) *Science in the National Curriculum*, London, HMSO.

Department of Education and Science (1990a) *Technology in the National Curriculum*, London, HMSO.

Department of Education and Science (1990b) *History for Ages 5 to 16*, London, HMSO July.

Department of Education and Science (1990c) *Modern Foreign Languages for Ages 11 to 16*, London, HMSO.

Department of Education and Science (1990d) *Geography for Ages 5 to 16*, London, HMSO.

Department of Education and Science (1991) *National Curiculum: Geography. Draft Statutory Order*, London, HMSO.

DICKHOFF, W. (1987) Drawing peace and war', *Interspectives*, **6**, pp. 37–43.

DIXON, B. (1977) *Catching them Young 2: Political Ideas in Children's Fiction*, London, Pluto Press.

DOISE, W., MUGNY, G. and PERRET-CLERMOND, A.N. (1975) 'Social interaction and the development of cognitive operations', *European Journal of Social Psychology*, **5**, pp. 367–83.

DOWNS, R.M. and STEA, D. (Eds) (1977) *Image and Environment*, Chicago, Aldine.

DUNN, A. (1988) 'A theoretical and practical investigation into the way in which primary school children perceive people from overseas', unpublished BEd long study, Scarborough, North Riding College.

EAMES, D., SHORROCKS, D. and TOMLINSON, P.D. (1990) 'Naughty animals or naughty experimenters? Conservation accidents revisited with video-stimulated commentary', *British Journal of Developmental Psychology*, **8**, pp. 25–37.

EDWARDS, V. (1983) *Language in Multicultural Classrooms*, London, Batsford.

ELKIN, J. and TRIGGS, P. (1985) *The Books for Keeps Guide to Children's Books for a Multicultural Society 8–12*, London, Books for Keeps.

ENGLISH TOURIST BOARD (jointly with Wales Tourist Board) (1989) *British Tourism Market 1988*, London, ETB.

EPSTEIN, D. and SEALEY, A. (1990) *'Where it really matters ...: Developing anti-racist education in predominantly white primary schools'*, Birmingham, Development Education Centre.

ESARTE-SARRIES, V. (1989) '"Onions and stripey tee-shirts" or how do primary pupils learn about France?', *British Journal of Language Teaching*, pp. 65–71.

ELLIOTT, G. (1980) *Oxford New Geography: A Course for Juniors 3*, Oxford, Oxford University Press.

ESCALONA, S.K. (1963) 'Children's responses to the nuclear war threat', *Children*, **10**, pp. 137–42.

ESCALONA, S.K. (1982) 'Growing up with the threat of nuclear war: some indirect effects on personality development', *American Journal of Orthopsychiatry*, **52**, pp. 600–7.

EUROPEAN COUNCIL (1988) Resolution of the Council and the Ministers of Education meeting within the Council on the European dimension in education of 24 May, 1988, (88/C 177/02) *Official Journal of the European Communities*, No. C177/5, 6.7.88.

EVANS-PRITCHARD, D. (1989) 'How "they" see "us": Native American images of tourists', *Annals of Tourism Research*, **16**, pp. 89–105.

FALCON, L.N. (1980) 'The oppressive function of values, concepts and images in children's books' in PREISWERK, R. (Ed.) *The Slant of the Pen: Racism in Children's Books*, Geneva, World Council of Churches, pp. 3–7.

FISHER, M. (1972) *Matters of Fact: Aspects of non-fiction for Children*, Leicester, Brockhampton Press.

FISHER, S. and HICKS, D. (1985) *World Studies 8–13: A Teacher's Handbook*, Edinburgh, Oliver & Boyd.

FITZGERALD, P. (1988) *The Beginning of Spring*, London, Collins.

FOUNTAIN, S. (1990) *Learning Together: Global Education 4–7*, Cheltenham, Stanley Thornes.

FRENKEL-BRUNSWIK, E. (1949) 'Intolerance of ambiguity as an emotional and perceptual personality variable', *Journal of Personality*, **18**, pp. 108–43.

FURTH, H.G. (1980) *The World of Grown-ups: Children's Conceptions of Society*, New York, Elsevier.

GENESEE, F., TUCKER, G.R. and LAMBERT, W.E. (1978) 'The development of ethnic identity and ethnic role taking skills in children from different school settings', *International Journal of Psychology*, **13**, pp. 39–57.

GERBER, R. (1981a) 'Children's development of competence and performance in cartographic language' in WILSON, P., GERBER, R. and FIEN, J. (Eds) *Research in Geographical Education*, Brisbane, Australian Geographical Education Research Association, pp. 98–124.

GERBER, R. (1981b) 'Competence and performance in cartographic language', *Cartographic Journal*, **18**, 2, pp. 104–11.

GERBER, R. (1982) 'An international study of children's perception and understanding of type used on atlas maps', *Cartographic Journal*, **19**, 2, pp. 115–21.

GERBER, R. (1984) A form-function analysis of school atlases' in HAUBRICH, H. (Ed.) *Perception of People and Places through Media*, Freiburg, Paedagogische Hochschule/International Geographical Union Commission on Geographical Education.

GILL, P. (1986) *A Year in the Death of Africa*, London, Paladin.

GILLMOR, D.A. (1974) 'Mental maps in geographic education: spatial preference of some Leinster school leavers', *Geographical Viewpoint*, **3**, pp. 46–66.

GOLDSMITH, E. (1984) *Research into Illustrations: An Approach and a Review*, Cambridge, Cambridge University Press.

GOODEY, B. (1973) *Perception of the Environment: an introduction to the literature*, Occasional Paper No. 17. Birmingham, University of Birmingham Centre for Urban and Regional Studies.

GOODEY, B. (1974) *Images of Place: Essays on Environmental Perception, Communications and Education*, Occasional Paper No. 30. Birmingham, University of Birmingham Centre for Urban and Regional Studies.

GOODMAN, M.E. (1964) *Race Awareness in Young Children*, Cambridge, MA, Addison-Wesley.

GORMAN, B. (1979) 'Seven days, five countries', *Urban Life*, **7**, 4, pp. 469–91.

GOUGH, H.G., HARRIS, D.B., MARTIN, W.E. and EDWARDS, M. (1950) 'Children's ethnic attitudes: relationship of certain personality factors', *Child Development*, **21**, 2, pp. 83–91.

GOULD, P. and WHITE, R. (1974) *Mental Maps*, Harmondsworth, Penguin Books.

GRACE, H.A. (1954) 'Education and the reduction of prejudice', *Educational Research Bulletin*, **33**, pp. 169–75.

GRACE, H.A. and NEUHAUS, J.O. (1952) 'Information and social distance as predictors of hostility towards nations', *Journal of Abnormal and Social Psychology*, **47**, pp. 540–5.

GRAFTON, T. (1984) *Starting Together: Development Education and Young Children*, Birmingham, Development Education Centre.

GRAHAM, J. and LYNN, S. (1989) 'Mud huts and flints: Children's images of the third world', *Education 3–13*, June, pp. 29–32.

GRAHAM, J. and LYNN, S. (1989) 'Third world images', *Child Education*, February, 11, pp. 24–34.

GRAHAM, M.D. (1951) 'An experiment in international attitudes research', *International Social Science Bulletin*, **3**, pp. 529–39.

GREIG, S., PIKE, G. and SELBY, D. (1987) *Earthrights: Education as if the Planet Really Mattered*, London, World Wildlife Fund and Kogan Page.

HADDON, J. (1960) 'A view of foreign lands', *Geography*, **45**, pp. 286–9.

HALSTEAD, M. (1988) *Education, Justice and Cultural Diversity: An Examination of the Honeyford Affair 1984–1985*, London, Falmer Press.

HALVERSON, N.D. (n.d.) *Geography via Pictures*, Washington, DC, National Council for Geographic Education.

HAMILTON, D.L. (1981) 'Stereotyping and intergroup behaviour: Some thoughts on the cognitive approach' in HAMILTON, D.L. (Ed.) *Cognitive Processes in Stereotyping and Intergroup Behaviour*, Hillsdale, NS, Erlbaum.

HAMILTON, D.L. and TROLIER, T.K. (1986) 'Stereotypes and stereotyping: An overview of the cognitive approach' in DOVIDIO, J. and GAERTNER, S. (Eds) *Prejudice, Discrimination and Racism*, New York, Academic Press.

HARNETT, P. and WELCH, G. (1986) 'Why teach children about Eskimos?', *Education 3–13*, **14**, 2, pp. 32–40.

HART, R. (1979) *Children's Experience of Place*, New York, Irvington.

HART, R.A. and MOORE, G.T. (1973) 'The development of spatial cognition: A review' in DOWNS, R.M. and STEA, D. (Eds) *Image and Environment: Cognitive Mapping and Spatial Behavior*, Chicago, IL, Aldine.

HARTMANN, P.G. and HUSBAND, C. (1974) *Racism and the Mass Media*, New York, Davis-Poynter.

HAUBRICH, H. (Ed.) (1984) *Perception of People and Places Through Media (Paper Collection of the Symposium of the Commission on Geographical Education of the 25th International Geographical Congress)*, Freiburg, Paedagogische Hochschule.

HAUBRICH, H. (1987) *Where and How I Live: 10-year-olds Write for the Children in the World*, published by the author at Birkenrain 34, D-7811 St. Peter, Freiburg, Germany.

HEATER, D. (1980) *World Studies: Education for International Understanding in Britain*, London, Harrap.

HEATER, D. (1984) *Peace Through Education: The Contribution of the Council for Education in World Citizenship*, London, Falmer Press.

HEIDER, F. (1958) *The Psychology of Interpersonal Relations*, New York, Wiley.

Helgren, D.M. (1983) 'Place name ignorance is national news', *Journal of Geography*, July-August, pp. 176–8.

HER MAJESTY'S INSPECTORATE (1989) *Aspects of Primary Education: The Teaching and Learning of History and Geography*, London, HMSO.

HEWSTONE, M. and JASPARS, J. (1984) Social dimensions of attribution' in TAJFEL, H. (Ed.) *The Social Dimension: European Developments in Social Psychology*, Volume 2, Cambridge, Cambridge University Press, pp. 223–98.

HIBBERD, D. (1983) 'Children's images of the third world', *Teaching Geography*, October, pp. 68–71.

HIBBERT, C. (1987) *The Grand Tour*, London, Thames Methuen.

HICKS, D. (n.d.) *Bias in Geography Textbooks: Images of the Third World and Multi-Ethnic Britain*, Working Paper No. 1, Centre for Multicultural Education, University of London Institute of Education.

HICKS, D. (1988) *Education for Peace*, London, Routledge.

HICKS, D. and TOWNLEY, C. (Eds) (1982) *Teaching World Studies*, London, Longman.

HICKS, E.P. and BEYER, B.K. (1968) 'Images of Africa', *Social Education*, **32**, pp. 779–84.

HOLLENBECK, A.R. and SLABY, R.G. (1979) 'Infant visual and vocal responses to television', *Child Development*, **50**, pp. 41–5.

HOLROYD, S. (1990) 'Children's development in socio-economic ideas: some psychological perspectives' in Ross, A. (Ed.) *Economic and Industrial Awareness in the Primary School*, London, Polytechnic of North London and School Curriculum Industry Partnership.

HOROWITZ, E.L. (1941) 'Some aspects of the development of patriotism in children', *Sociometry*, **3**, pp. 329–41.

HOROWITZ, M.J. (1978) *Image Formation and Cognition*, New York, Appleton Century Crofts.

HOUSE OF LORDS SELECT COMMITTEE (1990) European Schools and Language Learning in UK Schools, (Paper 48), April.

HUTCHINGS, M. (1990) 'Children's thinking about work' in Ross, A. (Ed.) *Economic and Industrial Awareness in the Primary School*, London, Polytechnic of North London and School Curriculum Industry Partnership.

INNER LONDON EDUCATION AUTHORITY (1981) *The Study of Places in the Primary School*, London, ILEA Learning Materials Service.

INNER LONDON EDUCATION AUTHORITY (1984) *Education in a Multiethnic Society; The Primary School*, London, ILEA Learning Resources Centre.

ISAACS, H.R. (1958) *Scratches On Our Minds*, New York, John Day.

JAHODA, G. (1959) 'Nationality preferences and national stereotypes in Ghana before independence', *Journal of Social Psychology*, **50**, pp. 165–74.

JAHODA, G. (1962) 'Development of Scottish children's ideas and attitudes about other countries', *Journal of Social Psychology*, **58**, pp. 91–108.

JAHODA, G. (1963) 'The development of children's ideas about country and nationality', *British Journal of Educational Psychology*, **33**, pp. 47–60 and pp. 143–53.

JAHODA, G. (1964) 'Children's concepts of nationality: a critical study of Piaget's stages', *Child Development* **35**, pp. 1081–92.

JASPARS, J.M.F., VAN DER GEER, J.P., TAJFEL, H. and JOHNSON, N.B. (1983) 'On the development of international attitudes in children', *European Journal of Social Psychology*, **2**, pp. 347–69.

JEFFCOATE, R. (1977) 'Children's racial ideas and feelings', *English in Education*, **11**, 1.

JOHNSON, N.B. (1966) 'What do children learn from war comics?', *New Society*, 7 July, pp. 7–12.

JOHNSON, N.B., MIDDLETON, M.R. and TAJFEL, H. (1970) 'The relationship between children's preferences for, and knowledge about, other nations', *British Journal of Social and Clinical Psychology*, **9**, pp. 232–40.

JOHNSTON, R.J. (1987) *Geography and Geographers: Anglo-American Human Geography since 1945*, London, Arnold.

JULKA, N. (1990) 'What's in a name', *Multicultural Teaching*, **8**, 2, p. 37.

JUNGKUNZ, T. and THOMAS, O. (1986) 'Young people's perceptions of other countries: Summary of pilot study findings', mimeo, Oxford, Oxford Development Education Unit, Westminster College.

KANTOR, R.N. *et al.* (1983) 'How inconsiderate are children's textbooks?', *Journal of Curriculum Studies*, **15**, 1, pp. 45–67.

KATZ, D. and BRALY, K. (1933) 'Racial stereotypes in 100 college students', *Journal of Abnormal and Social Psychology*, **28**, pp. 280–90.

KATZ, D. and BRALY, K. (1933) 'Racial prejudice and racial stereotypes', *Journal of Abnormal and Social Psychology*, **30**, pp. 175–93.

KATZ, P.A. (1976) *Towards the Elimination of Racism*, New York, Pergamon.

KATZ, P.A. and ZALK, S.R. (1978) 'Modification of children's racial attitudes', *Developmental Psychology*, **14**, pp. 447–61.

KELMAN, H.C. (1965) 'National and international loyalties' in KELMAN, H.C. (Ed.) *International Behaviour*, New York, Holt Rinehart & Winston.

KEMELFIELD, G. (1972) 'The evaluation of schools' broadcasting', *New Society*, 1 June, pp. 24–6.

KERNAN, C. (1982) *Television and the Socialization of the Minority Child*, New York, Academic Press,

KING, R. and VUJACOVIC, P. (1989) 'Peters Atlas: A new era of cartography or publisher's con trick?', *Geography*, **74**, 3, pp. 245–52.

KLEIN, M. (1985) *Reading into Racism*, London, Routledge & Kegan Paul.

KNIGHT, C. and RICE, M.J. (1984) 'Geographic knowledge and attitudes: The Americas' in HAUBRICH, H. (Ed.) *Perception of People and Places Through Media*, Freiburg, Paedagogische Hochschule.

KOSE, G. (1985) 'Children's knowledge of photography: A study of the developing awareness of a representational medium', *British Journal of Developmental Psychology*, **3**, 373–84.

KRUGMAN, H.E. (1965) 'The impact of television advertising: Learning with involvement', *Public Opinion Quarterly*, **39**, pp. 583–96.

KUTTZ, I. and UNGER-HAMILTON, C. (1984) *The Children's Guide to Paris*, London, Blackie.

KUYA, D. (1980) 'Racism in children's books in Britain' in PREISWERK, R. (Ed.) *The Slant of the Pen: Racism in Children's Books*, Geneva, World Council of Churches, pp. 26–46.

LAISHLEY, J. (1971) 'Skin colour awareness and preference in London nursery school children', *Race*, **13**, 1, pp. 47–64.

LAISHLEY, J. (1972) 'Can comics join the multi-racial society?', *Times Educational Supplement*, 24 November, p. 4.

LAMBERT, S. and WIEGAND, P. (1990) 'The beginnings of international understanding', *The New Era in Education*, **71**, 3, pp. 90–3.

LAMBERT, W.E. and KLINEBERG, O. (1967) *Children's Views of Foreign Peoples: a cross national study*, New York, Appleton-Century-Crofts.

LARSEN, O. (Ed.) (1968) *Violence and the Mass Media*, New York, Harper & Row.

LAWRENCE, H. (n.d.) *Little Folk in Many Lands*, London, Blackie.

LAWSON, E.D. (1963) 'Development of patriotism in children: A second look', *Journal of Psychology*, **55**, pp. 279–86.

LEGGE, J. (1988) 'Cold lands', *Junior Education*, December, pp. 24–5.

LEYENS, J-P. and CODOL, J-P. (1988) 'Social cognition' in HEWSTONE, M. *et al.* (Ed.) *Introduction to Social Psychology*, Oxford, Blackwell.

LIEBERT, R.M. and SPRAFKIN, J. (1988) (3rd edn) *The Early Window: Effects of Television on Children and Youth*, Oxford, Pergamon.

LINTON, T. (1990) 'A child's eye view of economics' in, ROSS, A. (Ed.) *Economic and Industrial Awareness in the Primary School*, London, Polytechnic of North London and School Curriculum Industry Partnership.

LIPPMAN, L. (1980) 'Racism in Australian children's books' in PREISWERK, R. (Ed.) *The Slant of the Pen: Racism in Children's Books*, Geneva, World Council of Churches, pp. 61–72.

LIPPMANN, W. (1922) *Public Opinion*, New York, Harcourt Brace Jovanovitch.

LIVERMAN, D.M. and SHERMAN, D.J. (1985) 'Natural hazards in novels and films: Implications for hazard perception and behaviour' in BURGESS, J. and GOLD, J. (Eds) *Geography, the Media and Popular Culture*, Beckenham, Croom Helm.

LONG, M. (1953) 'Children's reactions to geographical pictures', *Geography*, **38**, 2, pp. 100–7.

LONG, M. (1961) 'The reaction of grammar school pupils to geographical pictures', *Geography*, **46**, 4, pp. 322–37.

LOWENTHAL, D. (1961) 'Geography, experience and imagination: towards a geographical epistemology', *Annals of the Association of American Geographers*, **51**, pp. 241–60.

LOXTON, J. (1985) 'The Peters phenomenon', *The Cartographic Journal*, **22**, pp. 106–8.

LUTZ, H. (1980) 'Images of Indians in German children's books' in PREISWERK, R. (Ed.) *The Slant of the Pen: Racism in Children's Books*, Geneva, World Council of Churches, pp. 82–105.

LYNCH, J. (1987) *Prejudice Reduction and the Schools*, London, Cassell.

LYNCH, J. (1989) *Multicultural Education in a Global Society*, London, Falmer Press.

LYNCH, K. (1960) *The Image of the City*, Cambridge, MA, MIT Press.

McFARLANE, C. (1986) *Development Education in the Primary School, Books 1–3*, Birmingham, Development Education Centre.

McGARRIGLE, J. and DONALDSON, M. (1974) 'Conservation accidents', *Cognition*, **3**, pp. 341–50.

MANSON, G.A. and VUICICH, G. (1977) 'Towards geographic literacy' in MANSON, G.A. and RIDD, M.K. (Ed.) *New Perspectives on Geographic Education*, Dubuque, Iowa, Kendall Hunt, pp. 191–209.

MARCHANT, E.C. (Ed.) (1967) *Geography Teaching and the Revision of Geography Textbooks and Atlases*, Strasbourg, Council of Europe.

MARES, C. and HARRIS, R. (1987) *School Links International: Interim Report on the Evaluation of Pupil Attitudes*, Avon County Council and the Keep Britain Tidy Group Schools Research Project, Brighton, Brighton Polytechnic.

MARES, C. (Ed.) (1988) *Our Europe: Environmental Awareness and Language Development Through School Exchanges*, Wigan, The Tidy Britain Group.

Market Intelligence, December 1984, Mintel Publications.

MARSDEN, W.E. (1988) 'Geography in the primary curriculum: using the world's schools to promote empathy' in GERBER, R. and LIDSTONE, J. (Eds) *Developing Skills in Geographical Education*, Melbourne, Jacaranda Press, pp. 195–203.

MARSDEN, W.E. (1990) 'Primary school geography: The question of balance' in CAMPBELL, J. and LITTLE, V. (Eds) *Humanities in the Primary School*, London, Falmer Press, pp. 74–89.

MARSHALL, D. (Ed.) (1989) *Campus World 1989–1990*, Cambridge, Hobsons, on behalf of Campus 2000.

MARSHALL, T.H. (1950) *Citizenship and Social Class*, Cambridge, Cambridge University Press.

MAURER, R. and BAXTER, J.C. (1972) 'Images of the neighbourhood and city among black, Anglo and Mexican-American children', *Environment and Behaviour*, **4**, 4, pp. 351–188.

MEIJER, H. (1991) *Report on the Second Dutch — British Textbook Conference*, Utrecht, Information and Documentation Centre for the geography of the Netherlands.

MEIJER, H. (1983) 'Possible causes of errors in geography textbooks', *Internationale Schulbuchforschung*, **5**, pp. 301–9.

MEIJER, H. and HILLERS, E. (1981) 'International textbook revision in the field of geography: Some reflections on principles and methods', *Internationale Schulbuchforschung*, **3**, pp. 193–208.

MIDDLETON, M.R., TAJFEL, M. and JOHNSON, N.B. (1970) 'Cognitive and affective aspects of children's national attitudes', *British Journal of Social and Clinical Psychology* **9**, pp. 122–34.

MILLS, D. (Ed.) (1988) *Geographical Work in Primary and Middle Schools*, Sheffield, Geographical Association.

MILNER, D. (1970) 'Ethnic identity and preference in minority group children', unpublished PhD thesis, University of Bristol.

MILNER, D. (1983) *Children and Race: Ten Years On*, London, Ward Lock Educational.

MINGS, R.C. (1988) 'Assessing the contribution of tourism to international understanding', *Journal of Travel Research*, **27**, 2, pp. 33–8.

MORGAN, I. (Ed.) (1987) *The Holiday Which? Guide to Italy*, London, Consumer Association and Hodder & Stoughton.

MOORE, B. (1989) 'The "bad book box" — Racial bias and stereotype in children's books', *Multicultural Teaching*, **7**, 2, pp. 23–7.

MOORE, G.T. and GOLLEDGE, R.G. (Eds) (1976) *Environmental Knowing*, Stroudsburg, PA, Dowden, Hutchinson and Ross.

MORRIS, J.S. (1982) 'Television portrayal and the socialization of the American Indian child' in BERRY, G.L. and MITCHELL-KERNAN, C. (1982) *Television and the Socialization of the Minority Child*, New York, Academic Press.

MORRISSEY, M.P. (1984) 'Place recognition by Jamaican children' in HAUBRICH, H. (Ed.) *Perception of People and Places Through Media*, Freiburg, Paedagogische Hochschule.

MURPHY, D. (1965) *Full Tilt*, London, John Murray.

MURRAY, H.A. and MORGAN, C.D. (1945) 'A clinical study of sentiments', *Genetic Psychology Monographs, No. 32*, pp. 303 ff.

NATIONAL ASSOCIATION OF DEVELOPMENT EDUCATION CENTRES (1980)

NATIONAL COUNCIL FOR EDUCATIONAL TECHNOLOGY (1989) *Communique: The Newsletter of the NCET Communications Collaborative Project Special Edition*, July.

NESBIT, M. (1981) 'An investigation of the understanding of far places by 9–13 year old children' in BELL, P.G.E., CONVEY, A.L., DILKE, M. and HANNAM, R. (Eds) *Experiments in the Teaching and Learning of Geography*, Leeds, School of Education, University of Leeds, pp. 79–82.

NEWMAN, G. (1978) *Eskimos*, London, Franklin Watts.

NEBEL, J. (1984) 'German children's perceptions of France' in HAUBRICH, H. (Eds) *Perception of People and Places Through Media* (paper collection of the Symposium of the Commission on Geographical Education of the 25th Intenational Geographical Congress), Freiburg, Paedagogische Hochschule, pp. 220–41.

NIEMANN, H. (1987) 'Eindrucke aus Englischen primary schools', *Grundschule*, 4, pp. 32–8.

NORBROOK, D. (1985) *Passport to France*, London, Franklin Watts.

NORDENSTRENG, K. (1972) 'Policy for news transmission' in McQUAIL, D. (Ed.) *Sociology of Mass Communication: Selected Readings*, Harmondsworth, Penguin, pp. 386–405.

NOYES, E. (1979) 'Are some maps better than others?' *Cartographic Journal*, **16**, 2, pp. 72–7.

NUSSBAUM, J. (1979) 'Children's conceptions of the earth as a cosmic body', *Science Education*, **63**, 1, pp. 83–93.

NUSSBAUM, J. (1985) 'The earth as a cosmic body' in DRIVER, R., GUESNE, E. and TIBERGHIEN, A. (Eds) *Children's Ideas in Science*, Milton Keynes, Open University Press, pp. 170–92.

NUSSBAUM, J. and NOVAK, J.D. (1976) An assessment of children's concepts of the Earth utilising structured interviews', *Science Education*, 60, 4, pp. 535–50.

OJALA, J. (1978) 'Kahdeksan maailmaa' (tr. 'Eight worlds'), *Natura*, 1, pp. 17–22.

OOMEN-WELKE, I. (1988) 'Frieden fuer die Vaterlaender: Nationalhymnen von Schuelern gedeutet', *Praxis Deutsch*, 89, pp. 20–3.

OVERJORDET, A.H. (1984) 'Children's views of the world during an international media covered conflict' in HAUBRICH, H. (Ed.) *Perception of People and Places Through Media*, Freiburg, Paedagogische Hochschule, pp. 208–20.

PAIVIO, A. (1971) *Imagery and Verbal Processes*, New York, Holt Rinehart & Winston.

PAPE, H. *et al.* (1985) 'The so-called Peters projection', *The Cartographic Journal*, **22**, pp. 108–10.

PEARCE, P.L. (1980) 'A favorability-satisfaction model of tourists' evaluations', *Journal of Travel Research*, **14**, 1, pp. 13–17.

PEARCE, P.L. (1982) *The Social Psychology of Tourist Behaviour*, Oxford, Pergamon Press.

PELLY, D. (1990) 'In the face of adversity', *The Geographical Magazine*, January, pp. 16–18.

PERERA, K. (1988) 'Writing geography worksheets: Some linguistic considerations' in DILKES, J.L. and NICHOLLS, A. (Ed.) *Low Attainers and the Teaching of Geography*, Sheffield, Geographical Association, pp. 65–75.

PETCHENIK, B.B. (1983) 'A map maker's perspective on map design research 1950–1980' in TAYLOR, D.R.F. (Ed.) *Graphic Communication and Design in Contemporary Cartography*, Chichester, Wiley.

PETERSON, R.C. and THURSTONE, L.L. (1933) *Motion Pictures and the Social Attitudes of Children*, New York, Macmillan.

PHILLIPS, R.J., NOYES, E. and AUDLEY, R.J. (1978) 'Searching for names on maps', *Cartographic Journal*, **15**, 2, pp. 72–7.

PIAGET, J. (1929) *The Child's Conception of the World*, London, Kegan Paul.

PIAGET, J. with WEIL, A-M. (1951) 'The development in children of the idea of the homeland and of relations with other countries', *Institute of Social Science Bulletin*, **3**, pp. 561–78.

PIKE, G. (1984) *World Studies Resource Guide*, London, Council for Education in World Citizenship.

PIKE, G. and SELBY, D. (1988) *Global Teacher, Global Learner*, London, Hodder & Stoughton.

POCOCK, D.C.D. (1972) 'The city of the mind: a review of mental maps in urban areas', *Scottish Geographic Magazine*, **88**, pp. 115–24.

POCOCK, D.C.D. (1976) 'Some characteristics of mental maps: an empirical study', *Transactions of the Institute of British Geographers*, **1–2**, pp. 493–512.

PORTER, P.W. (1987) '"In Dunkelsten Afrika": Africa in the student mind', *Journal of Geography*, March/April, pp. 98–102.

PREISWERK, R. (Ed.) (1980) *The Slant of the Pen: Racism in Children's Books*, Geneva, World Council of Churches.

RAE, S. (1982) *The Blyton Phenomenon* London, Andre Deutsch.

REEDER, K. (1979) 'Pippi Longstocking' in STINTON, J. (Ed.) *Racism and Sexism in Children's Books*, London, Writers and Readers, pp. 112–8.

RELPH, E. (1970) 'An enquiry into the relations between phenomenology and geography', *The Canadian Geographer*, **14**, pp. 193–201.

RELPH, E. (1976) *Place and Placelessness*, London, Pion.

REMY, R.C., NATHAN, J.A., BECKER, J.M. and TORNEY, J.V. (1975) *International Learning and International Education in a Global Age,* New York, National Council for the Social Studies.

RICHARDSON, R. (1974) 'Tensions in world and school: An outline of certain current controversies', *Bulletin of Peace Proposals*, **5**, pp. 263–73.

RICHARDSON, R. (1982) 'Talking about equality', *Cambridge Journal of Education*, **12**, 2, pp. 35–42.

RICHTER, H. (1982) *Zur Psychologie des Friedens*, Hamburg, Reinbek.

RILEY, M.W. and RILEY, J.W. (1955) 'A sociological approach to communications research' in SCRAMM, W. (Ed.) *The Process and Effects of Mass Communication*, Chicago, IL, University of Illinois Press, pp. 389–401.

ROBERTS, D.F., HEROLD, C., HORNBY, M., KING, S., STERN, D., WHILELEY, S. and SILVERMAN, L.T. (1974) 'Earth's a big blue marble: A report of the impact of a children's television series on children's opinions', Unpublished manuscript, Institute for Communication Research, Stanford University, California.

ROBINSON, A.H. (1985) 'Arno Peters and his new cartography', *American Cartographer*, **12**, 2, pp. 103–11.

ROBINSON, J.P. and HEFFNER, R.A. (1968) 'Perceptual maps of the world', *Public Opinion Quarterly*, **32**, pp. 273–80.

ROSELL, L. (1968) 'Children's views of war and peace', *Journal of Peace Research*, **5**, pp. 268–76.

ROSS, A. (1990) *Economic and Industrial Awareness in the Primary School*, London, Polytechnic of North London and School Curriculum Industry Partnership.

ROTHBART, M. (1981) 'Memory processes and social beliefs' in HAMILTON, D.L. (Ed.) *Cognitive Processes in Stereotyping and Intergroup Behaviour*, Hillsdale, NS, Erlbaum.

ROWLES, G. (1980) 'Toward a geography of growing old' in BUTTIMER, A. and SEAMON, D. (Ed.) *The Human Experience of Space and Place*, London, Croom Helm.

RUTLAND, J. (1980) *Let's Go to France*, London, Franklin Watts.

SANDFORD, H. (1980) 'Directed and free search of the atlas map', *Cartographic Journal*, **17**, 2, pp. 83–92.

SANDFORD, H. (1981) 'Objective analysis of school atlases' in WILSON, P., GERBER, R. and FIEN, J. (Ed.) *Research in Geographical Education*, Brisbane, Australian Geographical Education Research Association, pp. 234–45.

SANDFORD, H. (1988) 'Guide to the selection of an atlas for young children' in MILLS, D. (Ed.) *Geographical Work in Primary and Middle Schools*, Sheffield, Geographical Association, pp. 298–303.

SAVELAND, R.N. (Ed.) (1980) *Place Vocabulary Research Project*, Athens, GA, Geography Curriculum Project.

SAVELAND, R.N. (1983) 'Map skills around the world: How to test and diagnose place vocabulary', *Social Education*, **47**, 3, pp. 24–31.

SCARFE, N.V. (1951) *A Handbook of Suggestions on the Teaching of Geography Towards World Understanding,* Paris, UNESCO.

SCHUG, M. (1990) 'Research on children's understanding of economics: implications for teaching' in Ross, A. (Ed.) *Economic and Industrial Awareness in the Primary School*, London, Polytechnic of North London and School Curriculum Industry Partnership.

SCHWARTZ, A.V. (1979) 'Mary Poppins Revised' in STINTON, J. (Ed.) *Racism and Sexism in Children's Books*, London, Writers & Readers, pp. 27–35.

SCHWEBEL, M. (1982) 'Effects of the nuclear war threat on children and teenagers: Implications for professionals', *American Journal of Orthopsychiatry*, **52**, pp. 608–18.

SCRUTON, R. (1986) 'Peace studies: No true subject' in O'KEEFFE, D. (Ed.) *The Wayward Curriculum: A Cause for Parents' Concern?*, London, Social Affairs Unit.

SECRETARY OF STATE FOR EDUCATION AND SCIENCE (1985) *Report of the Committee of Enquiry into the Education of Children from Ethnic Minority Groups ('Education for All')* (The Swann Report), London, HMSO.

SELMAN, R.L. (1980) *The Growth of Interpersonal Understanding*, New York, Academic Press.

SHERIF. M. (1966) *Group Conflict and Cooperation: Their Social Psychology*, London, Routledge & Kegan Paul.

SHERIF, M., MARVEY, O.J., WHITE, B.J., HOOD, W.R. and SHERIF, C.W. (1961) *Intergroup Conflict and Cooperation: The Robber's Cave Experiment*, Norman, OK, University of Oklahoma.

SHIPMAN, M., PHILO, G. and LAMB, R. (1986) *Television and the Ethiopian Famine: From Buerk to Band Aid*, Paris, UNESCO.

SIEGAL, A.W. and WHITE, S. (1975) 'The development of spatial representations of large scale environments' in REESE, H.W. (Ed.) *Advances in Child Development and Behaviour*, Vol. 10, New York, Academic Press.

SINGER, D.G. and SINGER, J.L. (1983) 'Learning how to be intelligent consumers of television', in HOWE, M.J.A. (Ed.) *Learning from Television: Psychological and Educational Research*, London, Academic Press, pp. 203–22.

SINGER, J.L. and SINGER, D.G. (1981) *Television, Imagination and Aggression: A Study of Pre-schoolers*, Hillsdale, NS Erlbaum.

SLATER, F. and SPICER, B. (Eds) (1980) *Perception and Preference Studies at the International Level*, Tokyo, International Geographical Union Commission on Geographical Education.

SLATER, J. (1990) *European Awareness Pilot Project 1988–1990*, London, Central Bureau for Educational Visits and Exchanges.

SMITH, A. (1989) *People of the World: Inuit*, Hove, Wayland.

SMITH, H.P. (1955) 'Do intercultural experiences affect attitudes?', *Journal of Abnormal and Social Psychology*, **51**, pp. 469–77.

SMITH, H.P. (1957) 'The effects of intercultural experience: A follow up investigation', *Journal of Abnormal and Social Psychology*, **54**, pp. 166–9.

SMITH, V.L. (1978) 'Eskimo tourism and marginal men', in SMITH, V.L. (Ed.) *Hosts and Guests*, Oxford, Blackwell.

SORRELL, P. (1974) 'Map design — With the young in mind', *Cartographic Journal*, **11**, pp. 82–90.

SPENCER, C., BLADES, M. and MORSLEY, K. (1989) *The Child in the Physical Environment*, Chichester, John Wiley.

SPENCER, D. and LLOYD, J. (1974) *A Child's Eye View of Small Heath, Birmingham*, Birmingham, Centre for Urban and Regional Studies, University of Birmingham.

SPICER, B. (1984) 'Methods of measuring students' images of people and places' in HAUBRICH, H. (Ed.) *Perception of People and Places Through Media*, Freiburg, Paedagogische Hochschule, pp. 124–9.

SPINK, M.M. and BRADY, R.P. (n.d.) *Pleasant Paths to Geography Book 1: The World We Live In*, Huddersfield, Schofield and Sims.

STILLWELL, R. and SPENCER, C. (1974) 'Children's early preferences for other nations and their subsequent acquisition of knowledge about those nations', *European Journal of Social Psychology*, **3**, 3, pp. 345–9.

STINTON, J. (Ed.) (1979) *Racism and Sexism in Children's Books*, London, Writers & Readers.

STOLTMAN, J.P. and FREYE, R. (1988) 'School atlases in the United States: An analysis of characteristics' in GERBER, R. and LIDSTONE, J. (Eds) *Developing Skills in Geographical Education*, Brisbane, International Geographical Union Commission on Geographical Education and the Jacaranda Press, pp. 165–72.

SUHL, I. (1979) 'Doctor Doolittle — The Great White Father' in STINTON, J. (Ed.) *Racism and Sexism in Children's Books*, London, Writers & Readers, pp. 19–27.

STORM, M. (1970) 'Schools and the community', *Bulletin of Environmental Education*, **1**, pp. 5–7.

SUMNER, W.G. (1906) *Folkways: A Study of the Sociological importance of Usages, Manners, Customs, Mores and Morals*, New York, Ginn.

TAJFEL, H. (1969) 'Cognitive aspects of prejudice', *Journal of Social Issues*, **25**, pp. 79–97.

TAJFEL, H. (1981) *Human Groups and Social Categories: Studies in Social Psychology*, Cambridge, Cambridge University Press.

TAJFEL, H. and FRASER, C. (Eds) (1978) *Introducing Social Psychology*, Harmondsworth, Penguin.

TAJFEL, H., JAHODA, G., NEMETH, C., CAMPBELL, J.D. and JOHNSON, N. (1970) 'The development of children's preference for their own country: A cross national study', *International Journal of Psychology* **5**, 4, pp. 245–53.

TARG, H.R. (1970) 'Children's developing orientations to international politics', *Journal of Peace Research*, 7, pp. 79–97.

THOMAS, K. (1971) *Religion and the Decline of Magic*, London, Weidenfeld & Nicholson.

TOLLEY, H. (1973) *Children and War*, New York, Teachers College Press.

TOWNSEND, J.R. (1987) *Written for Children*, Harmondsworth, Penguin.

TWITCHIN, J. (Ed.) (1988) *The Black and White Media Show Book. Handbook for the Study of Racism and Television*, Stoke-on-Trent, Trentham Books.

UNITED NATIONS (1948) *Universal Declaration of Human Rights*, Paris, United Nations.

UNITED NATIONS EDUCATIONAL, SCIENTIFIC AND CULTURAL ORGANIZATION (UNESCO) (1965) *International Understanding at School: An account of progress in Unesco's Associated Schools Project*, Paris, UNESCO.

UNITED NATIONS EDUCATIONAL, SCIENTIFIC AND CULTURAL ORGANIZATION (UNESCO) (1974) *Recommendation Concerning Education for International Understanding, Cooperation and Peace and Education Relating to Human Rights and Fundamental Freedoms*, Paris, UNESCO.

UNWIN, R.W. (1981) *The Visual Dimension in the Study and Teaching of History*, London, Historical Association.

VAN DER GAAG, N. and NASH, C. (1987) *Images of Africa* Oxford, Oxfam.

VERNA, G.B. (1981) 'A study of the nature of children's race preferences using a modified conflict paradigm', *Child Development*, **53**, pp. 427–35.

WAGENKNECHT, E. (1929) *Utopia Americana (Oz)*, Washington, DC, University of Washington Chapbooks.

WALMSLEY, D.J. (1982) Mass media and spatial awareness, *Tijdschrift Voor Economische en Sociale Geografie*, **73**, pp. 32–42.

WATKINS, B. and WILLIAMS, M. (1982) *Attitudes to Europe: A Study of Secondary School Pupils* mimeo.

WATSON, J. (1988) 'Peace education in Great Britain', *Interspectives*, 7, pp. 11–14.

WEBLEY, P. and CUTTS, K. (1985) 'Children, war and nationhood', *New Society*, 13 December.

WEINSTEIN, E.A. (1957) 'Development of the concept of flag and the sense of national identity', *Child Development*, **28**, 2, pp. 167–74.

WERTHAM, F. (1954) *Seduction of the Innocent*, New York, Rinehart.

WHITE, P. (1988) 'Countering the critics' in HICKS, D. (Ed.) *Education for Peace*, London, Routledge, pp. 36–53.

WHITEFORD, G.T. (1984) 'Perception of place: A dangerous homogenization? in HAUBRICH, H. (Ed.) *Perception of People and Places Through Media*, Freiburg, Paedagogische Hochschule.

WIEGAND, P. (1982) '"A biased view" (visual bias in geographical education)' in KENT, W.A. (Ed.) *Bias in Geographical Education*, London, University of London Institute of Education.

WIEGAND, P. (Ed.) (1985) *The Oxford Junior Atlas*, Oxford, Oxford University Press.

WIEGAND, P. (Ed.) (1987) *The Oxford Rainbow Atlas*, Oxford, Oxford University Press.

WIEGAND, P. (1988) *The Oxford Junior Atlas Skills Book*, Oxford, Oxford University Press.

WIEGAND, P. (1989) *The Oxford Rainbow Atlas Activity Book*, Oxford, Oxford University Press.

WIEGAND, P. (1990) 'Starting teaching distant places', *Primary Geographer*, May.

WIEGAND, P. (1991a) 'Does travel broaden the mind?', *Education 3–13*, **19**, 1, pp. 54–58.

WIEGAND, P. (1991b) 'A model for the realization of a school atlas', *Geography*, **76**, 1, pp. 50–7.

WIEGAND, P. (1991c) 'The known world of the primary school', *Geography*, **76**, 2, pp. 143–149.

WILLIAMS, J.E., BEST, D.L. and BOSWELL, D.A. (1975) 'The measurement of children's racial attitudes in the early school years', *Child Development*, **46**, pp. 494–500.

WILLIAMS, M. (1986) *Report, 29th Council of Europe Teachers' Seminar on 'Geography for international understanding in primary schools'* (held in Donaueschingen, 7–12 October, 1985) Strasbourg, Council of Europe.

WILLIAMS, M., BIILMANN, O., HAHN, R. and VAN WESTRHENEN, J. (1984) 'A cross-national study children's attitudes' in HAUBRICH, H. (Ed.) *Perception of People and Places Through Media*, Freiburg, Paedagogische. Hochschule, pp. 220–41.

WOLF, K. and FISKE, E. (1949) 'Variations in choice: Three stages in comic reading' in LAZARSFELD, P. and STANTON, F. (Eds) *Communications Research 1948–1949*, New York, Harper and Brothers, pp. 5–21.

WOLFORTH, J., POPESCU, D. and Belanger, F. (1984) 'North and South: Perceptions of Canadian schoolchildren' in HAUBRICH, H. (Ed.) *Perception of People and Places Through Media*, Freiburg, Paedagogische Hochschule.

WOOD, D. (1988) *How Children Think and Learn*, Oxford, Blackwell.

WRIGHT, D.R. (1983) 'International textbook research — past stagnation and future potential', *Curriculum*, **2**, 4, pp. 14–18.

WRIGHT, D.R. (1979) 'Visual images in geography texts', *Geography*, **64**, 3, pp. 47–61.

WRIGHT, D.R. (1982) 'Colourful South Africa? An analysis of textbook images', *Multiracial Education*, **10**, 2, pp. 22–32.

WRIGHT, D.R. (1983) 'They have no need of transport ... a study of attitudes to black people in three geography textbooks', *Contemporary Issues in Geography and Education*, **1**, 1, pp. 11–15.

WRIGHT, D.R. (1985) 'In black and white: Racist bias in geography textbooks', *Geographical Education*, **5**, pp. 13–17.

YOUNISS, J. (1980) *My Friends, My Parents and Me*, Chicago, IL, Chicago University Press.

YUSSEN, S.R. (1974) 'Determinants of visual attention and recall in observational learning by pre-schoolers and second graders', *Development Psychology*, **10**, pp. 93–110.

ZIMET, S.G. (1976) *Print and Prejudice*, London, Hodder & Stoughton.

Index

absolute location, 171
Africa, 68, 69, 91ff, 144
alphabet flashcards, 104–105
America, 90–91
animism, 47
artificialism, 47
artwork, 115–119, 182
assessment, 9
atlases, 126ff, 175–176
attitudes, 53ff
attitude surveys, 85
Australia, 68, 76ff, 87–89
Australian aborigines, 103
authenticity of place, 33–34

Brandt report, 13
Bronte family, 179

Campus 2000, 166–168
captions, 182
categorization, 79
Central Bureau for Educational
    Visits and Exchanges, 12, 162,
    165, 197
Centre for Global Education, 10,
    197
CEWC (Council for Education in
    World Citizenship), 8
children's literature, 96ff
CISV (Children's International
    Summer Villages), 162ff

citizenship, 17
colour (on maps), 133
comics, 135ff
Commission for Racial Equality, 197
Commonwealth Institute, 171
Council for Evnironmental
    Education, 15, 197
CWDE (Centre for World
    Development Education), 182,
    197

direct experience, 6
design of text books, 114
development education centres, 9,
    13, 182, 191, 197
development education, 13ff

Earth as a cosmic body, 43ff
education for economic and
    industrial understanding, 8, 58ff
egocentricity, 37ff
E-mail, 165ff
empathy, 186–187
English, 24–27, 178ff
environmental education, 15
Ethiopia, 68, 93, 142–144
ethnocentrism, 96, 104, 105, 125,
    141
ethnography, 162
Eurocentrism, 96, 104
European dimension in education,
    11ff

KING ALFRED'S COLLEGE
LIBRARY